ABUSED AND BATTERED
Social and Legal Responses to Family Violence

SOCIAL INSTITUTIONS AND SOCIAL CHANGE

An Aldine de Gruyter Series of Texts and Monographs

EDITED BY

Michael Useem • James D. Wright

Mary Ellen Colten and Susan Gore (eds.), **Adolescent Stress: Causes and Consequences**

Paul Diesing, **Science and Ideology in the Policy Sciences**

G. William Domhoff, **The Power Elite and the State: How Policy is Made in America**

Glen H. Elder, Jr. and Rand D. Conger, **Families in a Changing Society: Hard Times in Rural America**

Paula S. England, **Comparable Worth**

Paula S. England, **Theory on Gender/Feminism on Theory**

Paula S. England and George Farkas, **Households, Employment, and Gender: A Social, Economic, and Demographic View**

George Farkas, Robert P. Grobe, and Daniel Sheehan, **Human Capital or Cultural Capital?**

F. G. Gosling (ed.), **Risk and Responsibility**

Richard F. Hamilton and James D. Wright, **The State of the Masses**

Gary Kleck, **Point Blank: Guns and Violence in America**

James R. Kluegel and Eliot R. Smith, **Beliefs About Inequality: Americans' Views of What Is and What Ought to Be**

David Knoke, **Organizing for Collective Action: The Political Economies of Associations**

Dean Knudsen and J. L. Miller (eds.), **Abused and Battered: Social and Legal Responses to Family Violence**

Robert C. Liebman and Robert Wuthnow (eds.), **The New Christian Right: Mobilization and Legitimation**

Clark McPhail, **The Myth of the Madding Crowd**

Clark McPhail, **Acting Together: The Organization of Crowds**

John Mirowsky and Catherine E. Ross, **Social Causes of Psychological Distress**

Carolyn C. and Robert Perrucci, Dena B. and Harry R. Targ, **Plant Closings: International Context and Social Costs**

Robert Perrucci and Harry R. Potter (eds.), **Networks of Power: Organizational Actors at the National, Corporate, and Community Levels**

David Popenoe, **Disturbing the Nest: Family Change and Decline in Modern Societies**

James T. Richardson, Joel Best, and David Bromley (eds.), **The Satanism Scare**

Bernard C. Rosen, **The Industrial Connection: Achievement and the Family in Developing Societies**

Alice S. Rossi and Peter H. Rossi, **Of Human Bonding: Parent-Child Relations Across the Life Course**

Roberta G. Simmons and Dale A. Blyth, **Moving into Adolescence: The Impact of Pubertal Change and School Context**

David G. Smith, **Paying for Medicare: The Politics of Reform**

Walter L. Wallace, **Principles of Scientific Sociology**

Martin King Whyte, **Dating, Mating, and Marriage**

James D. Wright, **Address Unknown: The Homeless in America**

James D. Wright and Peter H. Rossi, **Armed and Considered Dangerous: A Survey of Felons and Their Firearms**

James D. Wright, Peter H. Rossi, and Kathleen Daly, **Under the Gun: Weapons, Crime, and Violence in America**

ABUSED AND BATTERED
Social and Legal Responses to
Family Violence

Dean D. Knudsen and JoAnn L. Miller
(*Editors*)

ALDINE DE GRUYTER
New York

About the Editors

Dean D. Knudsen is Professor of Sociology at Purdue University. He received his Ph.D. from the University of North Carolina. He has published numerous books and articles on family violence. His earlier works, including the co-authorship of *Spindles and Spires*, were in the sociology of religion field.

JoAnn L. Miller is Associate Professor of Sociology and a member of the Women's Studies Committee at Purdue University. She received her M.A. in Sociology from the College of William and Mary and the Ph.D. from the University of Massachusetts at Amherst. She has published numerous articles in the sociology of law field.

Copyright © 1991 Walter de Gruyter, Inc., New York
All rights reserved. No part of this publication may be reproduced or transmitted in any form or by any means, electronic or mechanical, including photocopy, recording, or any information storage and retrieval system, without permission in writing from the publisher.

ALDINE DE GRUYTER
A division of Walter de Gruyter, Inc.
200 Saw Mill River Road
Hawthorne, New York 10532

The paper used in this publication meets the minimum requirements of American National Standard for Information Sciences—Permanence of Paper for Printed Library Materials, ANSI Z39.48-1984.

Library of Congress Cataloging-in-Publication Data
Abused and battered : social and legal responses to family violence / edited by Dean D. Knudsen and JoAnn L. Miller.
     p.   cm. — (Social institutions and social change)
   Includes bibliographical references and index.
   ISBN 0-202-30413-2 (cloth). — ISBN 0-202-30414-0 (paperbound)
   1. Family violence—United States.   I. Knudsen, Dean D., 1932–
. II. Miller, JoAnn L., 1949-   .   III. Series.
HQ809.3.U5A29   1991
362.82'92—dc20   90-22716
                                                                CIP

Manufactured in the United States of America

10 9 8 7 6 5 4 3 2 1

Contents

List of Contributors   *vii*

Preface   *ix*

Introduction: Some Fundamental Issues   *xi*

PART I. CONCEPTUALIZATION AND EMPIRICAL STUDY

1. Family Violence Research: Some Basic
    and Applied Questions
    JoAnn L. Miller   5

2. Physical Violence in American Families: Incidence
    Rates, Causes, and Trends
    Murray A. Straus   17

3. Public-Health Conceptions of Family Abuse
    Jacquelyn C. Campbell   35

4. Variations in Defining Family Mistreatment:
    A Community Survey
    Stephen W. Webster   49

5. Criminal-Justice Processing of Violent and
    Nonviolent Offenders: The Effects of Familial
    Relationship to the Victim
    Sharon D. Herzberger and Noreen L. Channels   63

PART II. EFFECTS OF VICTIMIZATION

6. An Investigation of Child Sexual Abuse
    and Consequent Victimization: Some
    Implications of Telephone Surveys
    John E. Murphy   79

7. The Mixed Roles of Social Support and Social
    Obstruction in Recovery from Child Abuse
    Diana Gurley   89

8. The Admissibility of Expert Testimony
    on the Battered-Woman Syndrome
        Debra F. Kromsky and Brian L. Cutler   101

PART III. SOCIAL RESPONSES TO FAMILY VIOLENCE: BATTERERS AND THEIR VICTIMS

9. The Outcome of Participation in a Shelter-Sponsored
    Program for Men Who Batter
        Richard M. Tolman and Gauri Bhosley   113

10. Removal of the Perpetrator versus Removal
    of the Victim in Cases of Intrafamilial Child
    Sexual Abuse
        *Patricia Ryan, Bruce L. Warren, and
        Peggy Weincek*   123

11. Perceptions of Verbal Aggression in Interspousal
    Violence
        Teresa Chandler Sabourin   135

PART IV. LEGAL RESPONSES TO FAMILY VIOLENCE

12. Police Classification of Domestic-Violence Calls:
    An Assessment of Program Impact
        Richard K. Caputo   147

13. Legal Responses of Prosecutors to Child Sexual
    Abuse: A Case Comparison of Two Countries
        Bruce K. Mac Murray   153

14. Family Violence and the Courts: Implementing
    a Comprehensive New Law
        Eleanor Lyon and Patricia Goth Mace   167

15. Improving the Investigation and Prosecution
    of Child Sexual-Abuse Cases: Research Findings,
    Questions, and Implications for Public Policy
        Debra Whitcomb   181

16. Preventing and Provoking Wife Battery through
    Criminal Sanctions: A Look at the Risks
        David A. Ford   191

References   211

Index   231

List of Contributors

Gauri Bhosley

Crisis Center for South Suburbia
Chicago, IL

Jacquelyn C. Campbell

College of Medicine
Wayne State University

Richard K. Caputo

Director, Research Center
School of Social Work
University of Pennsylvania

Noreen L. Channels

Department of Sociology
Trinity College
Hartford, CT

Brian L. Cutler

Florida International University
Miami, FL

David A. Ford

Indiana University at Indianapolis
    and Family Research Laboratory
University of New Hampshire

Diana Gurley

Psychiatric Epidemiology Training
    Program
Columbia University

Sharon D. Herzberger

Department of Psychology
Trinity College
Hartford, CT

Dean D. Knudsen

Department of Sociology and
    Anthropology
Purdue University

Debra F. Kromsky

Dade County Advocates for Victims
Miami, FL

Eleanor Lyon

Research and Evaluation Services
Child and Family Services, Inc.
Hartford, CT

Patricia Goth Mace   Research and Evaluation Services
                                        Child and Family Services, Inc.
                                        Hartford, CT

Bruce Mac Murray   Department of Sociology
                                        Anderson University

JoAnn L. Miller   Department of Sociology and
                                               Anthropolgy
                                        Purdue University

John E. Murphy   Department of Sociology
                                        St. Cloud State University

Patricia Ryan   Institute for the Study of Child and
                                               Family
                                        Eastern Michigan University

Teresa Chandler Sabourin   Department of Communication Arts
                                        University of Cincinnati

Murray A. Straus   Family Research Laboratory
                                        University of New Hampshire

Richard M. Tolman   Jane Addams College
                                        University of Illinois, Chicago Circle

Bruce L. Warren   Institute for the Study of Child and
                                               Family
                                        Eastern Michigan University

Stephen W. Webster   Department of Sociology
                                        Kent State University

Debra Whitcomb   Education Development Center, Inc.
                                        Newton, MA

Peggy Wiencek   Institute for the Study of Child and
                                               Family
                                        Eastern Michigan University

Preface

Defining family violence is problematic. What do we know, with relative certainty, about spouse abuse, child abuse, or elder abuse? What can we do to help, and not harm, victims of family violence?

We know that familial and intimate violence kills, injures, and mutilates its victims physically and psychologically. We know that the social-science community, the legal community, and the public-health community must integrate their research and their intervention efforts so that we can broaden our current understanding of the causes and consequences of violence and abuse against family members. We know that too little is known about a problem that is too poorly defined and explained in contemporary American society.

Two decades of family violence research have generated information that is used by practitioners in legal, health, and social-service settings. Researchers borrow methods and theory for studying the family violence problem from the major academic disciplines. Explanations for the initiation of abuse, for perceptions of abuse at the community and individual level, and for the multiple responses to incidents of abuse are more comprehensive now than they were a decade ago.

Contributors to this volume represent sociologists, psychologists, public-health nurses, social workers, and legal analysts. Together they advance our knowledge about family violence along two critical dimensions: (1) they provide new and sophisticated insights regarding the etiology of the numerous forms of family abuse, and (2) they suggest innovative strategies for alleviating or mitigating the anguish resulting from violence and abuse.

This volume heralds the second generation of domestic abuse research. These studies and essays examine the *implications* of the victim- or offender-oriented legal and social responses that were engendered by the pioneers of family violence research. Contributors systematically address the intended and unintended consequences of programs and procedures designed to remedy the effect of intimate and familial brutality.

Brutality against children and partners is a tragedy that makes all its observers uncomfortable. We invite readers to join us and the numerous contributors to this volume on a distressing journey that we feel compelled to take.

We wish to acknowledge many people who have assisted in the development of this book. The Department of Sociology and Anthropology and Reece McGee provided a stimulating and supportive milieu in which to work. The editors at Aldine de Gruyter, Trev Leger and Richard Koffler, and managing editor Arlene Perazzini deserve sincere thanks. Special appreciation is also due Kay Solomon, Candy Lawson, and Evelyn Douthit, whose work was essential to completion of the book. Finally, we wish to thank our spouses—Lucille and Scott—and our children—Karen, Steve, and Jonathan—for their continued love and loyalty.

Introduction: Some
Fundamental Issues

Family violence in the United States is a multidimensional dilemma: complex and intertwining problems with insufficient remedies affect victims, their families, the courts, and social-service agencies. Nonetheless, lawmakers and social-policymakers strive to resolve the family violence problem. Reformers develop imaginative ideas, they try new laws, and they develop a variety of treatment or intervention strategies for correcting and preventing the violent and sexual abuse of vulnerable children, marital partners, siblings, and elderly parents.

Family violence researchers—regardless of differences in academic disciplines or preferred theoretical perspectives—can help to maximize the effectiveness of social programs designed to ease the pain of family violence. Researchers can chronicle the patterns of abuse. We can design studies to explain the persistence of family violence. We can execute evaluation studies. And we can inform policymakers and lawmakers about the unexpected as well as the expected consequences of schemes devised to heal victims and to stop the abuse. The contributors to this volume show us how to begin a new generation of research and social intervention.

I. The Current Predicament

What is the real magnitude of the family violence problem in this society? The work published herein indisputably exposes a high level of family violence in the United States. John E. Murphy, in "An Investigation of Child Sexual Abuse and Consequent Victimization: Some Implications of Telephone Surveys" reports that 18% of the women and 11% of the men he interviewed in Minnesota had, at least once in their lives, experienced a form of sexual abuse. Murray A. Straus, in his chapter "Physical Violence in American Families: Incidence Rates, Causes, and Trends," distinguishes an incidence rate from a prevalence rate in his 1975 and 1985 studies. He uses these studies to estimate recent increases in family violence. Employing the 1985 data, Straus estimates a 6.3% annual *incidence rate* of spousal violence. He estimates conservatively a 30% *prevalence rate* for American families that will experience battering over the course of a marriage. Further, giving us a second *prevalence* measure, he estimates that the severely violent family in the general population typically experiences five major assault events per year. These figures are comparable to other estimates (e.g., Frieze and Browne 1989; Garbarino 1989).

Incidence is "the number of new cases of a particular problem that are identified or arise in a defined geographical area during a specified period of time." Prevalence is "the number of existing cases [with a given condition] in a particular geographic area at a specified time" (Rossi and Freeman 1985:117). Together, these two indicators summarize the family violence problem. They can inform the legal and public-health sectors how to respond to the family violence problem. To illustrate: An incidence rate of battering in a particular county tells us how many perpetrators per month are likely to be court-ordered to a six-week batterers' therapy program. We need to examine the prevalence of family violence, however, when drafting comprehensive legislation intended to ameliorate in this society the "chronic illness" that we call family violence.

The current predicament is that there is too much family violence in the United States. For an earlier point in time, we would hesitate to make such a claim. Instead, we would question whether or not we could estimate accurately the magnitude of a problem that was not clearly defined legally or socially. Presently, for many forms of family violence (battery or child sexual abuse, for example), we see definitional consensus emerging. For those particular forms of abuse, we can indeed make magnitude estimates accurate enough to guide policy decisions. For other forms of family violence (elder neglect or spousal rape are prime examples), we still see too much disparity in relevant state laws to expect social consensus. Without social consensus in the definition of an offense, and without statutory consistency, we cannot measure or estimate with any precision or accuracy the magnitude of the problem.

II. Persistent Problems

Jacquelyn C. Campbell, in "Public-Health Conceptions of Family Abuse," shows us the utility of a public-health perspective for understanding a family suffering from abuse. Moreover, she proposes an approach for efficaciously responding to the spouse abuse problem. A person traumatized by an act of family violence needs help for healing the emotional wounds along with the medical help provided for healing cuts, bruises, and broken bones. Campbell, on the one hand, brings to the family violence research literature a somewhat new and urgently needed perspective—the public-health perspective (Spivak et al. 1989). On the other hand, she reminds us that the family violence problem is a persistent one. In doing so, she asks us to reflect upon the potential damage in the "generic process of Blaming the Victim [that] is applied to almost every American problem" (Ryan 1971:5) including spouse abuse and child abuse.

Contributors to this volume highlight three major failures in the legal system's response to family violence that stem from a victim-blaming process. These failures, if left unchecked, will ensure the persistence of the family violence problem in the United States.

One consequence of victim blaming is the all too persistent failure of the police, the criminal justice system gatekeepers, to help remedy the real problem of family abuse (e.g., Stith 1990). Richard K. Caputo, in "Police Classification of Domestic Violence Calls: An Assessment of Program Impact," finds that police can (and do) "misclassify" calls regarding domestic violence. A police department committed to ameliorating the family violence problem—rather than blaming the victim of violence—gives the legal system an opportunity to stop the revolving door nightmare. The well-known and well-publicized Minneapolis spouse abuse experiments (Sherman and Berk 1984; Berk and Sherman 1988; Berk et al. 1988; Sherman and Cohn 1989) verify the premise that police can affect recidivistic and abusive behavior. The legal system can indeed be efficacious in treating the family abuse problem. It can also exacerbate the persistence of the real problem by blaming the victim.

Sharon D. Herzberger and Noreen L. Channels, in "Criminal Justice Processing of Violent and Nonviolent Offenders: The Effects of Familial Relationship to the Victim," highlight another persistent problem that is associated with a victim-blaming approach to the family violence problem. In their research, they show that offenders who are accused of criminally violent acts against victims to whom they are related are more likely to be released on bail than others, and they are less likely to be convicted by a trial court judge. It is a persistent problem: blame the victim of spouse abuse and treat the perpetrator with as much leniency as possible. A victim-blaming approach will avoid any offender degradation associated with the criminal justice process. It tells the victim to prepare for more abuse. And it tells the courts and social-service agencies to expect manifestations of the battered-woman syndrome.

Bruce K. Mac Murray highlights a third persistent problem in the legal response to family abuse: prosecutorial discretion. Mac Murray compares the case screening and prosecution decisions characterizing two Massachusetts counties in his qualitative research, "Legal Responses of Prosecutors to Child Sexual Abuse: A Case Comparison of Two Counties." A 1983 law, i.e., the Massachusetts District Attorney Reporting Law, was designed to help prosecutors secure convictions in sexual-abuse cases. The law identified the district attorney as the key criminal justice actor for criminalizing child sexual-abuse cases. It did not, however, specify the criminal charges upon which individuals accused of sexual abuse should be prosecuted. Prosecutorial discretion was left unchecked and unstructured, thereby precluding uniformity in the prosecution of child sexual-abuse offenders. This style of law, one encouraging prosecutorial discretion, can permit an implicit victim-blaming approach through its failure to mandate a legalistic response to all cases of sexual abuse.

III. New Insights

Contributors to this volume illustrate and explain the persistence of family violence. They also give us new ideas, new insights that can inform the policymakers and lawmakers who struggle to remedy the problem. They tell us a story about persons who abuse and batter their spouses and children. They take us out of the trap set by victim blaming.

Two papers in this volume, David A. Ford's "Preventing and Provoking Wife Battery through Criminal Sanctioning: A Look at the Risks" and Richard M. Tolman and Gauri Bhosley's "The Outcome of Participation in a Shelter-Sponsored Program for Men Who Batter," give us provocative, new, and refined ideas on how the legal system and social services can increase or decrease the likelihood of continued spouse abuse. Both papers are focused on the batterer.

David A. Ford gives us an extraordinarily sophisticated understanding of how criminal sanctions meted out to men convicted of battery can deter or encourage future acts of violence. His research, substantively, is in the tradition of the Minneapolis spouse abuse experiment, which examined the role of *punishment certainty* in deterring future acts of domestic violence in another large city—Indianapolis. David Ford's research examines the roles of *punishment severity* and *anger* in recidivism. Ford urges us to continue our empirical search for appropriate levels of punishment severity. He gives us the analytic tools to begin the development of a punishment scheme that will stop the violence.

Making empirically based judgments about programs designed to treat batterers is extremely problematic. What indicates "success"? How can we collect data on the "outcome" of program participation? Evaluation researchers document the difficulty of gathering the data necessary to assess the effectiveness and efficiency of social programs (Burstein et al. 1985). Statisticians describe the difficulty of estimating the real effects of social programs (Judd and Kenny 1981). One major problem is the fact that many batterers do not complete programs (Gruzinski and Carrillo 1988); often the dropouts have the most severe problems (Hamberger and Hastings 1989).

Richard Tolman and Gauri Bhosley show us that we can evaluate empirically the effectiveness of treatment programs for batterers. To design this type of evaluation study requires inventiveness and researchers who can elicit trust from victims of abuse, whose trust in others is delicate if not lacking. In a creative and sensitive study, Tolman and Bhosley talked to victims of spouse abuse to find out whether or not the abuse stopped partly as a result of a shelter-sponsored batterers' treatment program. And they asked victims about fear and comfort in expressing anger. This study establishes the necessity to measure multiple indicators of program success whenever we attempt to appraise the utility of social intervention designed to stop family violence.

Diana Gurley's research, "The Mixed Roles of Social Support and Social Obstruction in Recovery from Child Abuse," invites us to listen carefully to the voices of women who were sexually abused as children. If we dare to listen, we can hear traumatized women telling us that they are victimized over, and over, and over again. Caregivers can hurt. Therapists can hurt, whenever they blame the victim. Diana Gurley gives us a unique study of the social support and social obstruction that family abuse victims experience. She shows us that we must dare to enter the nightmare of pain if we want to help stop it from recurring.

IV. What Can We Do?

As academics, we can do a lot. We can design cross-disciplinary research agendas to understand comprehensively the extent and consequences of all forms of family violence. We can continue our empirical and theoretical search to define precisely the separate forms or types of family abuse (e.g., Ellis 1987). We can conduct research that draws samples of victims and perpetrators from the general population and from the known clinical (and criminal) populations. In spite of the difficulties we can design and implement experimental and quasi-experimental studies. Experimental research is needed to examine empirically the critical cause and effect relationships regarding family violence that we argue theoretically.

We can design longitudinal studies for examining the long-term and unexpected consequences of family abuse. And we can design longitudinal studies to follow up perpetrators who undergo treatment, and who experience punishment for their crimes. Finally, we can develop cross-national inquiries of family abuse. Cross-national studies will show us the importance of cultural norms and values in the genesis and tolerance of violent and abusive families.

As advocates who want to terminate the family abuse problem, we can do a lot. The lack of information about the law, inadequate programs, and reticence of victims contribute to inaction (Martin 1989), but several things can be done to help victims and prosecute perpetrators. Debra Whitcomb, in "Improving the Investigation and Prosecution of Child Sexual-Abuse Cases: Research Findings, Questions, and Implications for Public Policy," summarizes a multiplicity of innovative techniques for the prosecution of family abuse cases. She also informs us that we need to continue the development of constitutional and effective means to prosecute the problematic child victim-witness case. Eleanor Lyon and Patricia Goth Mace, in "Family Violence and the Courts: Implementing a Comprehensive New Law," formulate (implicitly) a blueprint for lawmakers who want to draft legislation that can effectively respond to the problem of family violence in this contemporary society.

V. A Public Issue

Mary Ann Glendon, a jurist specializing in comparative family law, uncovers recent changes in this and other western societies: "Although the legal system has shifted its focus from families to individuals, society still relies on families to play a crucial role in caring for the young, the aged, the sick, the severely disabled, and the needy" (1989:306). The American family is the locus for love and support. And it needs help. Once, family life was private. The state regulated and governed family life least of all. The parent-child relationship was sacred. The husband-wife relationship was not to be monitored or controlled by government. Now family problems are public. No longer can we afford to keep the family violence problem hidden within the family's closet. But neither can we afford to allow legal actions or social services to go unexamined, or to continue without assessment of their impact on the family, and not only on individuals.

The research in this volume is an effort to focus attention on family violence, and to illustrate the implications of findings for legal, social, and public-health responses. But the studies presented here are only a beginning. There is much to be done if we are to attack the issue of family violence. And the time to do it is now.

PART I

Conceptualization and Empirical Study

The contributors to Part I address methodological and theoretical issues that are critical for the investigation and understanding of all aspects of family violence.

JoAnn L. Miller, in "Family Violence Research: Some Basic and Applied Questions," shows that the study of family violence is partly a consequence of U.S. social reform and population change characteristics of the 1960s and the 1970s. She examines how family violence research methods originated within, and are affected by, the established research traditions of the social sciences. She also discusses three issues that are distinctive to family violence inquiry: the visibility paradox, the difficulty of designing impact analyses, and the blurring of distinctions between basic and applied research. The essay concludes with a discussion of research ethics.

Murray A. Straus familiarizes the reader with the focal problems of family violence in contemporary U.S. society. His sociological studies, perhaps more than any other researcher's, are scrutinized thoroughly by academics and social-policy makers alike who need to estimate accurately the extent of the family violence problem in modern U.S. society.

Straus asks the fundamental question: "What do we know?" He takes us first to his 1975 nationwide survey and then to his 1985 study in order to summarize changes over time. He examines six measures of intrafamilial violence and concludes that American society has experienced a decrease in spouse battery and child abuse within the past ten years. We can currently observe, through Straus's most recent research, a 6.3% annual incidence rate for households experiencing at least one severe assault directed at an adult. Further, 2.3% of our nation's children are severely assaulted each year.

Straus considers several common features of U.S. families in his empirically-driven, theoretically-oriented explanation of the pervasive nature of intrafamilial violence. He maintains that the family is a primary source of affection and the principal arena for interpersonal conflict. Straus explains the normative nature of family violence, and he explains how it is learned through family interaction and maintained by gender inequalities.

1

Jacquelyn C. Campbell, a professor of nursing in the College of Medicine at Wayne State University in Detroit, brings us into the world of public health so that we may gain needed insights for approaching prevention and potential remedies for victims of family violence. She urges the helping professions to consider the importance of preventing the emergence of brutality within the family. She explains how the individual and family effects of violence entail physical, emotional, and behavioral responses. Campbell discusses the imperative of examining the often disparate bodies of knowledge pertaining to all forms of family violence. Finally, to check some of the myths regarding select forms of family violence, Campbell brings to the reader's attention some of the major findings from her own longitudinal research on battered women.

Stephen W. Webster approaches the difficult task of measuring characteristics of definitions for family abuse. He argues that community definitions of mistreatment are critically important to basic researchers who study the social construction of deviance, and to practitioners who face the problems of underreporting and overreporting incidents of abuse and neglect.

Most research on family abuse focuses primarily on professional definitions or clinical definitions of child abuse or spouse abuse. Webster's research uses a modified factorial survey design to discern the general population's conception of abuse, and its perceptions of reporting practices. A random sample of respondents judged vignettes describing family mistreatment for four victim types: child, elderly parent, husband, and wife. They rated the scenarios on scales measuring the seriousness and appropriateness of the behavior, the intent to harm, the extent of physical or psychological harm, and the likelihood of reporting the incident to authorities. Webster analyzes these factors and discusses the implications for the processes of recognition, reporting, substantiation, and treatment of family violence victims in this innovative research.

Sharon D. Herzberger and Noreen L. Channels, in "Criminal Justice Processing of Violent and Nonviolent Offenders: The Effects of Familial Relationship to the Victim," present a study that tracks violent and nonviolent criminal defendants through the early phases of the criminal justice process in Connecticut. They designed their research to examine empirically the effect of victim-offender relationship on pretrial detention and bail decisions.

Herzberger and Channels make a strong case for studying family violence in the context of the larger criminal-justice process. They argue that the extent to which existing criminal-justice policy is appropriate for family violence cases can only be ascertained through research that compares the treatment of family violence cases to the treatment of other violent (and nonviolent) cases.

Generally, Herzberger and Channels find that criminal defendants charged with violent crimes against victims to whom they are related are treated more leniently than others at the bail-setting stage of the criminal-justice process. They question the ethics, the legality, and the constitutionality of bail and other pretrial release decisions that reflect victim-offender relationship.

The reader will see, when considering the numerous conceptual and methodological issues raised by these authors, the difficulty and complexity associated with the study of family violence. Further, the reader will observe advances in theory and research over the past ten years that make future family violence studies capable of informing those likely to develop programs and social policy designed to alleviate some of the injury and trauma of family abuse.

Chapter 1

Family Violence Research: Some Basic and Applied Questions

JoAnn L. Miller

I. Introduction

About the time family violence research began, a passionate plea for objective social-science research with a moral purpose was made: "The rationalism which is the driving force behind social study, whether we admit it or not, is the faith that institutions can be improved and strengthened. . . . [T]o find the practical formulas for this never ending reconstruction of society is the supreme task of social science" (Myrdal 1962:1024).

The family violence field includes research designed to describe, predict, or explain the intentional use of force to inflict pain (Finkelhor et al. 1987:19) on a family member, whether the family member is a child, sibling, spouse, parent, or some other intimate living within the household. Studies on abused or neglected children were the first to reach audiences through professional journal publications, followed by studies on child sexual abuse, marital rape, and elder neglect and abuse.

II. Emergence of Research Topics

The appearance of most if not all of the particular family violence research topics in the professional journals can be traced explicitly to either a social-reform movement, or to a shift in the sociodemographic composition of the general population. The extraordinarily influential paper on the "battered child syndrome" (Kempe et al. 1962) appeared in the *Journal of the American Medical Association*. During an era of child welfare reform in the United States, the American Medical Association ostensibly took the lead in disclosing and distributing information on what was, until then, a secretly held shame.

5

The women's movement (Ferree and Hess 1985) helped proliferate a research literature on violence against wives. As one writer summarizes:

> Before the reemergence of the women's movement in the late 1960s, the social science literature was largely oblivious to the possibility that women were being assaulted in familial relations with men. It was generally assumed that marriage, especially middle-class marriage, was a "companionate," egalitarian, peaceful affair in which violence played no part. (Wardell et al. 1983)

Marital rape, a criminal offense in only a minority of states, was a subject for the popular press in the mid-1970s (Finkelhor and Yllo 1983) and for social-science research by 1980 (Straus et al. 1980; Russell 1980).

Elder abuse studies, achieving recognition with Burston's 1975 article on "granny bashing," are still primarily limited to exploratory, descriptive reports (Pillemer and Wolf 1986). To date, we have no comprehensive understanding of the etiology of elder neglect and abuse, a social problem that clearly corresponds to a relatively recent sociodemographic change, i.e., the aging of the U.S. population.

Family violence research topics are indeed disparate, covering victims ranging from infants to the elderly, and covering injury that ranges from scratches or scars—physical or emotional—to death. Changes in the U.S. population as well as the emergence of social-reform movements are also disparate factors. Nonetheless, what all family violence research topics share is their connection to social forces that summon or mandate inquiry.

III. Building from Established Research Traditions

The study of family violence developed within the academic disciplines of sociology, psychology, medicine, nursing, and the law. In addition, interdisciplinary programs, especially public-health, child development, and family studies, generated query. Drawing upon established research traditions (established methods and conventions for designing research, collecting and analyzing data), the study of family violence matured methodologically at a rapid pace. Partly as a result of its sophisticated methodologies, the field of family violence:

> has some impressive research accomplishments to boast for its short tenure. In three areas, quite a bit of research has been done: (1) A great deal is known about the prevalence of various types of family violence; (2) there is a fair bit of evidence about risk factors that are associated with family violence; and (3) a substantial body of knowledge exists concerning the effects of family violence on its victims. (Finkelhor et al. 1987:13)

Currently, the social-science approach to family violence research shares at least five features with the research traditions from which it was generated. The work in this volume shows clear examples of each.

A. Quantitative and Qualitative Methods

First, we find a substantial body of what are conventionally called "quantitative" and "qualitative" research designs being applied to the study of all types of violence within families. The prototypical quantitative study (see, e.g., Straus et al. 1980; Straus and Gelles 1990) administers the survey questionnaire to a probability sample of respondents representing the general population or a specified clinical population. The exemplary qualitative study (see, e.g., Greenblat 1983) uses intensive, face-to-face interviews to ascertain the meaning and effects of abuse.

The majority of work in this volume is quantitative, either only in the data collection method used or also in the data analysis method used. Some studies are based on the straightforward counting of events, while others provide multivariate analyses of nominal and interval-level-dependent variables. Caputo's work (in Part IV), for example, counts police calls and how they are classified to calculate a referral ratio for domestic-disturbance calls. The Herzberger and Channels study (in Part I) of bail decisions in Connecticut examines the nominal-level bail vs. detention decision, as well as the interval level amount of bail decision, with a multivariate analytical model.

Gurley's research (in Part II) on social support, and the study of Connecticut's Family Violence Prevention and Response Act of 1986 by Lyon and Mace (in Part IV), are qualitative studies that depend upon the face-to-face, in-depth interview for gathering the information needed to draw inferences regarding the consequences of intentions. Lyon and Mace let the voices of those who carry out the spirit of the law critique its implementation. Gurley examines how intimates can harm and help adult women recovering from the trauma of child abuse.

B. Definitions and Conceptualizations

Second, similar to the debates characterizing the application of social-science methods to most types of research problems, we find scholars disagreeing upon the definitions and conceptualizations of what constitutes family violence. Researchers at the Centers for Disease Control, for example, argue that persons related by "emotional intimacy" should be included in the operationalization of "family" in all family violence studies. Restricting "family" members to those who fit the legal definition in any epidemiologic study will result in a substantial and biased underestimate of the problem (Saltzman et al. 1990).

These types of disagreements, over defining "family" or deciding whether spanking a child is a form of child abuse or appropriate parenting behavior, influence the research design as well as the scope of the data collected (Finkelhor et al. 1986). Straus (in Part I) illustrates this issue clearly in his discussion of the extremely different incidence estimates of child abuse that are derived from two measures—the Child Abuse 1 Measure, which includes "hitting with an object," and the Child Abuse 2 Measure, which does not include it. Are 1.5 million children physically abused each year in the United States? Or is the true annual incidence rate closer to 6.9 million? It depends on which behaviors are included and excluded in the definition of what constitutes abuse.

Variation in the conceptualization of abuse is not a problem affecting research and researchers alone. Persons working in the helping professions and those making criminal-justice system decisions need shared definitions and conceptualizations of abuse. Kromsky and Cutler (in Part II) show the necessity of communicating a definition, and the manifestation of an abstract concept, i.e., the "battered-woman syndrome," to those who must make judgments about its effects. Campbell (Part I) maintains "a beaten child should suggest to us a possible incest victim, a battered mother, and abused siblings and grandparents." An exclusively medical response to the beaten child can only be unduly inadequate, according to Campbell, because it cannot approach the whole problem. Reconceptualizing child abuse and spouse abuse is a prerequisite for the appropriate social and public-health response to the nightmare shared secretly by millions of American families.

C. Methodological Advances

Third, the study of family violence, similar to any other social-science field of study, benefits from methodological or technological advances at the data collection stage. For example, "random-digit dialing" (Sudman 1983), a relatively new innovation in sampling techniques, was used by John Murphy (in Part II) to select respondents for his research on child sexual abuse and rape in Minnesota. Stephen Webster's study of community perceptions of familial abuse (in Part I) also uses this new sampling technique to select respondents representing the general population of northeast Ohio. "Computer assisted telephone interviewing" (Karweit and Meyers 1983) is a related and recent data collection innovation that can also be applied to family violence research.

D. Designing Causal Studies

Fourth, only a handful of comprehensive studies are designed to examine the causes of family violence (see Harrenkohl et al. 1983). In this volume, Herzberger and Channels (in Part I) track criminal defendants charged with violent crimes through the early stages in the criminal-justice process to uncover the causes of disparity in bail decisions that are partly due to offender-victim relationship. The design framing research that enables the emergence of empirically-based causal explanations is expensive, difficult to achieve, yet critically important to the field of family violence.

Research designs are as frequently restrained by limited funds and the immediate need for data as they are enhanced by theoretical concerns. We see cross-sectional designs and data collection methods dominating the field, requiring authors to rely upon a conceptual or theoretical framework for developing causal explanations that can be supported, although never disproved empirically. Work by Straus and by Campbell in this volume exemplify this mode of social science.

Straus provides a multidimensional theory of violence that is based largely on the unique and the unusual characteristics of the American family. Campbell develops a theory to explain intrafamilial violence and the public-health response it induces with theoretical strands from the disciplines of sociology, psychology, medicine, and public health. Both these theories examine family violence as a function of society—its institutions and its structures. Neither is formally testable, but both indicate appropriate methods and data for increasing the plausibility of the causal theories.

E. The Influence of Theory

Fifth, the methods used to study family violence, similar to the methods used to study any other social phenomena, are influenced by the particular theoretical or conceptual perspective that guides the researcher's thinking. A dramatic and important example of this point is provided by Wardell and her colleagues (1983) as they question the "scientific" validity of wife abuse studies guided theoretically by the notion that abused women suffer from psychological pathologies. Research designed from this type of psychological perspective attempts to observe empirically the differences between "pathological" wives who are beaten and those who are not. If pathological wives are the exclusive research subject in a study of abuse, only measured attributes of the victim will be found to predict or explain wife abuse. Stated differently, research designed theoretically to blame the victim will show that "blaming the victim" (Ryan 1971) is our best scientific and empirical explanation for wife abuse. If, however, the offender, or the relationship between the victim and the offender, is the subject for empirical measurement—premised on theoretical notions concerning violence, or husband-wife relationships in contemporary American society—empirical studies can generate explanations for abuse that are not restricted to blaming the victim.

In Part IV of this volume, David Ford challenges the well-established "deterrence theory" that guides research on punishing batterers for the purpose of reducing recidivistic behavior. He dares to examine the full range of possible responses to punishment. He produces an extremely refined perspective on the effects of sanctions in response to spouse abuse.

IV. Some Departures from Established Research Traditions

Although the family violence field has built its methodologies from established research traditions, it has also confronted methodological issues that are unusual if not unique to the field.

Three are particularly noteworthy: (1) the visibility paradox of family violence research, (2) the difficulty of designing evaluation studies or impact assessments, and (3) the blurring of the distinction between basic and applied research within the field of family violence.

A. Visibility Paradox

Unlike many of the phenomena studied by social scientists, the direct observation of an incident of family violence—be it child neglect, child sexual abuse, spouse abuse, spousal rape, or elder abuse—is improbable if not impossible for the researcher. Researchers can observe a wide array of private behavior, ranging from prayer in church to sexual behavior in public restrooms. Researchers normally cannot, however, observe family violence (or acts of stranger violence such as rape or homicide). Retrospective accounts and experimental simulations, although useful for gaining insights regarding behaviors and psychological dispositions, do not compensate fully for the inability to make direct observation of the phenomena under investigation.

Whereas family violence incidents are largely *invisible* to the researcher, the publications and research monographs written by those who study family violence are among the *most visible* in the social sciences. Similar to AIDS research, "family violence research does not tend to stay hidden in obscure professional journals. It often makes front page news, and is readily championed and manipulated by advocates for various points of view" (Finkelhor et al. 1987:115).

B. The Difficulty of Designing Evaluation Studies

Studies assessing the effectiveness of a program or intervention, sometimes called impact assessments (Rossi and Freeman 1985), are desperately needed yet extremely difficult to design within the field of family violence. Establishing treatment and control groups is ethically problematic but essential for evaluation research. Moreover, a family violence problem usually involves numerous "service providers," a factor that complicates the evaluation study design.

Consider, hypothetically, research designed to assess the success of a psychotherapy program for the sexually abused child. Imagine that police arrested the perpetrator and a child protective-services unit removed the child from her home. Police, the courts, protective services, a family therapist, and two psychotherapy programs—one in which the mother participates and one in which the father is being treated—have simultaneous influences on the "treatment" program designed to help the sexually abused child, as do the child's family dynamics and the family context. Stretching the net adequately to capture all or most of the influences on the child for the purpose of measuring program impact is virtually impossible. Ignoring the multidimensional nature of such treatment, however, can only lead to an inadequate research design.

Further, the crisis nature of intervention can preclude a research design that enables the assignment of research subjects to treatment and control groups. An extreme response to an incident of family violence, such as a woman leaving her home to enter a shelter or a child being taken into protective custody, as well as an immediate response may be necessary to avert severe harm or other trauma. This particular problem is not unique to the field of family violence research. It is, however, unusual and an extremely important consideration for this often politicized and often controversial field of social-science inquiry.

The evaluation studies in this volume underscore many of the problems researchers face, as well as the ingenious approaches they take to appraise a program or process designed to heal the injury or trauma of family violence.

In their study of the outcome of a batterers' program (in Part III), Tolman and Bhosley interviewed 53% of the batterers' victims to gauge the program's effectiveness. Where are the remaining 47%? Are some too severely injured to be surveyed? Did some refuse to participate in the study because they are not affected strongly by the battering incident? Have some left their homes or their hometowns in fear? How can we judge the true effects of a program if nearly half of the individuals designated for the study are missing? The Tolman and Bhosley evaluation study is a convincing one, partly because it examines several outcome measures that pertain to familial relationships. From the empirical findings they provide, policy and program designers can estimate the need for batterers' treatment programs.

Ford's research (discussed above) on the provocative vs. deterrent effects of arrest and adjudication in domestic-violence cases illustrates the necessity of evaluating a family violence prevention program by measuring its effects *indirectly.* He relies on measuring the defendants' perceived anger and the victims' perceptions regarding violence for the analysis designed to examine empirically the effects of criminal sanctions on ensuing acts of violence.

Whitcomb's evaluation of prosecutorial innovations for adjudicating child sexual-abuse cases (in Part IV) explicates the need to develop a unique research agenda to assess the effectiveness of each state or regional program. Effective adversarial proceedings that are structured by the simultaneous goals of protecting defendant rights and avoiding or minimizing the revictimization of a child are indeed difficult to achieve. As the states' trial courts struggle to design methods for protecting the defendant and the child victim-witness, the state and federal appellate courts rule on the constitutionality of using such methods as closed-circuit television for testimony and videotaped depositions (Greenhouse 1990). Concomitantly, evaluation researchers undertake the challenge of assessing these programs validly, ethically, and—out of necessity—innovatively.

C. The Blurring of Basic- and Applied-Research Distinctions

Traditionally speaking, social scientists distinguish between basic and applied research. Basic studies are those designed and conducted for the purpose of "understanding why things are as they are" (Hunt 1985:55). Applied studies are designed and implemented for the purpose of "learning how to solve practical problems" (1985:55). Ideally, social-policy and social-program decisions "should emerge from the continual testing of ways to improve the social condition" (Rossi and Freeman 1985:34). In other words, social-policy decisions should be informed by applied-research findings.

Within the field of family violence research, the distinction between basic and applied research is, at best, blurred. All family violence research, at least implicitly, and at least potentially, speaks to policymakers and social-program designers. In this volume, Sabourin (in Part III) examines the role of verbal aggression in relationships characterized by physical violence for the purpose of developing appropriate treatment programs. The Ryan et al. study (also in Part III) contends with the dilemma of deciding which family member ought to be removed from the home in cases of child sexual abuse. Surely research on these and most other family violence problems is intended to have application. And surely research in this field must take advantage of all the resources, i.e., the best theory and the best methods that the social and health sciences can offer.

V. The Need for Systematic Data

Family violence research is visible, politicized, and conducted, at least in part, for the moral purpose of correcting a brutal social problem. Evaluation studies are very difficult to design. For these reasons, there is an urgent need to collect systematic data on family violence.

Systematic data are collected in a uniform way, on a regular basis, and by a large-scale organized system (Finkelhor et al. 1987:21). The U.S. Census, the Uniform Crime Reports (UCR; compiled annually by the Federal Bureau of Investigation), or the National Crime Survey (NCS; conducted by the Census Bureau and sponsored by the Justice Department) are preeminent examples of systematic data. Somewhat limited and otherwise problematic (Martin 1983) but unbiased, systematic data provide researchers with the information necessary to analyze such phenomena as population and crime trends, as well as possible explanations for earned personal income or various forms of crime.

Child abuse statistics are collected annually by the individual states (Finkelhor et al. 1987), and until recently were analyzed by the American Humane Association. The UCR and the NCS supposedly capture selected incidents of family violence. For example, the UCR include homicide data and assault offenses that are committed by spouses.

We currently lack systematic data on all forms of family violence. The extant systematic data, with respect to their usefulness for family violence research, are seriously limited. All three forms (state, UCR, and NCS data) exclude large numbers of cases. No systematic collection method currently being used obtains nationwide, truly uniform data on family violence. The methods all suffer from potential under- and/or overreporting problems. Further, all current forms of family violence data depend upon local police, social-service agencies, hospitals, and local interviewers to make interpretations about the nature of the case that is reported (or not reported) to a central data collection center. The resulting compilations are, to use Finkelhor's words, "a serious obstacle for the field" of family violence research (Finkelhor et al. 1987:21). (Currently, at least three proposals for developing nationwide, systematic data collection are being deliberated.) We argue that unbiased, uniformly and routinely collected family violence data are necessary to advance knowledge about family violence trends and patterns, and to examine the etiology of the various forms of injury and harm sustained by victims of family violence.

VI. Research Ethics

No study conducted within any particular subfield of family violence can avoid major ethical concerns and questions. Some are typical within the social sciences, albeit exaggerated when applied to family violence research subjects. Others are unusual if not unique to the field of family violence. Generally speaking, two types of ethical concerns require the researcher's attention: (1) minimizing the risk of potential harm resulting from, or exacerbated by, the research experience, and (2) maximizing the likelihood that consent to research at least approximates informed consent.

A. Minimizing Risks of Harm

Noble intentions notwithstanding, all social scientists who depend upon either research subjects or recorded incidents of family violence may place their source of data at risk of harm subsequent to the research process. Suppose a researcher is conducting a retrospective, structured, face-to-face interview with an adult who was a victim of child sexual abuse. The interview can trigger emotional trauma, a form of harm that we must acknowledge is associated with the research process. Suppose further that information alleging spouse abuse, which is obtained from a local social agency or court records, is inadvertently disclosed by a research assistant. As a consequence, the already abused wife endures both emotional trauma when learning about the information disclosure as well as the potential for additional physical injury. Simply stated, even in retrospective studies, or even in those instances where previously recorded information is used as research data, the victim of family violence can be put in jeopardy of *more abuse and more harm* as a result of the research process. Data collection methods requiring the individual's participation, and especially those requiring information from or observation of the victim and/or the perpetrator, compel the utmost attention to whatever means are necessary to reduce, as much as possible, the likelihood of victim harm.

The researcher, promising confidentiality, can find her/himself facing a dilemma if she/he believes she/he is aware of likely harm to the research subjects. In the field of family violence, this situation is neither hypothetical nor, should we assume, uncommon. If failing to get the help necessary to prevent violence results in harm, and if disclosing the identity of the potential victim or the offender to local officials negates an agreement of confidentiality, which course of action can the researcher take to resolve the situation in an ethical way?

For those unusual studies that are designed to measure the effectiveness of "treatment" programs—whether treatment is the arrest of batterers or psychotherapy for child victims of sexual abuse—establishing treatment and control groups under quasi-experimental or experimental conditions can be especially troublesome. Consider, for example, a comparison of the potential effects of random assignment in a spouse abuse study (Sherman and Berk 1984) to those associated with a study of parolees previously convicted for property offenses (Rossi et al. 1980). On the one hand, not receiving "treatment" to prevent battery may result in the death of a spouse. On the other hand, not receiving "treatment" for reducing the recidivistic tendencies of a thief may result in personal financial loss. Although our society can indeed tolerate the personal and social costs due to the assignment method used in a study to reduce economically motivated crimes, our society cannot and should not tolerate the costs of human life or severe physical harm that can result from random assignment for certain forms of family violence research.

Borrowing from Richard Berk's (1987) argument regarding causal inference and random assignment, we must imagine the "what if" question to decide whether the benefits from the controlled experiment outweigh the potential costs of denying treatment. Stated differently, we must form "expectations about the likely result [of treatment or its absence, i.e., we must form expectations about behavior] under two or more conditions recognizing that the comparisons are virtually impossible to observe directly" (Berk 1987:184).

All told, it is a difficult task to minimize the various forms of harm that can result from researching family violence. Harm can range from shame or embarrassment to ostracism or death. Regardless of the degree of difficulty, it is critically important for the researcher to do all that is possible to minimize harm and its threat.

B. Maximizing Informed Consent

University committees on the use of human subjects, following federal guidelines, identify certain populations, such as prison inmates or psychiatric patients, as especially vulnerable populations. Why? One explanation is that informed consent is nearly impossible among vulnerable populations. The individual prison inmate approached to participate "voluntarily" in the research program perceiving, accurately or not, that her/his decision will reduce the duration of prison time is not consenting on a truly voluntary basis. The psychiatric patient, not capable of perceiving accurately or completely the possible consequences of an experimental program, is not "informed" adequately to give informed consent.

When considering family violence research participants, the abuser is somewhat analogous to the prisoner, and the abused, especially the child, is somewhat analogous to the psychiatric patient. The voluntaristic dimension of participation and the comprehension of the research project are potentially profound problems in family violence research. They are compounded once we account for the relational nature of family violence. All forms of family violence explicitly involve at least two persons, making attempts to achieve unequivocal informed consent for all possible research participants unusually difficult if not futile.

VII. Summary

Family violence research poses challenges and problems that reflect the limitations and innovations we see in social science and health care research generally. In addition, family violence research has additional problems, especially its visibility, evaluation design limitations, the lack of systematic data, and the ethical concerns of minimizing harm and achieving informed consent.

The field of family violence needs more researchers, more funds—especially from private foundations—and more research. Methodological constraints notwithstanding, the most substantial gap in the current body of research is the lack of systematic evaluation of social policies and social programs designed to ameliorate one of our nation's worst nightmares: the pervasive acts of violence and abuse committed with shame and secrecy in the social institution we hold sacred, the family.

Chapter 2

Physical Violence in American Families: Incidence Rates, Causes, and Trends

Murray A. Straus

I. Introduction

Violence is not the exclusive property of a few cruel or mentally ill parents or spouses. It occurs in millions of "normal" families. As long as the general public and legislators perceive family violence as a problem of a few "sick" persons, however, the financial support for the effort needed to end family violence will be inadequate. In addition, the risk— almost the certainty—of serious policy errors or omissions is increased by the lack of information on incidence and prevalence rates of violence among families in general. Research findings based on clinical samples of abused children aided by child protective services or family violence victims in a battered-women's shelter are indeed necessary. However, information obtained from studies of clinical populations may not apply to other abused children or spouses.

The difference between the implications of empirical findings based on a clinical population and those based on a cross section of the general population is illustrated by research on gender differences in domestic assaults. Findings from studies conducted in shelters for battered women or from studies of police reports indicate that physical abuse of spouses is overwhelmingly an act of *male* violence. Studies of the general population, however, show that wives hit husbands about as often as husbands hit wives. Women also initiate assaults just as often as men do (Stets and Straus 1990; Straus 1989), a fact unknowable from shelter statistics or police statistics.

When men are assaulted, they are *less likely* than women to be injured (Stets and Straus 1990). The police tend to record only those abuse cases in which there is an injury. In addition, men have greater economic resources than women, and therefore do not as often need the equivalent of a battered-women's shelter. Finally, male pride in physical strength and the shame in not being able to "handle the situation" inhibits filing a complaint with the police. The high level of domestic assaults by women is critically important information for primary *prevention* (Straus 1990b; Straus and Smith 1990), although it does not appear in shelter statistics or police statistics. Victim services and treatment efforts must continue to respond to violence by men. In addition, women must be alerted to the criminality and the danger to themselves that comes from assaulting a spouse.

II. What is Violence?

The question, How much violence takes place behind the closed doors of American households? is obscured by the principle of family privacy, and by certain paradoxes regarding the family.

A. Obstacles to Perceiving Family Violence

The family is a loving and supportive group, but—paradoxically—it is an extremely violent group. That does not mean that all families are loving and supportive, nor does it mean that all families are violent. Typically, love is most likely to be experienced in the context of one's family. Similarly, violence is more likely to occur at the hands of a family member than it is at the hands of anyone else. The likelihood of a man's being assaulted by a member of his family is more than 20 times greater than by someone who is not a family member. For women, the risk is more than 200 times greater (Straus et al. 1980:49).[1]

Even though the world outside the family is less violent than the world inside the family, paradoxically, the loving and supportive aspects of the family obscure an ability to perceive the violent aspect of family life and to face up to how much violence exists.

B. Definition and Measurement of Violence

Family violence estimates vary tremendously, depending on how the problem is defined and on the method used to measure it. The definition of violence used for the research reported in this chapter is derived from Gelles and Straus (1979:554): an act carried out with the intention or perceived intention of causing physical pain or injury to another person.

There are two elements in this definition: act and intention. The first, the act, is clear. One only has to imagine a husband who aims and shoots a gun at his wife. Fortunately, most men are bad shots and usually miss. Nonetheless, the shooting is a serious act of violence, even though no one is injured. Using the act as a defining criterion of violence results in a higher incidence rate than one based only on assaults that actually result in injury.

Consider intention—the second element of the definition. Suppose a husband and wife are moving a piece of furniture. It slips and breaks the wife's toe. This is not violence as defined above, because there is no intent to cause pain or injury.

1. Acts versus Injuries.   Child protection workers and staff members working in shelters for battered women often define violence in terms of the injuries sustained. A battered child means an injured child. For some purposes, measuring violence by injuries is appropriate, e.g., if the purpose is to estimate the need for medical services. However, such a measure greatly underestimates the total number of violent incidents. Only about 5% of physically abused children and 3% of physically abused women are injured severely enough to require medical care (Stets and Straus 1990; Straus 1980). Victims are suffering, both from the psychological impact and from the physical blows, but if injury alone were used as the basis for defining and measuring intrafamily violence, the rates of child abuse and wife abuse would be very low. These rates would fail to capture over 95% of the actual cases of violence.

2. Other Aspects of Violence.   One dimension that needs to be considered in order to understand violence is whether the violent act is legitimate according to either the legal norms (a parent slapping a child, for example), or the informal norms of society. Some violence is legitimate, whereas some (slapping a spouse, for example) is illegitimate. Another dimension is whether the violence is instrumental (to coerce someone to do or not do something), or expressive (to see the other person in pain).

3. Physical Violence is not the Only Type of Abuse.   The focus of this chapter is on physical violence, which does not imply that physical assaults are the only, or even the worst, types of abuse in families. A child or a spouse can be terribly hurt by verbal assaults (Straus et al. 1989; Vissing and Straus 1990). Some children and wives are sexually assaulted (Finkelhor 1986; Finkelhor and Yllo 1985), and theft by a family member is more common than theft by a stranger (Straus and Lincoln 1985).

III. How Violent Are American Families?

The incidence rates for two types of family violence have been known for many years—physical punishment of children and murder of a family member.

A. *Physical Punishment and Murder*

Child development researchers have studied the rate of physical punishment since the 1920s. These studies leave no doubt that physical punishment is nearly universal in American society. While it may seem inappropriate to include physical punishment as violence, it is an act *intended* to cause the child a certain degree of physical pain.

The Federal Bureau of Investigation has compiled statistics for murders of family members since the 1930s. Data are also available from other nations as well. In the United States, within-family killings account for about 25% of all homicides. In Canada, the figure is about 50%, and in Denmark about 66%. These data make it clear that an individual is far more likely to be murdered by a member of one's own family than by anyone else (Straus 1986, 1988).

In Denmark, the few family homicides that do occur are a large slice of a very small pie. On the other hand, the rate of within-family homicides in the United States is low partly because the U.S. murder rate is extremely high. However, even in Denmark, where homicide has nearly been eliminated, the one place where it tends to persist is within the family.

B. *The National Family Violence Surveys*

Information about physical punishment and homicide has been available for a number of years, but little has been known about the rates of violent acts that are more serious than physical punishment, but less serious than murder. To help fill that gap, the first National Family Violence Survey was conducted in 1975 (Straus et al. 1980), based on a nationally representative sample of 2143 American couples. A second survey was conducted in 1985. A representative sample of 6002 couples was surveyed, sufficiently large to allow a 20% change between the survey years to be statistically significant. The 1985 survey corrected for certain 1975 omissions by including single parents, and separated or divorced individuals if the marriage had ended within the previous two years.

Detailed information on how the 1985 study was conducted is given elsewhere (Straus and Gelles 1990), including information showing that the sample accurately represents the U.S. adult population. Some respondents from the National Family Violence Surveys withheld information about violent incidents, and even more respondents did not recall incidents. Consequently, the figures pertaining to violence are minimum rates. The true rates of family violence are higher by some unknown amount.

C. The Conflict Tactics Scales

Both the 1975 and the 1985 National Family Violence Surveys used the Conflict Tactics Scales or CTS (Straus 1979, 1990a) to measure violence, including subscales for both minor and severe violence. The items in the minor-violence scale are pushing, grabbing, shoving, throwing something, and slapping or spanking the spouse or child. The severe-violence scale consists of items that are more likely to cause an injury that needs medical treatment: kicking, biting, punching, beating up, choking, burning, threatening with a knife or gun, and using a knife or gun.

D. Incidence Rates

Table 1 shows the violence rates from the 1985 National Family Violence Survey. These rates are discussed in detail elsewhere (Straus and Gelles 1986, 1990). Thus, only a few key items are elaborated here.

1. Marital Violence. The rates for physical assaults between partners in a married or cohabiting relationship are shown in panel A of Table 1.[2] Sixteen of every hundred couples reported a violent incident during the year of the survey. If this statistic is accurate, an estimated 8.7 million couples experienced violence that year. However, these are lower-bound estimates, and the true figure is much greater—perhaps as high as one-third of American couples in any one year [see Straus et al. (1980:34–35) for an explanation]. On the other hand, 16 per 100 may overstate the situation, because as Table 1 shows, 3.4 million incidents were "severe" assaults that carry a high risk of causing an injury, such as kicking, punching, choking, or use of weapons.

2. Prevalence Rate. In contrast to the one-year incidence rates, prevalence rates are used to indicate the proportion of couples who, *over the course of the marriage,* experienced a violent altercation. The exact figure from the 1985 survey is 30%. However, that is probably even more of an underestimate than the incidence rates are, because violent events are often forgotten, particularly if they occurred only once and a long time ago. Again, assuming that the true rate is much higher, perhaps 60% of American couples experienced at least one physical assault over the course of the marriage.

3. Gender Differences in Marital Assaults. Wife battering has been the aspect of marital violence of most public concern. Women are the major victims when physical, economic, and psychological injury are examined (Straus et al. 1980; Stets and Straus 1990). Nevertheless, the data in Table 1 show that women assault their partners as often as men assault theirs. This is a serious problem, not only because violence is morally

Table 1. 1985 National Family Violence Survey: Annual Incidence Rates for Family Violence and Estimated Number of Cases Based on These Rates

Type of intrafamily violence[a]	Rate per thousand couples or children	Number assaulted[b]
A. Violence between husband and wife		
Any violence during the year (slap, push, etc.)	161	8,700,000
Severe violence (kick, punch, stab, etc.)	63	3,400,000
Any violence by the husband	116	6,250,000
Severe violence by the husband (wife beating)	34	1,800,000
Any violence by the wife	124	6,800,000
Severe violence by the wife	48	2,600,000
B. Violence by parents: child aged 0–17		
Any hitting during the year	Near 100% for young child[c]	
Very severe violence (child abuse 1)	23	1,500,000
Severe violence (child abuse 2)	110	6,900,000
C. Violence by parents, child aged 15–17		
Any violence during the year	340	3,800,000
Very severe violence	21	235,000
Severe violence	70	800,000
D. Violence by children aged 3–17 (1975 sample)		
Any violence against a brother or sister	800	50,400,000
Severe violence against a brother or sister	530	33,800,000
Any violence against a parent	180	9,700,000
Severe violence against a parent	90	4,800,000
E. Violence by children aged 15–17 (1975 sample)		
Any violence against a brother or sister	640	7,200,000
Severe violence against a brother or sister	360	4,000,000
Any violence against a parent	100	1,100,000
Severe violence against a parent	35	400,000

[a] Rates for part A are based on the entire sample of 6,002 currently married or cohabiting couples interviewed in 1985. [*Note:* These rates differ from those in Straus and Gelles (1986) because these are computed in a way that enabled the 1985 rates to be compared with the more restricted sample and more restricted version of the CTS used in the 1975 study.] Rates for part B are based on the 1985 sample of 3,232 households with a child age 17 and under. [*Note:* These rates differ from those in Straus and Gelles (1986) for the reasons given above.] Rates for parts C and D are based on the 1975 study because data on violence by children were not collected in the 1985 survey.

[b] These figures were computed by multiplying the rates in this table by the 1984 population figures as given in the 1986 Statistical Abstract of the United States. The population figures (rounded to millions) are 54 million couples, and 63 million children aged 0–17. The number of children aged 15–17 was estimated as 11.23 million, by taking 75% of the number of aged 14–17.

[c] The rate for three-year-old children in the 1975 survey was 97%.

wrong, but because it vastly increases the risk of women being attacked in retaliation (Straus 1989).

4. Chronicity of Assaults on Women. The annual incidence rates and the marital prevalence rates indicate how many couples experience an assault. The chronicity of violence—how often the violent acts occur—is also important. Among those women who reported an incident involving a severe assault by the husband, one-third reported only one incident. However, the distribution is very skewed; the average is five assaults during the year. These are very violent couples, but they are less violent than the couples in which the female partners sought help from a battered-women's shelter. Two studies of shelter population women using the CTS have found approximately 60 assaults during the year (Giles-Sims 1983; Okun 1986).

5. Community Samples and Clinical Samples. The substantial difference in the chronicity of violence between the violent couples in the National Family Violence Survey and the frequency of violence to which women in shelters have been exposed suggests that there is not only a "clinical fallacy," but probably a "representative sample fallacy" as well (Straus 1990b). The "battered women" in this sample are not as frequently battered as the women in shelters. The average of five incidents per year among the cross section of battered women in the National Family Violence Survey suggests that it is equally hazardous to generalize from a representative sample to a clinical population.

6. Child Abuse. Panel B of Table 1 shows the rates of physical abuse of children, using two related measures of child abuse. The Child Abuse 1 measure (very severe violence) includes only those acts that are undeniably abusive: kicking, biting, punching, beating up, choking, and attacking a child with a knife or gun. Table 1 shows that 2.3%, or an estimated 1.5 million American children, were physically abused in 1985. Moreover, these attacks occurred an average of seven times (median = 3.5 times).

The Child Abuse 2 measure (severe violence) includes the same acts measured in Child Abuse 1, and in addition includes hitting with an object. The incidence of child abuse derived using this measure is 11 out of every 100 children, or an estimated 6.9 million abused children. The Child Abuse 2 statistic is almost five times greater than the Child Abuse 1 statistic. Which measure is correct?

Many people object to "hitting with an object" as a measure of abuse because it includes traditionally approved objects, such as a paddle, hairbrush, or belt. If child abuse is the use of force beyond what is normatively permitted, then this is not child abuse. On the other hand, it can be argued that such violence is no longer normatively permissible. Sweden and other European countries have made any use of physical punishment illegal, and in the United States, a national committee with that goal was formed in January 1989. The resolution of this issue may depend on research that can identify what the norms really are.

7. *Summary.* The statistics presented provide evidence that the family is preeminent in violence. The risk of assault within the family is many times greater than the risk of stranger assault. This is particularly true for women. Using the figures on assaults from the FBI, the rate of nonfamily physical assault on women is less than 20 per 100,000 women, but the rate of intrafamily severe assaults on women is about 4,000 per 100,000 women, or about 200 times greater. If one were to count all the instances in which he "slapped" her, the figure would be much higher. The puzzle remains: How can the family be both a loving and supportive group, and at the same time such a violent group?

IV. The Social Causes of Family Violence

This chapter examines only a few of the multiple social causes of family violence, not because other types of causes, especially psychological causes, are unimportant. Rather, the division of labor in science and social science and constraints of space make such limitations necessary.

A. The High Level of Conflict Inherent in Families

The first of the social causes of family violence is the inherently high level of conflict that is characteristic of families. Conflict can be observed in all human groups, but it is especially prevalent in certain types of groups, and the family is one of them. There are several reasons for this.

1. *Wide Range of Activities.* First, the family is concerned with the entire range of activities and interests of its members, the "whole person" as the phrase goes. This is what most people want and value in family relationships. The difficulty is that it means that nothing is off limits, and therefore anything can be the focus of a conflict; the greater the number of issues of mutual concern, the greater the probability of conflict.

2. *Gender and Age Differences.* The family usually consists of both men and women, both the young and the old. Differences among them, which are rooted in traditional cultural orientations as well as in the historical experience of each generation, are a potent source of conflict. To a certain extent, men and women have different values and cognitive

orientations, different conceptions of power, and different world views (Gilligan 1982). The "battle of the sexes" is built into the family, in fact, in its most acute form. The generation gap is also most acute within the family. It expresses itself in many ways, for example, in clothing styles and whether rock or Bach is going to be played on the family stereo.

3. *Shared Identity.* The rock vs. Bach example also illustrates another reason why conflict is so frequent and so severe within the family—the shared identity of family members, and the resulting intensity of involvement. In addition, there is a presumed right to influence other family members. If one spouse comments that the other one's shirt and jacket colors do not go well together, he or she usually does it out of concern for the other and because they have a "shared fate." Moreover, the comment about clashing colors is not just an abstract esthetic judgment—there is an implicit expectation that a shirt or jacket of a different color will be chosen.

4. *Involuntary Membership.* Membership in the family is, to a considerable extent, not a matter of choice. A parent cannot order children out of the home, and children cannot just leave, even though most have probably thought about doing that at one time or another. The involuntary membership therefore blocks using one of the most frequent solutions for human conflicts—leaving.

Leaving a martial relationship continues to be difficult for spouses, even in this era of high divorce rates: It is expensive; there is guilt; there are still some good things about the marriage; one must tell parents, friends, and other relatives, and, finally, there is the well-being of the children. So even when the conflict seems to be unresolvable, people stay and put up with conflict that they would otherwise stop by leaving.

5. *Family Privacy.* Another characteristic of the family that accounts partially for the high level of conflict is family privacy. Privacy insulates conflicts within the family from both social controls and social supports that can serve to reduce or resolve the conflict. For example, family members say nasty things to each other in private that they would never say in public.

6. *Conflict and Violence.* Hotaling and Straus (1980) describe a number of other characteristics of the family that engender a high level of conflict (e.g., stress, organizational features of marriage, sexist attitudes). All of these add up to produce a high level of conflict, which in turn increases the risk that one or another member of the family will try to win the conflict by hitting, or will just hit out of anger over the conflict. As the amount of conflict increases, the assault rate also increases dramatically.

B. Gender Inequality

A second major cause of family violence is gender inequality, particularly, male dominance (Straus 1977; Coleman and Straus 1986). Male dominance is manifested in many obvious and subtle ways, such as the fact that men earn more than women in the United States and that the husband is usually considered the head of the household.

The idea of the husband as the head of the household is at the root of a great many assaults on wives. It frequently means that when the couple cannot agree, the husband will have the final say. There are millions of women who believe in that principle—more women than men opposed the Equal Rights Amendment. However, sooner or later within the marriage, an issue will arise that, principle or not, is so important for the wife that her way must prevail. This is double trouble: there is the issue at hand, and, according to the husband, the wife is reneging on the implicit terms of their marriage contract.

The issue then becomes transformed into a moral question for this hypothetical man. This rationale produces moral indignation on the part of men, and provides a powerful justification for violence. In fact, most violence in the family or elsewhere is carried out for what the violent person thinks is a morally correct purpose. This happens, for example, in the stereotypical movie Western, where someone "insults my girl" and is justifiably hit on the head with a whiskey bottle. Or it is seen on the television daytime soap opera, where her husband says something outrageous and she "slaps the cad."

The direct, linear relationship found between inequality and violence in the National Family Violence Survey analysis (Straus et al. 1980:192) indicates that the greater the departure from gender equality, the greater the risk that physical force will be used to maintain the power of the dominant person.

Egalitarian couples have the lowest rates of violence, and husband-dominated couples have the highest rate of spouse abuse. As Coleman and Straus (1986) have shown, male dominance is related to violence even when the wife believes—sometimes fervently—that the husband should be the head of the family. The violence rates in wife-dominant couples are also higher than the rate in egalitarian couples, but not as high as in husband-dominant couples.[3] In addition, one has to keep in mind that there are fewer wife-dominant than husband-dominant couples.

C. Norms That Permit Intrafamily Violence

Almost all human behavior is influenced by the rules of society that specify appropriate behavior in specific situations—what anthropologists and sociologists call *cultural norms*. Every society also has its rules about violence. As with other rules, those regulating violence vary from situation to situation.

1. Violence by Parents. In American society, violence by parents is permitted, and to a certain extent required (Carson 1986). Parents not only have the legal right to hit, but they are expected to do so if the child persistently misbehaves. This right was reaffirmed when a number of states passed child abuse laws. Those statutes say that nothing in the law should be taken as denying the right of parents to use ordinary physical punishment. A certain irony exists here: legislation that was passed to protect children from assault simultaneously puts the weight of the state on the side of hitting children "when necessary."

These laws are not merely obsolete statutes. Most American parents support the use of physical punishment and almost all administer it, at least to small children. Ninety percent of the parents who participated in the National Family Violence Survey approved of physical punishment. These findings are consistent with those from two other recent national surveys (Lehman 1989).

2. Violence by Spouses. The marriage license also is a hitting license. This right was a formal part of the common law until just after the Civil War in the United States (Calvert 1974). Blackstone's (1778) definitive codification of the English common law gave husbands the right to physically "chastise" an errant wife. This rule has not been recognized by the courts for more than a century, but it has lived on de facto in the actions (and nonactions) of the police, prosecutors, and victims. Until it was changed in 1977, the training manual for domestic-disturbance calls published by the International Association of Chiefs of Police essentially recommended that hitting a spouse be treated as a "private matter" and that arrests should be avoided.

Despite the new laws passed during the 1980s, and despite increased police action, the implicit hitting license remains. The major change has been a reduction in the severity of violence that is tolerated.

The informal social norms have changed much less than the law has. Almost a third of American men and a quarter of American women perceive that it is normal for a husband or wife to slap the other "on occasion" (Straus et al. 1980:47), admittedly under very general or unspecified circumstances. If we had specifically asked whether it would be all right to slap a spouse because the dinner was not prepared correctly, the percentage of those approving would probably have dropped to near zero. Conversely, if we had asked about a wife slapping a husband if she came home and found him in bed with another woman, approval would probably increase to at least 60–70%.

Since everyone is against violence "in principle," it is often difficult to perceive that there are norms permitting violence between a couple, as the following example demonstrates. After a lecture, a prominent sociologist objected to my claim that the family is an extremely violent group. He argued that figures showing a 16% violence rate indicate that 84% are *not* violent. In response, I said that if "only" 16% of the faculty had hit other faculty members or students that year, it would be sufficient to conclude that there is *much* violence on campus. The questioner naturally rejected my conclusion. He was implicitly using a different set of norms for families than for universities. The norms of American society absolutely prohibit violence in one setting and tolerate it in the other. This is extremely important because violence, like other crimes, is more likely to occur when the offender believes that detection, arrest, or sanction is unlikely (Gelles 1983; Gelles and Straus 1988).

The distinctiveness of the cultural norm that makes the marriage license a hitting license is illustrated by a recognition that more conflict does not necessarily lead to more violence in all situations. There is a huge amount of conflict in academic departments—novels have been written about it—but neither in novels nor in real life is there physical violence. Yet physical violence occurs in 45% of high-conflict families. There are some very rare exceptions to the rule, but violence does not occur in 45% of high-conflict academic departments. An occasional slap of one professor by another would simply not be tolerated, but an occasional slap within the family is likely to be tolerated. This tolerance is a partial explanation the persistence of family violence.

D. Family Training in Violence

A limitation to the theory presented so far is that it does not explain why the norms for families permit violence, whereas the norms for other groups prohibit it. Part of the explanation lies in the fact that in the family there is a "hidden curriculum" that teaches violence. It starts in infancy with physical punishment. Over 90% of parents surveyed by the National Family Violence Survey report that they hit toddlers in the 3–4-year group (Wauchope and Straus 1990). Over 20% of the parents surveyed report hitting an infant, and approximately 33% continue hitting even when the children are aged 15–17. Again, these are lower-bound estimates, once more illuminating the notion that being hit by a parent is an almost universal experience of children in the United States.

Most of this violence is ordinary physical punishment carried out by a loving and concerned parent. A ten-month old child picks up a stick and puts it in his mouth. The parent takes it away and says, "No, no, don't do that. You'll get sick. Don't put dirty things in your mouth." Unfortunately, children crawling on the ground are almost certain to do it again! Eventually, the parent is likely to come over to the child and gently slap his hand, again saying, "No, don't do that."

The problem is that these actions also teach the child the principle that those who love you are those who hit you. This lesson starts in infancy, when the deepest layers of personality are presumably being formed. It continues for half of all American children until they physically leave home. Moreover, the principle is easily reversed to "those you love are those you can hit." Ironically, the fact that hitting is done by a loving and careful parent makes it worse. Not only do children learn that those who love you hit you, but that it is morally right for them to do so. In one pilot study we found that toddlers have a clear conception of the moral rightness of hitting. The children were shown pictures of an adult hitting a child and were asked to say what was happening. Without exception they said it was because the child in the picture had done something wrong.

The important point for understanding family violence is that this principle extends into adult life. It is a direct transfer from the script learned early in life, through physical punishment.

The hypothesis that the more physical punishment experienced as a child, the greater the probability of hitting one's spouse, was tested with data from the National Family Violence Survey. Each respondent was asked how often he/she was physically punished at about age 12 or 13. The results support the hypothesis. The more a husband was physically punished as a child, the greater was the probability he would assault his wife as an adult. The same effect of physical punishment is also found among wives (Straus 1983).

E. Violence Has Multiple Causes

As developed thus far, the family violence theory has pointed to the high level of conflict in families, the inequality between men and women, cultural norms that permit intrafamily violence, and family training in violence as the risk factors that increase the probability of violence. A number of other risk factors need to be incorporated, such as alcoholism (Kaufman-Kantor and Straus 1987), poverty, and other types of stress (Straus 1980b). The level of violence in the larger society also has a potent influence (Baron et al. 1988).

No single risk factor by itself puts a family at high risk of violence. The weakness of any one factor is illustrated by the finding that individuals who experienced frequent physical punishment as children are more than twice as likely to assault their spouse than those who did not (11 vs. 5%). At the same time, the 11% figure also indicates that 89% of spouses who *did* experience a great deal of physical punishment at age 13 did *not* assault their spouse during the year of the survey. The same type of interpretation applies to each of the other risk factors. For example, more violence occurs in male-dominant marriages, but most male-dominant marriages are not physically violent.

None of the elements in this theory (or in anyone else's theory) is by itself determinative. It takes the combined effect to produce a high probability of violence. This can be illustrated by reflecting upon some of the risk factors discussed above. Let us envision a hypothetical family in which the husband grew up experiencing a lot of physical punishment. That is one risk factor. If the wife had a similar experience, it is another risk factor. If the husband observed his parents engaging in physical fights, that adds to the risk. If he believes he ought to have the final say in family decisions, that further adds to the risk. Suppose he also drinks heavily and is unemployed and therefore under stress. In combination, these factors add up to a prescription for violence.

The statistical analysis that demonstrates this theory was conducted by creating a simple (unweighted) checklist score for each of the 2,143

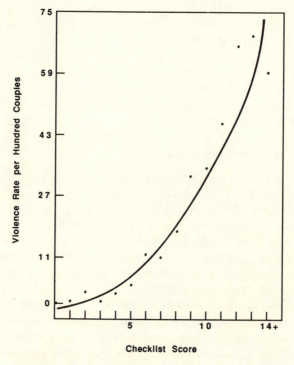

Figure 1. Couple violence rate by checklist score.

couples in the 1975 National Family Violence Survey. One point was assigned for the presence of any of the six risk factors in the example of the preceding paragraph, and also for the presence of 13 other risk factors. Figure 1 (from Straus et al. 1980:204) shows for each risk factor score group the percentage of couples who reported a violent incident during the year. The horizontal axis is the checklist or risk factor score; the vertical axis is the rate of couple violence.

As Figure 1 shows, couples with low risk factor checklist scores have a violence rate that is nearly zero. Thereafter, as the checklist scores increase, the rate of violence increases exponentially. About 70% of the couples in the highest risk categories reported a violent incident during the year. Similar results were obtained using a checklist of risk factors found to be associated with physical abuse of children (Straus et al. 1980:212). These are truly remarkable findings.[4]

V. Trends in Family Violence

One of the fortunate outcomes from the last 15 years of research on family violence is that it has revealed causal factors that, for the most part, can be changed if society is so inclined.

A. The Campaign against Child Abuse and Wife Beating

On the remedial side of the change effort, we have created a vast network of child protective services (CPS). To be sure, these services are not nearly enough, but they are far greater than what existed in 1960 when state-funded CPS departments did not even exist as a separate entity. Also, there are now about a thousand shelters for battered women in the United States. Most shelters are underfunded and inadequately staffed, but the situation is better than in 1973, when no shelters existed. Arrest and prosecution of wife batterers are now common, even though most cases are still ignored (Kaufman-Kantor and Straus 1990).

B. Changes That Help Prevent Family Violence

On the primary prevention side of the effort (Straus and Smith 1990), parent education programs have continued to grow throughout the past 50 years, even though at a snail-like pace. Gender inequality is being reduced, but at a rate that can be gauged by the fact that the wages of women with full-time employment are about a third less than men's. There has been a tremendous growth in family counseling and therapy. This has no doubt aided couples in resolving the inevitable conflicts of married life, but these services still reach only a fraction of the population, and hardly any of the low-income population, where the known incidence of wife beating is relatively high. Racial segregation is now legally dead, informal discrimination has been reduced, and there is a growing Afro-American middle class. But, there is also a growing Afro-American underclass whose situation is worse than ever. Contraception is now widespread, so there are fewer unwanted children, who are at high risk of abuse, but the United States still has the highest teen pregnancy rate of any industrial country. These and other changes have implications for violence reduction (Straus and Gelles 1986, 1990).

C. Changes in Six Measures of Violence

Clearly, the existing treatment and prevention programs leave much to be desired. Nevertheless, writing in 1981, I suggested that the cumulative effect of the changes discussed above was likely to be a reduction in the incidence of child abuse and wife beating (Straus 1981). In 1985 the second National Family Violence Survey provided an opportunity to test that idea. Somewhat to our surprise, it revealed evidence consistent with the hypothesized decrease (Straus and Gelles 1986).

Figure 2 shows the percentage change in six measures of violence from the National Family Violence Survey, and changes in two other measures of violence that occurred between 1975 and 1985.

The data on child abuse show that the rate of physical abuse of children decreased by 47% between 1975 and 1985. That decrease is exactly opposite to what has been the experience in CPS during this same period. Cases *increased* threefold between 1976 and 1985. The two figures do not contradict each other. The increased rate of cases reported to CPS is a measure of public *intervention* intended to help children. It indicates that between 1976 and 1985, three times as many Americans took the major step of reporting a suspected case of child abuse, a sign that more Americans are starting to do something to reduce this phenomenon. To the extent that those efforts are successful, this could be one of the factors that accounts for the lower rate of child abuse found in the 1985 National Family Violence Survey.

Intrafamily homicides are also plotted in Figure 2 (from Straus 1986) and show a similar decrease during this period. This consistency with the decrease in child abuse is important because homicides are the most accurate of all statistics on violence. The third largest decrease was the number of severe assaults by husbands of their wives—what is often called wife beating. Next is the rate of violent crime, as measured by the National Crime Survey (NCS), conducted each year by the U.S. Department of Justice.

None of the trend lines for other types of violence show changes large enough to be statistically significant. However, the very fact that they

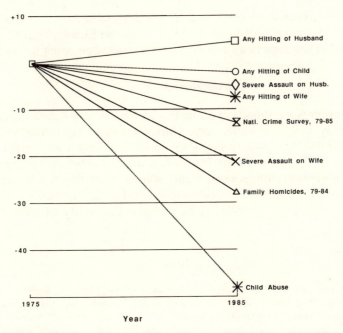

Figure 2. Percentage increase or decrease in violence rates from 1975 to 1985.

did not change much is extremely important. Part of the reason is that none of those forms of violence have been the object of the extensive and sustained effort that has been focused on child abuse and wife beating (Straus and Gelles 1986). The campaign against child abuse has been in place the longest (since the mid-1960s) and has had the most resources directed to it. The campaign against wife beating started a decade later, and has had fewer resources. Consistent with this, the rate of wife beating has declined, but not as much as the rate of child abuse has. Figure 2 shows the rate of assault by wives of husbands and the rate of physical punishment of children. Neither of these has been the object of an extensive public campaign and, consistent with that, neither has declined.[5]

Figure 2 documents impressive gains, and also many aspects of family violence for which no progress has been made. Moreover, even child abuse and wife beating—two forms of violence where large reductions seem to have occurred—remain tremendous problems. The rates for 1985 (shown in Table 1), i.e., the rates *after* the presumed decrease, indicate that more than one of six American couples engaged in a phys- ical assault during the year of the survey—an estimated total of 8.7 million couples, of which 3.4 million made severe assaults (kicking, punching, choking, attacks with weapons). Despite the large decrease in child abuse, more than one out of ten children were *severely* assaulted by a parent that year, a total of 6.9 million children. Clearly, violence is still endemic in the American family. The task ahead remains formidable.

Acknowledgments

This chapter is a publication of the Family Violence Research Program of the Family Research Laboratory, University of New Hampshire, Durham, NH 03824. A program description and publications list will be sent on request. The work of the Family Research Laboratory has been supported by grants from several organizations, including the National Institute of Mental Health (R01MN40027 and T32MN15161), a National Science Foundation (SES8520232), and the University of New Hampshire.

Notes

1.   These estimates are based on comparing the National Family Violence Survey rate with the National Crime Survey (NCS) rate. They probably exaggerate the greater risk of intrafamily assault for men because the NCS vastly underestimates assaults by intimates inside the family and by friends and acquaintances outside the family. For example, most barroom brawls and street fights that young men get into are not included in the NCS data.

2.   Table 1 combines married couples and unmarried cohabiting couples. The violence rates for the latter are much higher (Yllo and Straus 1981; Stets and Straus 1990). However, since the cohabitors are only a small part of the total, it does not importantly affect the rates shown in this table.

3.   The tendency of men in male-dominant relationships to use violence even more than do women in female-dominant relationships results from the combination of several factors. First, it is more practical for men to use physical force to back up their position because of their greater average physical size and strength. Second, male dominance is often a normatively approved type of couple relationship (Coleman and Straus 1986), whereas female dominance is rarely held to be the desirable state of affairs. Thus, when a man is challenged, he is more likely not only to be frustrated, but as noted above, also to have the moral indignation that is typically used to justify violence. Third, male values in American society make men more amenable to the use of force to achieve some desirable end.

4.   However, the 70% violent figure conversely means that 30% of those with a larger number of risk factors were not violent. This is partly because of the inevitability of measurement error, and partly because the risk factors included in the figure represent a test of a theory concerning the social causes of family violence. If psychological factors had also been included among the risk factors, the prediction of violence might have been even greater.

5.   In addition to the public campaigns and provision of services for children and battered women, many other changes in American society between 1975 and 1985 probably also contributed to the decrease in child abuse and wife beating. These are discussed in Straus and Gelles (1986).

Chapter 3

Public-Health Conceptions of Family Abuse

Jacquelyn C. Campbell

I. Introduction

In 1985, the U.S. Surgeon General gathered a group of experts to make recommendations to the nation on violence and public health (Koop 1986). Since that time, awareness of interpersonal violence as a health care problem, not just as a criminal-justice issue, has increased.

We have realized that the long-term answers to family violence are found in prevention efforts, rather than in curative or punitive reactions. The efforts to prevent violence must be initiated before the problem starts or immediately following early detection and intervention (Mercy and O'Carroll 1988). The helping professions need to take responsibility for these proactive efforts. This approach requires social-system change—change within the health care system and within the American social system at large.

In this chapter, I summarize health care system research on family violence. I present theoretical premises that explain why health care professionals and other professionals tend to respond to family violence in certain ways. Using data from a longitudinal study of battered women, I illustrate how family members respond to violence in a normative framework. And I conclude the chapter with suggestions for how the health care system can be helpful to violent families.

II. Health Care System Successes and Failures

The health care system brought the problem of child abuse to the public's attention. Helfer and Kempe (1976) not only documented the magnitude of the problem and its presenting characteristics, but initiated the efforts for mandatory reporting and health care education pertaining to child abuse.

35

One major contribution from public health research is the description of the types and patterns of physical injuries associated with abused children (Kempe and Helfer 1980), battered women (Stark et al. 1981), and abused elders. The injuries sustained by abused children have received the most intense scrutiny in an effort to help medical personnel distinguish abuse from various types of accidents. A characteristic pattern of proximal injuries—especially to the head, neck/face/throat, trunk, and sexual organs—became clear from record review studies in abuse cases of all ages (Pahl 1979). For all groups, sexual abuse frequently accompanied physical abuse. This is best documented in battered-women studies (Campbell 1989b; Finkelhor and Yllo 1982; Shields and Hanneke 1983; Russell 1982). All survivors of family violence tend to have injuries at multiple sites, in various stages of healing.

Researchers find that victims of family violence also manifest a wide range of physical symptoms that are not obviously related to family violence injuries—such as headaches, menstrual problems, chronic pain, and digestive and sleeping disturbances (Briere and Runtz 1987; Campbell 1989a; Conte and Schuerman 1987; Goldberg and Tomlanovich 1984; Hilberman and Munson 1978; Stark et al. 1981; Walker 1979, 1984a); for children specifically encopresis and enuresis (bowel and bladder incontinence) have also been identified (Newberger and Bourne 1978). High levels of communicable diseases have been documented by studies on shelters for battered women and their children (Hollencamp and Attala 1986).

Most authors have characterized these kinds of symptoms as evidence of psychopathology, even though similar symptoms are described in studies of survivors of rape and other violence, as well as in studies of widows and divorcees (Burgess and Holmstrom 1974; Kitson et al. 1980, 1982; Parkes and Brown 1972). Few analysts have considered the possibilities of old injuries causing such symptoms as headaches and other forms of chronic pain. And even fewer have considered the effects of stress on the immune system, which has been documented in studies of the effects of marital disruption (Kiecolt-Glaser et al. 1987). Rather than being conceptualized as hysterical or psychosomatic, such symptoms can be considered a part of a normative physical stress reaction. Such responses to stress are common to those who have experienced emotional trauma, e.g., physical attack by a stranger or a disruption of strong attachment bonds.

A. Failures in Recognizing, Reporting, and Intervening

Health care professionals—in fact, most professionals—tend to think of child abuse as an isolated phenomenon rather than as a part of more pervasive dynamics. Too often we fail to recognize that a beaten child should suggest to us a possible incest victim, a battered mother, and abused siblings and grandparents within the family. The child represents to us a potential future child or wife abuser if a careful and long-term intervention is not implemented for that child.

Recognizing and reporting elder abuse presents other difficulties. Phillips and Rempusheski (1985) examined nurses' decisions to report elder abuse cases. The nurses attempted to consider numerous factors regarding elder abuse. They considered the difficulties of establishing elder abuse, and the emotional trauma of the abuse, as well as the trauma of placing elders in a nursing home. Most difficult of all, the nurses tried to balance the elders' stated wishes (usually not to report) with their concerns for the elders' safety and well-being. All told, the nurses' decisions are very problematic.

Reporting any abusive incident can be limited to filling out the appropriate forms and sending them to the appropriate agency, but it ideally takes the form of insistent, persuasive, personal, and repeated reporting. Health care professionals must work *with* protective services. Empirical evidence supports the contention that when resources are sufficient to respond to all reports, protective services achieve impressive substantiation rates (Knudsen 1988). Health care professionals must also communicate their intention to report so that the family can trust the health care professional as well as the protective workers.

B. Spouse Abuse and Incest

The failure of the health care system to assess systematically the extent of wife abuse and incest is well documented. An important study of an inner-city emergency department was completed in Detroit (Goldberg and Tomlanovich 1984). Researchers found that 22% of all adult patients were there because they had experienced violence in their primary, most intimate relationship, and most of those persons were at the hospital for a medical complaint rather than trauma. The majority of patients stated that they would have liked to have services related to the violence (e.g., referrals, counseling). However, they also stated that they had *not* been asked about abuse. Hospital chart review studies also show that battering is generally not discussed, even when the pattern of injuries is clearly indicative of interpersonal violence (Stark et al. 1979).

When emergency personnel are trained to recognize and inquire about possible battering, the number of emergency patients diagnosed as battered rises dramatically, as documented in at least two recent studies (McLeer and Anwar 1989; Tilden and Shepherd 1987). However, a study conducted in a major hospital in Pennsylvania found that two years after training, workers' identification of battery victims decreased to close to pretraining levels (Kurz and Stark 1989). Surely we cannot

conclude that family violence decreased in the city. Rather, we must look
to the ongoing health care system problems. Just as simply "teaching"
an abusive parent realistic developmental expectations for a child does
not change the parent's perception of her/his own child, a health care
professional just knowing the facts is not enough to change perma-
nently the reporting practices within the health care system.

C. Attitudes of Professionals

A series of studies of health care professionals' attitudes about battered women (Davis and Carlson 1981; Rose and Saunders 1986; Shipley
and Sylvester 1982) helps us understand the lack of reporting. Frequently, health care professionals accept the myths about battered wom-
en and blame them for remaining in the relationship.

Although health care professionals do not blame survivors for their
victimization, there is dislike for certain behaviors. Health care providers are "unhappy" with sexual-abuse survivors within and outside
the family who do not resist "enough." Even professionals find it difficult to comprehend how it is possible for the abused child to want to
return to abusive parents. We also tend to be angry when abusive parents have another baby after the abused child has been removed. We do
not recognize that the parents are acting out of very normal grief for the
loss of the child. Battered women who do not leave their abusers are
especially suspect. Kurz (1987) published a classic study that describes
the subtle blaming of and distancing from battered women that goes on
in the emergency department. Stark et al. (1979) have enlightened us
about the labeling, the inappropriate treatment, and the lack of referral
that all too often affect battered women.

III. Theoretical Perspectives

Health care professionals are neither evil nor ignorant. What happens
to them when confronted by family violence? Three theoretical perspectives are helpful for understanding the response of professionals to family violence. Each offers a potential explanation for the inadequate response to family abuse that we observe among numerous health care
professionals.

A. Just-World Hypothesis

The just-world hypothesis was first advanced by Lerner and Simmons
(1966), who suggested that individuals tend to believe basically that
good things happen to good people and bad things happen to bad

people. This belief helps make ours a safer and less frightening world, because we think of ourselves as basically good and therefore protected. If a person has been victimized by family violence, a horrible thing to contemplate, we have a need to make some sense of that fact. We prefer not to see the horrible thing in the first place. This lack of recognition or denial is based on fear and a sense of powerlessness. When family violence is unmistakable, however, we need to figure out why that particular person is victimized. If bad things happen to bad people, then the person must have done something wrong.

B. Blaming the Victim

Blaming the victim for the victimization is easy when the victim is of a certain type—against which we feel biased already. It is easier for us to blame and distance ourselves from women or minority group members, for example; we may be already biased against those segments of the population. Conversely, the more the person reminds us of ourselves, the harder it is to recognize fault, or even the violence at all. White middle-class health care professionals are not likely to recognize an abused, white middle-class victim.

William Ryan (1971) articulated this process in his classic *Blaming the Victim*. Ryan's contribution helps us understand how victim blaming precludes blaming the system in which this violence is perpetuated. If the battered woman is to blame for tolerating the violence against her, then our society is less at fault for perpetuating the notions that power, aggression, and dominance are the marks of a successful man and a successful nation. We do not need to worry about a society that tolerates the abuse of children—we say that abused adolescents provoke violent behavior from their parents.

Consider another example—the "collusive" mother—the family member who has somehow always been considered the most despicable in incest cases. In spite of research evidence to the contrary (e.g., Faller 1988), health care professionals remain eager to uncover the mother's role in the sexual abuse of her daughter. The child may not be blamed, but another female family member is denigrated. There is only an inadequate understanding of normal maternal responses to a horrible dilemma.

C. Labeling

The third perspective, borrowed from deviance theories, is especially relevant to researchers and those in the helping professions. The labeling perspective articulated by Schur (1980) helps us understand how making survivors or perpetrators of family violence into objects to be studied or neatly diagnosed phenomena helps us further distance ourselves from the victims. Consider the implications of the diagnosis "battered-woman syndrome," which has been suggested by some medical experts for all abused wives. Other experts are equally concerned about diagnosing and labeling sexual-abuse survivors (Briere and Runtz 1987; Conte and Schuerman 1987). If an individual, by virtue of having been abused some time in the past, is labeled with an official medical or psychiatric diagnosis, the assumption of "pathology" becomes concrete. The family violence survivor is officially "sick" and the onus of responsibility is on the sick to become well. Responses to trauma become "symptoms" rather than the survival strategies or normative reactions. Family violence survivors become a "deviant group," to be studied and "fixed" (Loseke and Cahill 1984). The abuser and true cause of trauma remain undiagnosed.

The Finkelhor and Pillemer (1988) research conducted in Boston indicates that the largest group of abused elders are battered women grown old. The deviant-group approach labels these women as pathological for staying in the marriage as long as they did, rather than looking at the social forces that kept them there. As Wardell and associates (1983) have pointed out, researchers are trained to compare the group under study with "normal" groups on all the measures hypothesized to uncover differences. Researchers publish the observed differences, rarely if ever the similarities, and the resulting literature begets long lists of "characteristics" that label battered women, violent families, incest survivors— all of which serve to make the victims seem more deviant, more different, less like "us."

IV. Reframing Research

Health care professionals and researchers struggle to comprehend fully the behavior of family violence survivors, especially in terms of their continued attachment to the abuser. Why does a battered woman stay in the abusive relationship? To ask this question implies that she should leave rather than stay. A battered woman is in most danger of being killed by her partner when she leaves (Campbell 1981; Hart 1988). Furthermore, my own longitudinal study and Bowker's (1983) research have documented the variety of strategies used by some battered women to end the violence and maintain their relationships.

In cases where the violence does not end, it is normal and healthy for a battered woman to consider the whole tapestry of her existence and her significant others over a long period of time before ending her most important attachment relationship (Campbell 1989b; Landenburger 1988). Constraints that make leaving difficult include cultural sanctions (Torres 1987), an intense attachment to the abuser (Strube and Barbour 1983), and the lack of financial and other resources (Pagelow 1981; Strube and Barbour 1983). Gilligan's (1982) research shows that the process by which women make moral decisions involves weighing more heavily the consequences that affect others than the consequences that affect themselves. Thus, we see concern for her children to be a major issue in the woman's decision making (Lichtenstein 1981). Yet the majority of battered women do *not* stay in abusive relationships. In my study of battered women, two-thirds of those who returned for a second interview had either left the abusive relationship or had been successful in ending the violence. Okun's (1986) research also suggests that the majority of abused women eventually leave their relationship if it remains continuously violent. In both studies the pattern of leaving and returning many times before making a final break was observed. Rather than interpreting this behavior as a sign of weakness (e.g., Giles-Sims 1983), it can be viewed as a normal behavioral pattern, influenced by the quality of social support and assistance the woman receives (Bowker 1983; McKenna 1987). The leaving and returning is purposeful, intended to (1) pressure the abuser into meaningful change, (2) test external and internal resources, (3) evaluate how the children respond to the absence of their father.

Similarly long processes of dissolution of attachment relationships have been observed by researchers studying spouses of alcoholics (Jackson 1954; Lemert 1960), divorced and separated women (Hackney and Ribordy 1980; Hamen 1982; Weiss 1975), and persons experiencing anticipatory grief (Kubler-Ross 1969; Marris 1974). A grieving framework is useful for explaining some of the responses, including denial, a response frequently articulated by battered women (e.g., Ferraro and Johnson 1983). This coping mechanism has been renamed "forgetting and minimizing" by Kelly (1989) in her exploration of responses to sexual violence (rape, incest, and battering). The women in Kelly's study saw this response as being generally very useful, rather than problematic, as often implied by researchers.

An examination of clinical reports uncovers the reluctance of abused children and elderly family members to leave their families. Erroneously, some health care professionals perceive this response as pathological rather than normal. Merely realizing the normal grief and realistic fear—of foster homes for the children and nursing homes for the elders—makes these responses seem understandable and even healthy.

A. Social Isolation

In child abuse literature, social isolation is theorized as a causative factor of family violence. Violent family members, however, may be purposely keeping the family isolated in order to hide the abuse. This theme is clearly described in studies of wife abuse, wherein abusive husbands forbade their wives access to various helping agencies (Okun 1986). A woman who participated in my research was told by her battering partner to terminate the visits of a public-health nurse. The nurse had been assigned the family due to its high risk for child abuse. The abusive husband convinced the neighbors to watch for the nurse and any other visitors while he was at work, explaining that he did not want people meddling in his private business. This exemplifies clearly an induced isolation.

The pattern of isolation may also be in response to a judgmental support network that has been approached for assistance, but found unhelpful (Hoff 1984). Bowker (1983) discerns a pattern of battered women trying first an informal support network for help with the violence, but later turning to a more formal network, such as police, lawyers, and shelters.

B. Psychological Responses to Battering

More empirical work has been completed on the psychological responses to abuse in battered women than in either child abuse or elder abuse survivors. The body of literature on emotional responses to incest is generally cast in terms of long-delayed responses, rather than immediate ones. The psychological responses that are described and explored most frequently in the research literature include the cognitive responses of attributions and problem-solving abilities, and the emotional responses of lowered self-esteem and depression. Psychological difficulties are assumed to be an effect of violence for survivors of child abuse. This cause-and-effect sequence was established empirically in research on battered women outside the mental-health system (Hoff 1984; Rounsaville 1978).

C. Attributions

The cognitive formulations used to explain events predict long-term outcomes in a variety of situations. Frieze (1979) was the first to extend this approach to the study of battered women. She found that her respondents tended to respond initially to battering with an internal attribution of causality. As the abuse continued, these women focused on external attributions, a finding replicated by Giles-Sims (1983). As time passed, the battered women (as described by Miller and Porter 1983) blamed themselves less for causing the violence but more for allowing the abuse to continue. However, in opposition to much of the descriptive work of battered women, only a minority (approximately 20%) of the women in either the Frieze or Campbell (1989a) studies actually blamed themselves for the abuse occurring. In contrast, the Jehu (1989) study of a clinical sample of victims reports that the majority of adult survivors of repeated childhood sexual abuse by a person known to them blamed themselves.

Some analysts argue that internal attributions (self-blame) may either be adaptive for survivors of violence as a way of maintaining control over their lives (Miller and Porter 1983) or contributory to chronic learned helplessness (Abramson et al. 1978). Research to date has not been definitive, concerning either battered women or other survivors of family violence. However, we do know that there is insufficient evidence to assume that self-blame is either widespread among survivors of family violence or always pathological (Conte 1985).

D. Problem-Solving Techniques

Both descriptive studies (Hilberman and Munson 1978; Walker 1979) and those using paper and pencil vignettes (Claerhout et al. 1982; Launius and Jensen 1987) find that battered women manifest trouble in problem solving. Academic difficulties have also been reported in studies of abused children (Conte and Schuerman 1987; Hoffman-Plotkin and Twentyman 1984). Finn (1985) compared coping strategies of 56 battered women with instrumental norms and found battered women are significantly less likely than others to use three active coping methods (social support, reframing and spiritual support). However, Finn fails to consider

1. the possibility of the batterer enforcing isolation (Okun 1986),
2. the avoidance of nonsupportive network members can be adaptive (McKenna 1987),
3. reframing may minimize the physical danger and may therefore not be useful in a battering situation (Edleson and Brygger 1986), and
4. battered women often report clergy to be unhelpful (Dobash and Dobash 1979).

It is interesting to note that the Finn study turned up no significant difference between groups on the fourth coping mechanism measured, i.e., mobilizing to acquire and accept help.

In contrast, other researchers describe a variety of approaches used and a variety of factors considered by battered women—clearly suggestive of appropriate decision making (e.g. Bowker 1982; Dobash and Dobash 1979; Frieze 1979). In my study, the battered women ($N = 97$) had thought of or attempted significantly more solutions to their relationship problems than the control group of women ($N = 96$), who were not abused but were also having problems in an intimate relationship (Campbell 1989a).

Undoubtedly, some battered women, children, and elders are so frequently and so severely beaten and controlled that their ability to solve problems is severely and chronically affected. Techniques of coercive control by batterers are described clearly by Okun (1986). This extreme difficulty in problem solving could be explained by the "post–traumatic stress disorder," identified by the American Psychiatric Association (1987) to include symptoms of memory impairment or trouble concentrating. However, this response seems to be at the extreme end of a continuum—a conclusion supported by the empirical association between severe intellectual difficulties and severe abuse among children (Dietrich et al. 1983). Yet problem-solving difficulties have also been noted in widows and divorcees, in which case they were explained as normative responses to loss (Berman and Turk 1981; Glick et al. 1974). Such problems could also be explained as one of the deficits of learned helplessness or as one of the cognitive aspects of depression.

E. Depression

Depression has been observed clinically and derived by the use of research instruments in many studies of battered women, adult survivors of incest, and abused children (Briere and Runtz 1987; Conte 1985; Hilberman and Munson 1978; Murphy et al. 1988; Rounsaville 1978; Walker 1984a; Wolfe and Mosk 1983). Depression is also apparent among survivors of other forms of violence, and among divorcees and widows (Berman and Turk 1981; Bowlby 1980; Janoff-Bulman and Frieze 1983). Interestingly, depression is found disproportionately often among young, unemployed, and divorced women in the population at large (Radloff 1980). Since battered women and adult incest survivors are also found most often in these sociodemographic groups, it is difficult to make conclusions about whether depression in adult female survivors of family violence stems from abuse or from other factors. Walker (1979, 1984b) advanced *learned helplessness* as a theoretical concept to explain depression in battered women. Although her subsequent research generally supports the theoretical model, Walker also finds that women who had left the abusive relationship scored higher on the depression measure than those still living with the batterer. This ostensibly anomalous finding may indicate a problem with Walker's assumption that battered women remaining in the abusive relationship exhibited learned helplessness. Perhaps the depression experienced by the women who left was a result of grief rather than learned helplessness.

In my study, I compared the learned-helplessness model with the grief model (Campbell 1989a) in a multivariate analysis. I found that both models were equally applicable to battered women, but both left almost half the variance unexplained. This considerable variance unaccounted for may be a result of these models failing to consider more than the individual's situation. The wider contextual influences that contribute to both healthy and unhealthy responses to violence are seldom systematically included. Furthermore, only a small minority of the battered women exhibited all aspects of the syndrome of learned helplessness—depression, low self-esteem, apathy, and difficulty in problem solving.

F. Self-Esteem

Descriptive and qualitative studies of battered women (e.g., Lichtenstein 1981; Walker 1979) and incest survivors consistently mention low self-esteem as a characteristic of these populations. One study, however, did not. Kelly (1989) reported that a greater proportion of the incest and battering survivors in her qualitative study felt more independent and stronger—rather than "insecure-in-self"—as a result of the abuse.

Studies using depression measurement instruments rather than clinical descriptions or interviews have also generated conflicting results. Methodological differences, including different measurement instruments and different sampling designs, may account for the contradictions. The majority of studies have found battered women and adult survivors of childhood sexual abuse to score lower than nonabused persons on the same instrument that measures self-esteem or ego strength (Briere and Runtz 1987; Campbell 1989a; Drake 1985; Mahon 1981; Rosewater 1988; Star 1980). However, Arndt (1981) found nonsignificant differences between groups of battered women and others. Walker (1984a) reported that battered women scored higher than a sample of "normal" women on an investigator-developed self-esteem instrument, but this was the only study to find a difference in that direction.

In order to resolve these kinds of discrepancies, researchers attempt to make comparisons that control for responses to the other emotional issues inherent in family violence. The purpose for the comparison is to identify precisely those responses that are explicitly connected to violence. Thus, many researchers are accepting the notion that an appropriate comparison group for intimate partners experiencing violence is other couples in marital discord (Goldstein and Rosenbaum 1985) rather than normative groups. Using this kind of approach, I found no significant difference in mean levels of self-esteem in may comparison of battered women with other women who considered leaving an intimate relationship, even though both groups were below instrument norms (Campbell 1989a). Similarly, DiPietro (1987) found no significant difference in measures of self-esteem among incest survivors and among other young women in treatment for various family problems.

Low self-esteem is assumed to be a characteristic of battered women and other survivors of family violence in the literature on the subject that is not based on empirical research. Yet the actual evidence is clouded by methodological issues and a failure to take contextual variations into account. For instance, both the Shields and Hanneke (1983) and Campbell (1989b) studies found sexual abuse to have a direct, detrimental effect on battered women's self-esteem, independent of severity and frequency of physical beatings.

In summary, the research on the responses to family violence can be interpreted as a mere compilation of the ways in which a certain group of people manifest "sickness" and what makes them "more sick" than others. Or, the responses can be seen as how normal people respond to an extreme physical and emotional trauma, and yet are able to survive. Gondolf and Fisher (1988) and Landenburger (1988) take this approach when documenting survivor mechanisms and a recovering process from abuse.

V. Summary and Conclusions

There is a great deal that we are beginning to know about family violence. We in the health care system, in the criminal-justice system, and in the other helping professions are beginning to recognize and own the problem. We are having some trouble dealing with the horrible realities, the betrayal inherent in violence by one who is supposed to love, added to the physical and emotional brutality. We tend to distance ourselves from the survivors so that we don't have to feel as frightened and as responsible as a society.

Yet there is a new approach we can try that may help. We can try to catch the violence early, before it becomes an escalating pattern with devastating consequences. That entails asking about violence, whatever the context in which we see people, and dealing with it in a way that makes it clear we see society and perpetrators to blame, not the survivors. We also can think of victims as survivors, as healthy until proven otherwise, as strong and resourceful and read to resolve the problem if given respect and facilitation. We can see them as really just like us—behaving just like we would in a similar situation.

Those of us who are researchers need to document those strengths, to look carefully for what works in families, what makes the majority of the poorest families in the inner city not substance abusers or people abusers (Gelles and Straus 1988). Then we can build on what works. All of us can work for system and societal change, so that we reward those who are kind and gentle. This optimism can be called naive and idealistic in today's hard world. Yet we can see the differences in attitudes toward smoking that have emerged in recent years. The change hasn't affected everyone's life yet, but we are a long way from where we were ten years ago. We can do it with family violence, too.

Chapter 4

Variations in Defining Family Mistreatment: A Community Survey

Stephen W. Webster

I. Introduction

Lay persons in the community constitute a major source of reported cases of child abuse, wife battering, and the mistreatment of elderly family members (American Humane Association 1984). Thus, community definitions of family mistreatment are important for an understanding of the dual problems of unsubstantiated reports—which mislabel abuse—as well as the failure to report suspected mistreatment.

The earlier research on family mistreatment concentrated on professional definitions of child abuse (Giovannoni and Becerra 1979; Snyder and Newburger 1986; O'Toole et al. 1987). Moreover, the limited research on community definitions is largely limited to perceptions of child abuse (Gil and Noble 1969; Giovanonni and Becerra 1979; Finkelhor 1984). Little research has been conducted on community definitions of family mistreatment when elderly persons or spouses are the victims.

The research presented in this chapter uses a community-based survey designed to measure definitions of family mistreatment across four victim types, the influences of five interrelated dimensions of mistreatment—seriousness, intent, inappropriateness, physical harm, and psychological harm—and the respondents' perceived likelihood of reporting family mistreatment to the appropriate authorities. Specifically, it addresses the following questions:

1. Do community definitions or potential reporting behaviors vary across four victim types (child, elderly, husband, wife)?
2. Are community definitions or potential reporting behaviors associated with the sociodemographic characteristics of the respondents?

3.   How are community definitions of family mistreatment associated with potential reporting behaviors?

II. Defining Family Mistreatment

Definitions of family mistreatment share a level of ambiguity common to other types of deviance, such as criminal behavior or mental illness. To reduce the potential for ambiguity in definitions across victim types, several dimensions of family mistreatment must be considered.

Numerous factors, such as the perceived legitimacy of the incident, the instrumentality of the abuse, the intent to harm, the consequences of the abuse (physical vs. psychological, mild vs. severe), and the seriousness of an abusive incident, are important dimensions used by lay respondents when defining family mistreatment (Steinmetz 1977; Gelles and Straus 1979; Borkowski et al.1983; Finkelhor 1984; Utech 1987). Indicators of these various dimensions are measured in this study, which is designed to reflect community definitions of family mistreatment.

A. Variations by Victim Type

Mistreatment of family members is not viewed as a generic problem, but rather in terms of different types according to the status of the victim. As Finkelhor states, "each problem has its separate set of agencies, separate set of theories, and separate history of how it was 'discovered'" (1983b:17). This diversification and specialization has generated distinct bodies of research that are limited to a single victim type. However, O'Toole and Webster (1988) report that respondents alter their definitions of family mistreatment according to victim type; comparable behaviors are judged to be most serious for children, closely followed by the elderly, wives, and husbands. Finkelhor (1983b) suggests that judgments of seriousness are associated with both the victim's level of dependence and the victim's lack of power within the family. This indicates the importance of the structure and function of the family in shaping definitions of family mistreatment.

B. Variations by Respondent Characteristics

Most of the research on community definitions of family mistreatment is limited to investigations of child abuse (Giovanonni and Becerra 1979; Finkelhor 1984). Some researchers indicate that definitions vary by sociodemographic characteristics of respondents, especially education, income, social class, ethnic background, and gender. Others (Steinmetz 1977; Gelles and Straus 1979; Finkelhor 1983; Utech 1987) suggest that respondents who share common family norms share common definitions of family mistreatment.

C. Reporting Family Mistreatment

Knowledge about the criteria lay respondents use to define family mistreatment is crucial, but information regarding the probability of a respondent reporting the behavior is also crucial for understanding the problems of under- and overreporting. Empirical studies (e.g., Borkowski et al. 1983; Finkelhor 1984) indicate that many of the information dimensions that are used in identification are also relevant to reporting. Reporting behavior for family mistreatment appears to vary with sociodemographic characteristics of the respondents, as it does for other forms of deviant and nondeviant behavior.

III. Research Methods

A survey of adult residents in two northeast Ohio counties was conducted using telephone interviews. A random sample was drawn using a random-digit dialing method to select households. The adult whose birthday was closest to July 4 was asked to participate in the survey. Respondents provided background information—their age, sex, marital status, number of children, education, occupation, income, and religious affiliation.

Using a modified factorial survey design in which examples of family mistreatment were described along with different perpetrator and victim types, the interviewer read twenty randomly selected vignettes derived from Giovannoni and Becerra (1979). The respondent was asked to judge each vignette on six different scales: seriousness, inappropriateness, intent to harm, extent of physical harm, extent of psychological harm, and the likelihood of reporting the behavior to the appropriate authorities. Each scale was read as a semantic differential scale scored from 1 to 9. This scaling allows comparability to previous ratings of many of the same vignettes (Garrett and Rossi 1978; Giovannoni and Becerra 1979; Misener 1986; O'Toole and Webster 1988). An example is provided in Figure 1.

This procedure allows analysis of the effects of type of behavior, severity, and victim/perpetrator characteristics, without the need for each respondent to rate a large number of vignettes containing all possible combinations of factors.

The vignettes chosen reflect behaviors of varying severity across eight categories of family mistreatment: physical abuse, sexual abuse, emo-

Least serious	1	2	3	4	5	6	7	8	9	Most serious
Appropriate behavior	1	2	3	4	5	6	7	8	9	Inappropriate behavior
Accidental	1	2	3	4	5	6	7	8	9	Intentional
Mild physical harm	1	2	3	4	5	6	7	8	9	Severe physical harm
Mild psychological harm	1	2	3	4	5	6	7	8	9	Severe psychological harm
Unlikely to report	1	2	3	4	5	6	7	8	9	Likely to report

Figure 1. Vignette: The parent hit the child with a stick.

tional abuse, medical neglect, nutritional neglect, supervision, cleanliness, and housing, each of which is relevant to all four victim types—child, elderly, husband, wife. A complete listing of the vignettes is given in the appendix.

For the elderly parent as victim, respondents were told that the vignettes describe a 70-year-old parent and the son or daughter. For the child as victim, the respondents were told that the vignettes describe a seven-year-old child. This allows comparability with previous research and standardizes the characteristics of the perpetrator and victim, which affect definitions of mistreatment.

Pretesting indicated that most respondents rated 20 vignettes in about 15 minutes; thus, six versions of the interview schedule were constructed to cover all 96 possible vignette combinations (three vignettes each, for eight categories of abuse/neglect, across four victim types).

The sociodemographic profile of the survey respondents suggests it is typical for the geographical region. The respondents are middle-aged (about 50% are between 30 and 50 years of age), married (56%), Protestant (48%), raised in a small town or medium-sized city (52%), have two children (56% have between one and three children), and family incomes between $20,000 and $30,000 (28%). The respondent sample, relative to the general population, has a disproportionate number of women (72%), and a slightly higher level of educational attainment (average of 14 years). These latter two characteristics were unexpected given the random selection procedure used. Generalizations are qualified by these limitations.

IV. Findings

A. Variations by Victim Type

The first research question focuses on variation in judgments of seriousness, inappropriateness, intent, physical and psychological harm, and the likelihood of reporting across the victim types. Table 1 summarizes the responses to the six semantic differential scales averaged across

Table 1. Mean Semantic Differential Scores Averaged Across All 20 Vignettes

	Child	Elderly	Husband	Wife
Seriousness	7.90	7.92	5.85	6.71
(S.D.)	(.97)	(1.2)	(2.07)	(1.86)
Inappropriateness	8.24	8.20	6.84	7.23
(S.D.)	(.83)	(1.08)	(1.79)	(1.75)
Intent	7.73	7.98	7.29	7.10
(S.D.)	(1.29)	(1.20)	(1.62)	(1.67)
Physical harm	6.76	7.12	5.24	6.13
(S.D.)	(1.55)	(1.65)	(1.99)	(1.80)
Psychological harm	7.52	7.74	5.90	6.37
(S.D.)	(1.23)	(1.33)	(2.01)	(1.93)
Likelihood of reporting	6.29	6.48	3.90	4.70
(S.D.)	(1.96)	(2.22)	(2.20)	(2.28)

all vignettes relevant to a particular victim type. As with earlier studies, average aggregate responses are skewed toward the high end of the five dimensions of family mistreatment. The perceived likelihood of reporting, however, generates responses that cluster toward the middle of the scale. The highest aggregate averages are for perceived intent and for inappropriateness of the behavior described in the vignettes. The lowest average score is for the likelihood of reporting the behavior to authorities.

In comparing scores, the general pattern is that aggregate scores are highest for elderly parents as victims, followed by child as victim, and then wife. Husband as victim elicits the lowest average rating. Exceptions to this pattern are for inappropriateness, where the average aggregate score for child as victim is higher than that of elderly parent, and for intent, where the average aggregate score for husband as victim is higher than for wife as victim. This pattern suggests that comparable abusive or neglectful behaviors are perceived by respondents as being *more inappropriate* when they involve children as compared to the elderly, and *more intentional* if the husband, rather than the wife, is the victim. All differences in average aggregate scale scores between victim groups are statistically significant at the .05 level with one exception, i.e., the average seriousness scores between child and elderly parent as victims.

It is obvious that judgments of seriousness, inappropriateness, intent, physical and psychological harm, and the likelihood of reporting vary by victim type. This is consistent with earlier research focusing only on seriousness (O'Toole et al. 1985). In that study, the same vignettes were judged by a student sample to be most serious for elderly parent as victim (7.43), followed by child (7.38), wife (6.92), and husband (6.55).

These findings may partly be the consequence of requiring respondents to make judgments across victim types, since other research focusing only on child abuse and neglect found somewhat lower average seriousness ratings for child as victim (e.g., Giovannoni and Becerra 1979; Garrett 1982; Snyder and Newberger 1986). Prior research has not included ratings of vignettes for inappropriateness, intent, extent of physical or psychological harm, or the likelihood of reporting by community respondents or professionals, precluding further comparisons.

B. Variations by Respondent Characteristics

The second research question addresses the effects of respondent characteristics on judgments of seriousness, inappropriateness, intent, physical and psychological harm, and the likelihood of reporting. We find that women tend to form more severe judgments than men across the five dimensions of family mistreatment.[1] Women also perceive that they are more likely to report an abusive incident. This pattern holds for child, elderly parent, and husband as victims; for wife as victim the pattern is reversed—men form more severe judgments.

In general, Protestants appear to have the highest average aggregate scores, followed by Catholics, and by those with other or no religious affiliation. While the married and widowed respondents have higher average aggregate scores across the six scales than do the divorced and single respondents, only a small number of these are statistically significant differences.

Results of one-way analysis of variance tests for gender differences (male, female), religious affiliation (Protestant, Catholic, other, none), and marital status (married, divorced, widowed, single) for each of the five dimensions of family mistreatment along with potential reporting behavior by victim type reveal relatively few statistically significant differences in respondent judgments. Using .05 as the level of significance, only 1 of 24 gender comparisons was statistically significant. Women judged physical harm to be greater for a child victim. One religious affiliation difference is significant—respondents with no affiliation had highest scores when rating intent of abusing an elderly parent. Three differences across marital type are significant—all for the husband victim: in all cases, single respondents had the lowest scores for seriousness, inappropriateness, and reporting likelihood.

The few statistically significant differences in respondent judgments of the five dimensions of family mistreatment and reporting behaviors suggest that while respondents who are women, Protestants, or married may generally rate the vignettes higher on the five dimensions of family mistreatment and likelihood of reporting, the patterns of response indicate that respondent characteristics do *not* strongly influence their judgments about family mistreatment.

To examine the effects of other respondent characteristics, correlations indicating relationships between several factors, such as size of place raised (country, farm, town, small city, large city), number of children, years of education, occupational prestige, family income, age—and each of the six scales was calculated. The results are reported in Table 2.

The direction of the correlations involving each sociodemographic variable is generally consistent across the five dimensions of family mis-

Table 2. Correlations of Scales with Sociodemographic Characteristics by Victim Type[a]

	Place	Children	Education	Prestige	Income	Age
Seriousness						
(C)	.018	.066	−.127*	−.096	−.016	.089
(E)	−.160*	.028	−.192*	−.094	−.188**	.066
(H)	−.045	.038	−.216**	−.124*	−.132*	.187
(W)	−.147*	.104	−.064	−.017	−.006	.187
Inappropriateness						
(C)	.051	.032	−.042	−.086	.015	.078
(E)	−.100	.027	−.110	−.047	−.103	.033
(H)	−.108	.075	−.244**	−.188**	−.129*	.204
(W)	−.089	−.016	.080	.025	.073	.126
Intent						
(C)	−.116	.116	−.057	.011	.037	.104
(E)	−.151*	.072	−.203**	−.016	−.042	.069
(H)	−.104	.038	−.201**	−.136*	−.019	.135
(W)	−.042	.049	−.055	.016	.059	.153
Physical harm						
(C)	.062	.032	−.082	−.065	.004	.059
(E)	−.107	.074	−.133*	−.056	−.192**	.045
(H)	−.082	.061	−.221**	−.110	−.140*	.151
(W)	−.114	.049	−.011	−.018	−.063	.040
Psychological harm						
(C)	.045	−.057	.031	−.032	−.009	.058
(E)	−.048	.034	−.154*	−.065	−.170*	.003
(H)	.009	−.031	−.163*	−.132*	−.140*	.103
(W)	−.057	−.031	.024	−.032	−.134*	.135
Reporting likelihood						
(C)	−.059	.082	−.003	−.041	−.003	.058
(E)	−.073	.084	−.101	−.104	−.096	.068
(H)	−.032	.046	−.106	−.108	−.116	.067
(W)	−.081	.064	−.026	−.085	−.079	.076

*p < .05.   **p < .01.

[a] (C), child; (E), elderly; (H), husband; (W), wife.

treatment and potential reporting behavior, as well as across victim types. Number of children and age are directly correlated with the scales, while size of place raised, years of education, occupational prestige, and income are inversely correlated with the six scales.

Age and social-class indicators (i.e., education, occupational prestige, and income) are most strongly associated with judgments regarding the five dimensions of family mistreatment. However, the direct effects of age are limited to the spouse (husband or wife) as victim. The inverse effects of education and income are limited to elderly parent, and husband as victim types. Occupational prestige is related only to the husband as the victim. Size of place raised and number of children are only weakly associated with the five dimensions of family mistreatment and the four victim types.

The correlations between these sociodemographic variables and the likelihood of reporting are weak. The social-class indicators, especially years of education and income, and age have statistically significant effects, and these effects are limited to elderly parent and husband as the victim.

The results presented in Table 2 confirm the conclusion drawn from the earlier analysis. Sociodemographic characteristics of respondents have little effect on judgments of the five dimensions of family mistreatment and the likelihood of reporting. The correlations presented in Table 2, even when they are statistically significant, generally account for less than 5% of the variance in the six aggregate scale scores.

C. Intercorrelations among Scales

The third and final research question concerns the intercorrelations of the five dimensions of family mistreatment and potential reporting behavior. Table 3 summarizes the correlations among the six semantic differential scales and, as expected, they are all highly correlated with one another (all are significant at $p < .001$).

Perceived seriousness is most highly correlated with perceived inappropriateness for all four victim types, and with physical and psychological harm when elderly parent or husband is the victim. Inappropriateness is also strongly correlated with perceptions of physical and psychological harm when either an elderly parent or a husband is the victim.

For all of the associations regarding the five dimensions of family mistreatment and potential reporting behavior, the largest involve seriousness, and physical and psychological harm. These correlations with

Table 3. Correlation Coefficients among Semantic Differential Scales, for Victim Types

	Seriousness	Inappropriateness	Intent	Physical harm	Psychological harm
Inappropriateness					
(C)	.8389				
(E)	.8546				
(H)	.7514				
(W)	.7362				
Intent					
(C)	.5082	.5191			
(E)	.5084	.5592			
(H)	.4785	.5795			
(W)	.5111	.4958			
Physical harm					
(C)	.5131	.4138	.3756		
(E)	.7473	.6879	.4057		
(H)	.8134	.6023	.4642		
(W)	.5942	.4879	.5011		
Psychological harm					
(C)	.5781	.5708	.5197	.5436	
(E)	.8055	.7465	.4685	.7942	
(H)	.7977	.6764	.4906	.7849	
(W)	.5091	.5253	.4557	.5756	
Reporting likelihood					
(C)	.3869	.2979	.3630	.5626	.4755
(E)	.5655	.5007	.3001	.5882	.6467
(H)	.6107	.3908	.3003	.6753	.6174
(W)	.4224	.3591	.3523	.5489	.5233

potential reporting behavior are highest for elderly parent or husband as victim.

V. Discussion

It is clear from these findings that definitions of family mistreatment vary significantly by victim type—child, elderly parent, husband, or wife. Given the longer history of acknowledging child abuse and neglect as a social problem (Pfohl 1977) as compared to elder abuse (Pedrick-Cornell and Gelles 1982), and the greater social visibility of child abuse and neglect, our finding that comparable behaviors are seen as *more* severe for the *elderly parent* as victim rather than for the child as victim is unexpected. In addition, while the judgments for abuse of a wife victim are more severe than for a husband victim the average vignette scores for descriptions of wife as victim are closer to those for husband as victim than they are to those for child or elderly parent as victim. However, the relative severity of judgments across all five dimensions of family mistreatment may be better explained by the varying degrees of dependence or lack of power in the family than by victim type per se (Finkelhor 1983b). This interpretation suggests that community members have a greater concern with abuse and neglect of the elderly and of husbands than one might have expected, given their lower visibility as social problems, but expected as a function of their relative status within the family.

Victim type also had a sizable effect on potential reporting behavior. The perceived likelihood of reporting was greatest for vignettes describing an elderly parent as the victim, followed closely by those describing a child as the victim. There is a substantial decrease in likelihood of reporting when the wife is described as the victim, and another decrease is observed when the husband is the victim. Dependent status in the family and implied vulnerability can again explain respondents' potential reporting behaviors. Respondents may infer that self-reports by children and the elderly are less likely than by husbands or wives, thus requiring the respondent to report the perceived abuse or neglect to the appropriate authorities.

The few significant effects of sociodemographic characteristics on the five dimensions of family mistreatment are social-class indicators such as education, occupational prestige, and income, consistent with earlier research on child abuse (e.g., Giovannoni and Becerra 1979; Pelton 1981; Besharov 1986). A possible explanation for the observed inverse association between social class and perceptions of child abuse and neglect is the greater salience of the described behaviors for respondents in lower class positions. However, empirical support for the effects of social class is very weak and largely limited to judgments of behaviors with either the elderly parent or the husband as victim. These findings are inconsistent with those from previous studies (Giovanonni and Becerra 1979; Borkowski et al. 1983) and pose an important question regarding attitudes about reporting: How can these be measured?

As anticipated, the intercorrelations among the five dimensions of family mistreatment—seriousness, inappropriateness, intent, and physical and psychological harm—are uniformly high and statistically significant. This finding validates previous research that has relied on seriousness as the sole indicator of community and professional definitions of family mistreatment; but it also points to the relevance of all five dimensions when measuring perceptions of family mistreatment, and it indicates their efficacy across all four victim types.

VI. Significance

This research provides valuable knowledge in three areas. First, information from a community survey indicates that definitions of family mistreatment vary significantly by the status of the victim in the family. Comparable behaviors were judged to be more severe when dependent family members were involved, either an elderly parent, or a child. Second, information regarding potential reporting behavior may explain the lower substantiation rate of lay reports of family mistreatment in comparison with professional reporting rates. Potential reporting behavior was found to vary by victim type, with some minor effects of respondent characteristics on reporting for victim type. Third, community definitions of family mistreatment are multidimensional and appear to be highly correlated with potential reporting behavior. The five dimensions of family mistreatment examined in this research are highly intercorrelated, indicating the relevance of each to community definitions across victim types and to reporting behaviors.

Appendix
(Vignettes)

(Asterisks denote items deleted from husband and wife mistreatment instruments.)

1.   On one occasion, the (   ) and the (   ) engaged in sexual intercourse.   (*sexual abuse*) (included only on child abuse and elderly abuse instruments)

1a.   On one occasion, the (   ) forced his/her (   ) to engage in sexual intercourse.   (*sexual abuse*) (included only on wife abuse and husband abuse instruments)

*2.   The (   ) repeatedly suggested to the (   ) that they have sexual relations.   (*sexual abuse*)

3.   On one occasion the (   ) fondled the (   ) genital area. (*sexual abuse*) (included only on child abuse and elderly abuse instruments)

3a.   On one occasion, the (   ) has forcibly fondled the (   ) genital area.   (*sexual abuse*) (included only on wife abuse and husband abuse instruments)

4.   The (   ) usually punishes the (   ) by striking him/her in the face with his/her fist.   (*physical abuse*)

5. The (   ) banged the (   ) against the wall while shaking him/her by the shoulders. (*physical abuse*)

6. The (   ) struck the (   ) with a wooden stick. (*physical abuse*)

7. The (   ) are constantly screaming at their (   ), calling him/her foul names. (*emotional mistreatment*)

8. The (   ) keep the (   ) locked in. They feed and bathe the (   ) and provide basic physical care. (*emotional mistreatment*)

9. The (   ) ignore their (   ) most of the time, seldom talking with him/her or listening to him/her. (*emotional mistreatment*)

10. The (   ) regularly fail to feed their (   ) for periods of at least 24 hours. (*nutritional neglect*)

11. The (   ) fail to prepare regular meals for their (   ). The (   ) is on a special diet. (*nutritional neglect*)

12. The (   ) brought their (   ) to the hospital three times for being underweight. (*nutritional neglect*)

13. The (   ) live with their (   ) in an old house. Two windows in the living room where the (   ) spends most of his/her time have been broken for some time, and the glass has very jagged edges. (*housing*)

14. The (   ) live in an apartment with their (   ). They have few furnishings, a bed where the (   ) sleep, and two mattresses where the (   ) sleep. (*housing*)

15. The (   ) live with their (   ) in a small two-room apartment. They have lived there for several months. (*housing*)

16. The (   ) usually leave their (   ) on a filthy, sodden mattress. (*cleanliness*)

*17. The (   ) do not wash their (   ) at all. (*cleanliness*)

18. The (   ) do not see that their (   ) has clean clothing. (*clothing*)

19. The (   ) ignored the fact that their (   ) was obviously ill, in pain, and not eating. (*medical neglect*)

20. The (   ) have not given their (   ) medication prescribed by a physician. (*medical neglect*)

21. The (   ) have repeatedly failed to keep medical appointments for their (   ). (*medical neglect*)

22. The (   ) regularly left their (   ) alone all night. (*supervision*)

23. The (   ) regularly left their (   ) alone inside the house during the day. Often they did not return until almost dark. (*supervision*)

*24. The (   ) regularly left their (   ) with their neighbors, without knowing who would assume responsibility and be in charge. (*supervision*)

Note

1.   Because so few differences regarding gender, religion, and marital status are statistically significant, they are not reported in tabular form.

Chapter 5

Criminal-Justice Processing of Violent and Nonviolent Offenders: The Effects of Familial Relationship to the Victim[1]

Sharon D. Herzberger and Noreen L. Channels

I. Introduction

Despite the enactment of laws against spouse and child abuse and the development of relevant social movements, historically the prosecution of cases of family violence has been rare (Pleck 1989). Today, criminal-justice processing of such cases is equally unlikely. While there is no consistent evidence that police are less likely to arrest in cases of family violence than nonfamily violence (cf. Elliott 1989), prosecution of family violence cases is infrequent (Lerman 1986). Researchers attribute low rates of prosecution to the unreliability of the victim's testimony, lack of cooperation from witnesses, and requests from victims to drop charges (Boland et al. 1983; Forst and Hernon 1985). Some criminal-justice and social-service officials encourage less legal intervention to maintain family privacy and to avoid exacerbating an already stressful situation (Zimring 1989).

Although the criminal-justice system handles only a small proportion of the cases of family violence, researchers and policy officials have begun to study how the cases that do enter the system are treated. This study contributes to this effort and has two purposes.

First, while most studies of criminal-justice processing of family violence have concentrated on the decision to arrest or to prosecute the offender, the primary focus of this study concerns the factors that affect bail decisions and the likelihood of securing pretrial release. The importance of bail decision making has been demonstrated repeatedly in the criminal-justice literature. Alleged offenders who are detained in prison before their trial are more likely to be convicted and incarcerated (Herzberger and Channels 1988; Wheeler and Wheeler 1980) and to receive longer prison sentences (Goldkamp 1979; Lizotte 1978; Wheeler and Wheeler 1980, 1982) than those who secure release from pretrial detention. Furthermore, there is evidence that bail decision makers permit legally irrelevant factors, such as minority group membership and socioeconomic status, to affect their judgments about bail (Frazier et al. 1980; Herzberger and Channels 1988; Spohn et al. 1981–82). Thus, we decided to examine how relationship to the victim, which is also legally irrelevant to bail, affects bail setting. The influence of relationship to the victim on bail decisions is particularly interesting because, should the alleged offender be released on bail, he or she may return home to the victim.

Second, the study compares the treatment of family violence cases to the treatment of other violent and nonviolent criminal cases. Some researchers argue that the traditionally isolated study of family crimes has stymied efforts to determine the extent to which, and the ways in which, treatment of family violence cases is different from other cases, and the extent to which existing criminal-justice policy is appropriate to the realities of family violence (Elliott 1989; Fagan 1988; Fagan and Wexler 1987). Furthermore, treating family violence separately brings the danger that researchers will fail to take into account the existing paradigms, statistical procedures, and appropriate controls that social scientists employ to study the treatment of other offenders. In the present study we were able to examine the treatment of family violence cases within the larger criminal-justice context. We are able to isolate the effects of the relationship to the victim from the effects of the other contributing factors. We can also compare our findings on the influence of family violence to a host of existing findings on other violent crimes and begin to explore the policy implications.

An additional advantage of this study is that we examine the treatment of alleged offenders longitudinally. We track what occurs to the offenders at each stage of the bail decision-making process and how each decision affects the likelihood of pretrial release.

II. Research Methods

A. Sample

The data we analyze are derived from a sample of cases pertaining to individuals arrested for a felony and interviewed by a bail commissioner between May 1983 and April 1984. We obtained complete information on 1,323 cases.

B. Data

The Connecticut Office of Policy and Management provided the initial information on the cases through its Offender Based Transaction Statistics (OBTS) system. To the OBTS data, we added information obtained from the Department of Corrections, the Bail Commission, and from the 1980 census. We coded numerically information about the crime for which the criminal suspects were arrested, their previous convictions, and their personal characteristics (see the appendix). We also coded the bail and pretrial release decisions pertaining to the cases and the length of time served in prison before trial, using information from the individual's corrections file.

We distinguish between violent and nonviolent suspects by using the felony charges filed against the alleged offender. Violent criminal suspects are those charged with homicide, all forms of sexual or physical assault, and risk of injury to children, and those who caused a personal injury during the course of a crime. We classify all other cases as nonviolent. A total of 1,020 cases pertain to nonviolent suspects, whereas 303 pertain to violent suspects. Offender-victim relationship was derived from the bail commissioner's interview form. The specific relationship was not coded. Thus, although we presume that most violent family offenders are spouses or ex-spouses (cf. Elliott 1989), those noted to have a relationship with the victim could include other primary family members, cohabiting "family" members, and those with less proximal relationships (e.g., uncle, grandfather).

III. Findings

Panel A of Table 1 shows the characteristics of the sampled criminal suspects, who are either related or unrelated to the victim of their crime. We display characteristics separately for those charged with violent or nonviolent crimes. An examination of the entries shows that the groups appear to differ from each other in the number of prior crimes, and in ethnicity, gender, and marital status. This demonstrates the importance of controlling for these variables in regression analysis. Few individuals in the sample are charged with nonviolent crimes against a related victim. Thus, analysis of this group can produce only tentative results. We urge caution when drawing generalizations from this subsample.

Panel B of Table 1 shows the decisions made at each step of the bail-setting process for the four subgroups in our sample. The table shows the proportion of the entire subgroup that secured pretrial release, the proportion of those required to post bond, the amount of bail, and the

Table 1. Characteristics and Outcomes for Unrelated and Related Violent and Nonviolent Offenders[a]

	Violent suspects				Nonviolent suspects			
	Unrelated		Related		Unrelated		Related	
A. Characteristics								
Average offense severity[b]	4.70	(276)	4.56	(61)	4.41	(976)	4.09	(11)
Average number of counts	2.38	(276)	2.23	(61)	2.19	(976)	2.00	(11)
Average prior severity[b]	1.11	(276)	1.07	(61)	1.23	(976)	1.00	(11)
Average number of priors	4.37	(276)	3.64	(61)	4.86	(976)	3.55	(11)
Status[c]	.41	(276)	.34	(61)	.50	(976)	.27	(11)
Black (%)	41.7	(276)	49.2	(61)	37.3	(976)	45.5	(11)
Hispanic (%)	17.8	(276)	14.8	(61)	20.7	(976)	9.1	(11)
Married (%)	10.1	(276)	23.0	(61)	9.8	(976)	0.0	(11)
Female (%)	10.1	(276)	23.0	(61)	7.9	(976)	18.2	(11)
Median income ($)	13,160.6	(206)	12,310.0	(51)	13,618.4	(696)	14,588.2	(10)
B. Outcomes								
Released pretrial (%)	76.7	(258)	76.7	(60)	70.8	(889)	80.0	(10)
Required to post bond (%)	76.1	(276)	63.9	(61)	74.3	(975)	54.6	(11)
Final bail ($)	11,613.8	(210)	7,116.7	(39)	6,867.1	(719)	2,550.0	(06)
Bonded subsample released pretrial (%)	69.1	(194)	64.1	(39)	61.7	(661)	60.0	(05)

[a] Numbers in parentheses are the number of suspects in each category.

[b] Coded on 1–7 scale.

[c] Currently on parole, probation, or having outstanding warrant coded 1, others coded 0.

proportion who posted bond and secured pretrial release. Generally, for both violent and nonviolent offenses, suspects related to their victims appear to receive less severe treatment.

We used multiple-regression techniques to investigate the extent to which the offender's relationship to the victim affects bail decisions and pretrial release, controlling for other relevant predictors, and separately for violent offenders (Table 2) and nonviolent offenders (Table 3). Ordinary least-squares (OLS) regression was performed with the continuous dependent variable, i.e., the amount of bond required. Logistic regression was performed with the remaining dependent variables, which are dichotomous. In all analyses, the variable most pertinent to the theme of this study is "related," and most of the discussion is confined to this.

A. Violent Offenses

Release from pretrial detention reflects several criminal-justice decisions. In Connecticut, all offenses are "bailable." The police, a bail commissioner, or sometimes a judge decides whether to demand a financial bond to secure release or whether the individual may be released on recognizance or through a surety bond. If the alleged offender is required to post a financial bond, the decision maker must set the bond amount. The individual who secures the needed amount is then released.

In the first column of Table 2, we analyze the factors influencing release from pretrial detention for the entire violent subgroup. Individuals with a less serious criminal history, women, married suspects, and those for whom a bail commissioner set the final bail amount (as opposed to the judge) are more likely to secure release from pretrial detention. Furthermore, individuals required to post lower bond amounts are more likely to be released. The relationship between the offender and the victim does not significantly affect the likelihood of release: approximately three-quarters of the defendants who are either related or unrelated to their victims secure release from jail to await trial.

While an identical proportion of suspects related to the victim and unrelated to the victim secures pretrial release, the process through which the two groups achieve this end varies. Column B of Table 2 presents an analysis of the factors that predict whether alleged offenders will be required to post a financial bond. The results demonstrate that suspects related to their victims tend to be less likely ($p < .07$) than others to be so required. Columns C and D present analyses based only on the subsample of alleged offenders who are required to post a financial bond. The results show that, among this subsample, suspects who are related to their victims post a substantially smaller bond amount

Table 2. Factors Influencing Bail Decisions of Violent Offenders[a]

	A. Pretrial release b	B. Bond required (nonfinancial, financial) b	C. Final bond amount ($) b	D. Pretrial release (w/bond) (no, yes) b
Related		-0.62 (.34)	-15,650.55*** (4,268.25)	-1.35* (.59)
Severity		0.61*** (.16)	20,504.9*** (2,537.05)	
Number of counts		0.32** (.12)	4,305.9*** (1,131.09)	0.34 (.19)
Prior severity	-1.01*** (.26)		7,776.5*** (2,102.76)	-0.83** (.31)
Number of priors				
Status			8,682.71** (3,126.99)	
Judge	-1.02* (.44)	0.93** (.29)	23,406.09*** (4,930.12)	

Black suspect		0.59 (.31)	15,557.17*** (3,849.27)	
Hispanic suspect		0.87 (.45)	23,222.53*** (4,791.69)	
Married suspect	2.53** (.92)		14,963.37*** (4,441.96)	2.72** (.88)
Female suspect	2.11* (1.06)		-13,716.50** (4,639.65)	
Final bond amount	-0.00005*** (.0000)	—	—	-0.00005** (.0000)
Probability of exclusion	—	—	127,139.30*** (24,358.55)	—
Intercept		-3.33*** (.91)	-152,247.70*** (24,222.96)	
N	318	337	249	233
x^2, F	x^2 (12) = 79.61	x^2 (11) = 54.48	F (12,236) = 7.72	x^2 (13) = 60.30
p	.0001	.0001	.0001	.0001
R^2	.22	.10	.28	.18

*$p < .05$.   **$p < .01$.   ***$p < .001$.   All others, significant at $p \leq .10$.

[a] A dash means that the variable was not included in the analysis. Numbers in parentheses are standard errors.

than those who are unrelated. Despite this, we find that among suspects who are required to post bond, those related to their victims are *less* likely than unrelated suspects to secure release from pretrial detention (Column D).

Thus, the consequences of relationship to the victim of a violent offense are complex. Related offenders tend to be as likely as offenders unrelated to their victims to secure release on recognizance. However, *if required to post a bond*, albeit a smaller one, suspects related to their victims are more likely than unrelated suspects to remain in pretrial detention. The outcome—release from pretrial detention—is the same, whether or not one is related to the victim of a violent offense. However, the route through which this outcome is achieved substantially favors the alleged offender who is related to the victim of a violent crime.

B. Nonviolent Offenses

We repeated the analysis of violent cases on the sample of nonviolent cases. The results are summarized in Table 3. The analysis reveals that related suspects charged with nonviolent crimes are more likely to be released than unrelated suspects (80 vs. 71%). However, when controlling for other variables in a multivariate analysis, the suspect's relationship to the victim does not significantly affect the probability of release for the nonviolent offender.

When we analyze the stages of the release action, we find that offender-victim relationship does not significantly influence the decision to require a financial bond. Among those required to post a financial bond, offender-victim relationship does not affect the amount of bond or the likelihood of securing release from pretrial detention. There is no evidence to conclude that relationship to the victim of a nonviolent offense significantly affects the alleged offender's progress through the early stages of the criminal-justice system.

IV. Discussion

This study shows the importance of studying the treatment of suspects who are related to their victims in a comparative context. Violent crimes against a family member are handled differently at the bail-setting stage than the same crimes against unrelated victims. Although related and unrelated offenders are equally likely to obtain release from pretrial detention, suspects who are related to their victims and are charged with a violent offense are treated more leniently. Related suspects tend to be released on recognizance more often than unrelated ones and, if required to post a bond, are required to post a lesser amount.

In contrast to decision making for violent offenders, relationship to the victim of a nonviolent crime does not significantly influence bail decisions or pretrial release. However, as noted previously, the small sample of nonviolent offenders related to their victim renders problematic any firm conclusions about their treatment by criminal-justice officials. We should be especially cautious about concluding that relationship to the victim does not influence such decisions. Table 1 shows that related nonviolent offenders receive the leniency accorded related violent offenders with respect to requiring a financial bond and the amount of the bond, and Table 3 shows that the coefficients for the relationship variable are in the same direction as for violent offenders.

The differences in the treatment of related and unrelated *violent* suspects suggest several topics for further investigation. First, we need to study why bail commissioners and judges pay attention to the suspect's relationship to the victim of a violent offense. Given the questionable constitutionality of pretrial detention (Wheeler and Wheeler 1982) and the relative inability to predict either rearrest during the pretrial period or failure to appear for trial (Goldkamp and Gottfredson 1979; Gottfredson and Gottfredson 1986), the use of legally irrelevant factors, including relationship between the offender and the victim, to determine bail requirements seems particularly questionable. The bail decision-making process may allow considerable discretion and subjectivity of judgment. Bail setting usually follows arrest quite rapidly, and decision makers do not always have access to complete information about prior offenses and the characteristics of the present offense. This may promote reliance upon legally irrelevant factors, such as relationship to the suspect. Also, bail decision makers may believe, as many others do (cf. Elliott 1989), that related offenders are more likely to have their charges dismissed. If true, they may see little reason to hold the suspect in pretrial detention.

Second, we need to investigate why these decision makers may be more likely to release related offenders accused of violent crimes on recognizance and, if they decide to require a financial bond, to require less bond. Given the prevailing beliefs about the likelihood of a repeat offense for family offenders and the likelihood of retaliation if the victim contributes to the arrest, the tendency to be lenient is inexplicable. We might speculate that officials are attempting to reduce the financial and emotional strain on the household that would result from the offender's pretrial detention. However, this rationale also should apply to the handling of nonviolent crimes against relatives. Here also the absence of a family member may cause stress; yet there is no firm evidence that

Table 3. Factors Influencing Bail Decisions of Nonviolent Offenders[a]

	A. Pretrial release b	B. Bond required (nonfinancial, financial) b	C. Final bond amount ($) b	D. Pretrial release (w/bond) (no, yes) b
Related				
Severity	−.09 (.05)	.19* (.08)	2,499.25*** (591.65)	.21 (.12)
Number of counts	−.59*** (.13)	.30*** (.08)	985.90** (377.61)	
Prior severity		.27* (.11)		.41* (.17)
Number of priors	−.06*** (.01)		355.66*** (88.32)	.04* (.02)
Status	−.46* (.18)	.34* (.17)	1,926.80 (1,131.70)	
Judge	−.95 (.23)	.89*** (.16)	5,730.07** (2,185.92)	

Black suspect				
Hispanic suspect				.58* (.27)
Married suspect	.68 (.35)	-.66** (.24)		
Female suspect		-.53* (.27)		
Final bond amount	-.00007*** (.00000)	—	—	-.00005*** (.00000)
Probability of exclusion		—	19,327.78 (11,316.92)	4.01 (2.43)
Intercept	2.76*** (.65)	-1.00* (.49)	-16,157.90* (7,108.89)	.06 (1.46)
N	899	986	725	666
χ^2, F	$\chi^2(12) = 201.12$	$\chi^2(11) = 123.11$	$F(12,712) = 3.82$	$\chi^2(13) = 128.22$
p	.0001	.0002	.0001	.0001
R^2	.19	.10	.06	.14

a See notes to Table 2.

officials consider relationship when they make bail decisions about non-violent offenders.

Perhaps those who set bail for family violence cases are ambivalent about the role of the legal system in such "family matters" and decide that arrest alone is sufficient warning or punishment. Or, perhaps they anticipate that cases are eventually likely to be referred to counseling or social-service agencies for intervention (cf. Elliott 1989; Lerman 1986). Also, Giovannoni and Becerra (1979) found that while social workers, pediatricians, and police officers tend to see acts of child abuse as serious, attorneys rate these acts less severely. The authors suggest that one explanation for this difference may be the attorney's lack of immediate contact with the victim. To judges and bail commissioners, the victim is also absent, which may enable these bail decision makers better to tolerate violent family offenders.

Third, we need to understand why suspects in cases of family violence are less likely to obtain the required financial bond and to be released. Attorneys may recommend that their clients stay in prison to avoid contact with the victim or until they "cool off." Alternatively, spouses or other relatives, with or without an attorney's urging, may refuse to deliver the needed bond amount and thereby effectively keep the alleged offender in prison. We know that family offenders are likely to repeat their crimes (Klaus and Rand 1984) and that arrest is likely to reduce the chances of further violence, at least for a short period after the offense (Sherman and Berk 1984). Thus, the cooling-off period may be deemed more important than when the same crime has been committed against an unrelated victim.

The differential importance of relationship in violent and nonviolent offenses shown in this study needs to be replicated. However, we can suggest why later research may find the same results. First, while most violent offenders were charged with or convicted of assault, nonviolent offenders were mainly charged with or convicted of burglary, larceny, or drug offenses. Although first-degree burglary and first-degree assault are both B felonies, and thus equally severe in one sense, the crimes differ in many other ways. It is not surprising that criminal justice officials would make different decisions and contemplate different factors in each case. Furthermore, physical evidence of the crime may be more available for nonviolent offenses, reducing the need to rely upon the testimony of witnesses. In nonviolent cases, then, the problems of faulty or unenthusiastic eyewitness testimony may be obviated and relationship to the offender may not matter.

Second, individuals who commit nonviolent offenses may have different relationships with their victims than violent offenders. Because an individual is unlikely to be charged with breaking and entering, or with removing property from his or her own home, it is likely that more distant relationships are involved in these nonviolent crimes. When victims are not immediate family members, judges and other decision makers may be more willing to treat unrelated and related offenders equally, or may not have a preference to have the matter resolved in a nonlegal setting. Thus, they may base decisions more on the characteristics of the crime and ignore relationship to the offender.

Future studies of this issue should correct for the sample size deficiency by including a larger number of nonviolent, related suspects. In addition, future studies need to distinguish reliably between offenses against adults vs. children and the type of relationship between the offender and victim (Mickow 1988). Finally, since we may expect more discretion in decision making about misdemeanor charges, a study that includes misdemeanor arrests may provide an interesting comparison to the present research.

Appendix. Variables Used for Regression Analysis

Dependent Variables

Type of bond: nonfinancial = 0, financial = 1
Amount of bond: in dollars
Pretrial release: no = 0, yes = 1

Independent Variables

Related to victim: no = 0, yes = 1
Offense severity: most severe current charge coded from 1 to 7
Number of counts: at arraignment or at disposition, as relevant
Prior severity: severity of prior convictions within the last five years; none = 0, misdemeanor = 1, felony = 2
Number of priors: total number of known prior convictions
Status: none = 0, currently on parole, probation, or having an outstanding warrant = 1
Judge: source of final bail decision; bail commissioner = 1, judge = 2
Black suspect: no = 0, yes = 1
Hispanic suspect: no = 0, yes = 1
Married suspect: single = 0, other = 1
Female suspect: male = 1, female = 2

Note

1. This project was supported by a grant from the Hartford Institute of Criminal and Social Justice.

Part II

Effects of Victimization

In Part II researchers summarize work on three distinct family violence problems. Their work has two features in common. First, each addresses the possible long-term consequences of intrafamilial abuse or violence. John E. Murphy establishes empirically the relationship between child abuse and the likelihood of adult victimization. Diana Gurley focuses upon the long-term process of recovering from childhood physical or sexual abuse. Debra F. Kromsky and Brian L. Cutler investigate the knowledge that police officers, attorneys, and potential jurors have of the battered-woman syndrome, a psychological response to repeated incidents of violence.

Second, each author addresses methodological issues and challenges that are critically important to the field of family violence. Murphy's study illustrates the utility of innovative methods for selecting sample survey respondents and the use of telephone interviews. Gurley's study demonstrates the utility of ethnographic research. Kromsky and Cutler show the need to communicate social-science knowledge of phenomena to individuals who must respond to the effects of familial violence.

Consider, first, John Murphy's study. Research studying the problem of child sexual abuse tends to focus either upon incidence rates or prevalence rates. The data generally used to judge the extent of the child abuse problem do not reflect the true magnitude of the problem. Why? Because to draw representative samples, various data-gathering techniques, including telephone surveys, are required. Until John Murphy conducted his research in Minnesota, social scientists believed that random-digit dialing to sample child abuse victims are prohibited.

Subjects for the Murphy study are drawn from random-digit dialing numbers generated by a computer program. The interview schedule consists of 65 questions and takes between 10 and 15 minutes to complete. Questions concerning sexual abuse, date, and spouse abuse are included in the interview schedule.

A total of 777 interviews were completed for this particular study. Murphy shows that, overall, approximately 18% of the women and 11% of the men interviewed by phone had experienced at least one form of sexual abuse. Data also reveal that child sexual victimization is related to later experiences within a physically or sexually abusive dating relationship. Murphy discusses the implications for these findings and the implications for using innovative data-gathering techniques, such as random-digit dialing, within the field of family violence research.

Diana Gurley's study describes the ways in which relationships help and obstruct the recovery from childhood trauma, including sexual abuse. Themes of social support and social obstruction are specified, contrasted, and used by Gurley to examine recoveries from battering or sexual abuse. Her findings suggest that in addition to functional support (tangible aid, information assistance, belonging) relationships can also function negatively for people in abusive environments. Research participants report that their relationships were both helpful and hurtful, simultaneously and over time.

Gurley's research participants also report negative qualities of nonbattering relationships that echoed and reinforced their experiences with battery and sexual assault. For this reason, Diana Gurley urges researchers to attempt to observe social obstruction and the extent to which hurtful behavior in nonbattering relationships exacerbates the consequences, especially the long-term consequences, of battery and sexual abuse.

Debra Kromsky and Brian Cutler deliberate the importance of the battered-woman syndrome in their study, "The Admissibility of Expert Testimony on the Battered-Woman Syndrome." They show how the syndrome is used in legal cases in which a battered woman seeks to prosecute the batterer, or in which she is the defendant charged with killing or battering her partner. In both types of cases expert witnesses testify about the battered-woman syndrome for the purpose of corroborating the battered woman's testimony. Such testimony has the additional function of educating the jury on the multidimensional trauma resulting from battering.

Kromsky and Cutler administered a knowledge test to samples of survey respondents drawn to represent jury-eligible individuals, attorneys, and police officers. They find, on average, that people do have some knowledge about the characteristics of battered women. No respondent group, however, demonstrated complete knowledge of the syndrome. Certainly, the reader sees the need for developing systematically accurate, empirical information that can be communicated clearly to those individuals who must assess the consequences of family abuse in America's courtrooms.

Chapter 6

An Investigation of Child Sexual Abuse and Consequent Victimization: Some Implications of Telephone Surveys

John E. Murphy

I. Introduction

Research on child sexual abuse tends to focus either upon incidence rates or upon prevalence rates. Incidence rates are the number of cases occurring in a given time period (usually a 12-month period) that are officially reported to state agencies (Finkelhor 1986). We commonly acknowledge that incidence rates do not reflect the true magnitude of the problem. Because the majority of child sexual-abuse cases are unreported, they are not reflected in an incidence rate (Finkelhor and Hotaling 1983). Consequently, some very recent research concentrates on the prevalence of child abuse within the general population. Prevalence rates are based on victim or offender self-reports. They are estimates of the proportion of the general population that was sexually abused as children, and are reported as a percentage.

A comprehensive review of the prevalence studies by Finkelhor (1986) found only 15 studies published between 1960 and 1986. Eleven are based on probability samples of the general population. A great deal of variation in prevalence rates is found. Rates for women range from 6 to 62%, and for men the range was between 3 and 16%. A more recent community-based prevalence study, which was not included in Finkelhor's review, found that 12% of women and 3% of men in the general population report child sexual abuse (Murphy 1987).

The data on rape, including date rape and marital rape, suffer from the same reporting problems as the child sexual-abuse data. Because most victimization goes unreported, the estimated incidence of rape is a gross underestimate of the true rape rate.

There is a substantial need for empirical investigation regarding this problem before valid generalizations can be drawn from the disparate findings documented in the literature on child abuse and rape. Moreover, there is a strong need for community-based studies on date rape (Murphy 1987). Finally, we not only need to investigate the prevalence of child sexual abuse, date rape, and marital rape within the general population, but we also need to examine the links among these three forms of sexual victimization. To date, no research has examined whether experiencing child sexual abuse increases the likelihood of one's sexual victimization in dating and marital relationships. The study summarized in this chapter responds to these needs. It also tests a method of data collection seldom used in sexual abuse research—the telephone interview.

II. Telephone Surveys

Surveys of representative samples of respondents are necessary in family and related research (Kitson et al. 1982; Miller et al. 1982). If we cannot generalize empirical findings, accurate descriptions and predictions pertaining to the extent of victimization within the general population are impossible. Finkelhor (1986) argues that self-report studies, based on probability samples, yield the most useful and generalizable data. Bradley and Lindsay (1987) claim a need for the use of nonbiased, representative samples, especially when studying child abuse.

The telephone survey is one data collection technique that lends itself to research in which the accessibility of respondents is difficult, yet the need for a representative sample is imperative (Murphy 1987). Telephone research has three strong general advantages over more traditional methodologies:

1. It is faster and more economical than traditional research methodologies.
2. It has the potential of reaching approximately 95% of all households (Miller et al. 1982).
3. It can be an especially useful technique when studying low-base-rate phenomena in the family and the general population (Gelles 1983) because of its ability to reach large numbers of people quickly and efficiently.

However, as Gelles and Straus (1988) point out, telephone surveys miss transients and those without telephones in the population. These two groups are also consistently missed by other techniques, and the telephone appears to impose no greater sampling error in this respect than most other techniques.

Recent methodological work has shown that telephone surveys not only have response rates similar to, or higher than, the more commonly used methods (Gelles 1983; Groves and Kohn 1979; Harris and Associates 1979; Murphy 1987), but the data are highly reliable and valid (Sudman 1983; Gelles 1983; Hochstim 1977). In fact, Gelles (1983) argues that telephone surveys have several advantages over other methods when reaching sensitive family issues: anonymity is assured; other persons cannot hear or see the questions being asked; and the respondent does not have to worry about reactions of other family members to the topic being discussed. These advantages are especially important for the researcher who wishes to avoid further traumatizing victims by inadvertently disclosing a victimization experience when the victim wishes to keep it a secret.

There are two major ethical problems regarding the telephone survey that must be addressed: confidentiality and the potential retraumatization of victims. These ethical concerns are most pronounced in sexual-abuse research. For obvious reasons, confidentiality must be assured. If done correctly, telephone research can help to assure and maximize confidentiality. The random-digit dialing technique provides the researcher and interviewer with only a telephone number and area code. The interviewer will not know the name of the person being interviewed, what the respondent looks like, or where the individual lives. These are advantages that face-to-face interviews, and even mailed questionnaires, do not have. If telephone numbers are kept separate from the answer sheets and destroyed immediately after the data have been entered, little opportunity remains for a respondent's identity to be disclosed.

The possibility of retraumatizing a sexual abuse victim must be a concern for all researchers, regardless of the methodology used. Finkelhor states: "Researchers need to give careful thought to how their research design, interview, questionnaire, follow-up and recruitment procedures might cause inadvertent injury to research subjects" (1986:221). Any random selection procedure invades a person's privacy. The respondent, therefore, must be presented with the right to refuse to participate in the research. This can be accomplished by stating the purpose of the study at the beginning of the telephone interview, and asking the respondent if he/she wishes to participate. Additionally, it is wise to indicate that there is no need to answer any question that makes the respondent feel uncomfortable. This gives the research subject power over the research process itself. Strict adherence to the "norm of informed voluntary consent" mitigates the negative aspects of invasion of privacy (Kelman 1972). The telephone may even help to facilitate this process. Victims of sexual abuse often suffer from feelings of lack of control over their environment. The anonymity and distance provided by the telephone can help the respondents feel they have control over the process—they can easily hang up, thereby relieving any anxiety they may feel about being forced to participate.

III. Research Methods

For this research we used phone interviews to gather information regarding sexual abuse as a child, past and present sexual abuse as adults in dating and marital relationships, as well as information on the past and present family and relationship experiences. Subjects were drawn from a random sample of Minnesota adults who were 18 years of age or older at the time of the interview. Random-digit dialing was used to select telephone numbers. This is a technique in which telephone numbers for the telephone exchanges in the geographical area being surveyed are randomly generated by a computer program. As a result, all presently working numbers have an equal chance of being contacted, including new, changed, or unlisted numbers that would not appear in a telephone directory. A random method of selection based on age and sex was used to assure randomness of respondents within each household. The selection process alternated randomly between men and women and older and younger respondents. In order to contact hard-to-reach respondents, each number was called up to four times over different days, and appointments were made to interview the designated respondents at their convenience. The interviews were carried out over a five-day period, Sunday through Thursday.

The interview schedule consisted of 65 questions and took between 10 and 15 minutes to complete. The survey was an omnibus survey regarding views on, and experiences with, various political, social, and family issues. Twenty-five of the 65 questions were about family and abuse experiences. These questions occurred about one-third of the way through the interview schedule. They were preceded by a transition statement informing the respondent that he or she was now going to be asked some questions about family and personal life. Respondents were also assured that the interview was completely anonymous and that they should feel free not to answer any question that made them feel uncomfortable.

For the purpose of this study, child sexual abuse was defined as experience with one, or all, of the following behaviors before the age of 18:

1. an adult exposing himself to the child;
2. an adult touching or fondling breasts or sexual parts of the child's body when he/she was not willing;
3. having to touch an adult's body in a sexual way when the child did not want to;
4. an adult sexually attacking the child or forcing the child to have sexual intercourse;
5. an adult taking nude photographs of the child or performing a sexual act in the child's presence;
6. experiencing oral or anal sex with an adult.

Date and spouse abuse were defined as a respondent's experience with pushing, slapping, shoving, kicking, biting, hitting, punching, or beating up in his/her dating or marital relationships (either as a victim or a perpetrator). Date and marital rape were defined as the respondent's feeling that one had been forced to have sexual intercourse with a date or marital partner when unwilling.

IV. Findings

In all, 777 interviews were completed (418 persons refused). For samples of this size, the error due to sampling and other random effects is estimated to be 4% at the 95% level of confidence. Typical for telephone surveys, women were slightly oversampled, and the data were statistically weighted to compensate for this.

Sixty-five percent of all eligible respondents completed the survey. The response rates for the various family and sexual abuse questions within the survey varied between 94 and 98%.

A. Child Sexual Abuse

Ninety-seven percent of the respondents completing the entire interview answered the questions on child sexual abuse. Of those,

- 8% ($N = 63$) reported that a man exposed himself to the respondent as a child;
- 9% ($N = 67$) reported an adult touching sexual parts;
- 4% ($N = 29$) reported that they were forced to touch an adult's body in a sexual way;
- 3% ($N = 21$) stated that they were sexually attacked or forced to have intercourse with an adult;
- 3% ($N = 27$) reported an adult taking nude photographs; and
- 3% ($N = 21$) reported having engaged in oral or anal sex with an adult.

For the total sample, the overall rate of experience with at least one of the six categories of sexual abuse was 14% ($N = 108$). A larger proportion of women (18%) than men (11%) reported some form of child sexual abuse.

Ninety-seven percent of all respondents ($N = 753$) indicated that they had dated someone of the opposite sex. Of these, 94% ($N = 708$) answered the questions regarding whether they had been in a physically or sexually abusive dating relationship:

- 12% ($N = 87$) said they had been victims of physical abuse;
- 11% ($N = 76$) indicated they were the perpetrators of the abuse;
- 7% ($N = 48$) reported having been forced to have intercourse with a date (11% of the women, 2% of the men).

Overall, 19% ($N = 139$) of those who had dated had either been a victim or a perpetrator in a physically or sexually abusive dating relationship.

Seventy-six percent of the sample ($N = 591$) was involved in a current dating or marital relationship. Data regarding those persons who are currently either dating or married were combined into one category to ensure large enough subsamples for statistical analysis. Of this group,

- 9% ($N = 54$) indicated that they had been victims of physical abuse;
- 11% ($N = 65$) reported that they were perpetrators of an abusive act;
- 3% ($N = 20$) said they had been forced to have sexual intercourse with the present partner (5% of the women and 2% of the men).

Overall, 15% ($N = 88$) of those currently in an intimate relationship reported being a victim or a perpetrator in physical or sexual abuse.

B. Abuse in Past Dating Relationships

The data were analyzed to determine if experiencing child sexual abuse was related to later victimization in the victim's subsequent dating and martial relationships. The analysis suggests strongly that child sexual victimization is related to adult experiences with a physically or sexually abusive partner. Forty-five percent of those who had been sexually abused as a child, compared to 15% of those who were not, reported having been in a physically and/or sexually abusive dating relationship in the past ($\chi^2 = 47.36$, $df = 1$, $p < .000$). Specifically, 24% of those who had been sexually abused, compared to 10% of those who had not, reported being a victim of physical abuse. Twenty-nine percent of those who had been sexually abused, compared to 7% of those who had not, reported physically abusing their partners. Victims of child sexual abuse were five times more likely to be raped by their dates (21% compared to 4%) than were nonvictims ($\chi^2 = 38.31$, $df = 1$, $p < .000$).

C. *Abuse in Current Dating or Marital Relationship*

Experiencing child sexual abuse was also related to being in a present dating or martial relationship that was physically and/or sexually abusive. Child sexual-abuse victims were more than twice as likely as nonvictims (28% compared to 13%) to be in a presently physically and/or sexually abusive relationship ($\chi^2 = 11.24$, $df = 1$, $p < .001$). Further, victims of child sexual abuse were more than twice as likely as nonvictims (18% compared to 8%) to have been physically abused by their present partners. They were more than twice as likely (22% compared to 9%) to have physically abused their present partners. Although the numbers are too small to draw valid statistical inferences, we can observe that victims of child sexual abuse were twice as likely as nonvictims to report having been raped by their present partner (7% compared to 3%).

V. Conclusions

This research revealed a significant rate of self-reported child sexual abuse in the Minnesota population. All told, 14% of the adult respondents reported being sexually abused as a child (18% of the women, 11% of the men). The data also show that victims of child sexual abuse are much more likely than others to have entered into physically and/or sexually abusive past and present dating or marital relationships. Victims are three times more likely than nonvictims to have been in a physically and/or sexually abusive dating relationship in the past. When past date rape was singled out for analysis, child sexual-abuse victims were found to be five times more likely than nonvictims to have been raped by their past dating partners. The data pointed to a similar, but not as strong, relationship for the current dating or marital relationships. Child sexual abuse victims were twice as likely as nonvictims to be in currently physically and/or sexually abusive relationships. They were also twice as likely as nonvictims to have been raped by their present partners.

The association found in this study, showing a link between a person's sexual abuse as a child and later physical and sexual abuse in adult dating and marital relationships, requires explanation. Perhaps adults who were sexually abused as children are more vulnerable to abusive partners. It may also be that they come from homes in which it appears to the victim that one or both parents are physically or emotionally unavailable to them (Murphy 1988), thereby depriving them of an important socialization and support system.

Whether this phenomenon is "cause" and "effect" has yet to be determined. One possible explanation suggests that abused children may use withdrawal and detachment to cope with their circumstances (Egeland et al. 1987). This could explain why some victims tend to report less affection from their parents, and less time spent with their parents. Consequently, victims may be unlikely to receive positive, protective socialization from the parents. This could result in increased vulnerability.

The child sexual-abuse victim may self-impose isolationism into adulthood, thereby increasing the likelihood of revictimization. Inadvertently (or otherwise) the victim becomes prey for those who may be abusive, because they lack the necessary external social and emotional support provided by positive interpersonal relationships.

VI. Discussion

The fact that the present study found prevalence rates of child sexual abuse that differ from other community-based studies requires explanation. As Gelles and Straus point out: "Survey research is not a study of behavior; it provides us information on what people say to us about their behavior" (1988:211). Therefore, it is imperative that the methods used and the questions asked be as effective as possible so that the ensuing data reflect reality as closely as possible. In an earlier paper (Murphy 1987), I contend that the differences in prevalence rates found in the various studies may be explained by four factors: methodology, definitions, the number of screen questions used, and the response rates. The method in the present study utilized the telephone interview to gather data. Finkelhor (1986) points out that this data collection method tends to produce prevalence rates that are lower than those obtained from other methods, especially the face-to-face interview. In general, studies that concentrate solely on sexual abuse or related issues tend to report higher prevalence rates than do studies that investigate child sexual abuse along with a variety of other topics. This may be due to the notion that child sexual-abuse studies may give the respondent time to adjust to the subject matter along with the opportunity to recall information they might not have remembered in a less focused interview.

The definitions of child sexual abuse and the screen questions used in operationalizing definitions also affect the reported prevalence rates. Bradley and Lindsay (1987) contend that three major models of abuse are used in research: psychiatric, sociological, and social-situational. Depending on the perspective used, each study operationalizes abuse differently, and thus results in differing response rates. Therefore, caution is mandated when comparing findings from studies using various perceptions and definitions, because these studies may be measuring different aspects of child sexual abuse. Studies that use more encompassing definitions tend to have the highest reported prevalence rates (Finkelhor 1986).

One final issue requires discussion. All research, regardless of subject matter, must be sensitive to the need for protecting the well-being of its subjects. Abuse research must be especially sensitive to the potential for retraumatizing victims who participate willingly as research subjects. Despite its importance, there is a dearth of information regarding how— and if—abuse research may actually retraumatize victims. However, informally gathered evidence would suggest that this typically is not the case, at least for those who consent to the interview. The 1985 national telephone survey on family violence conducted by Gelles and Straus (1988) found that victims were more likely to *want* to be reinterviewed than nonvictims. In this study, we found that response to the abuse questions was as high or higher than responses to other questions on the survey. Interviewers were asked to rate the respondents' cooperation at the end of the interview. The categories ranged from "very good" to "poor." Those persons who reported having been sexually abused as a child were rated as more cooperative than those who were not abused. Caution should be used in interpreting these data. Cooperation should not be equated with the lack of trauma. Nevertheless, we may suggest that this points to the fact that a well-designed and implemented interview can, in some ways, be nonthreatening to victims of child sexual abuse. It is imperative that future research focus on this question.

Chapter 7

The Mixed Roles of Social Support and Social Obstruction in Recovery from Child Abuse

Diana Gurley

I. Introduction

This chapter examines the ways intimate relationships help and obstruct recovery from childhood trauma. It includes a thematic analysis of ethnographic data obtained from women who, as children, were sexually abused and battered by family members. When asked how their relationships with others affected their ability to deal with difficult times, the women described behaviors that had been helpful to them, but they also specified behaviors that obstructed their healing and impeded their recovery from trauma. The themes of social support and social obstruction that arose from their conversations are described and compared.

II. Stress and Social Support Research

Since 1956, when Selye produced a conceptual framework for understanding how stress affects somatic health, researchers have attended to the ways in which life events lead to psychological distress and in turn to the ways psychological distress leads to various physical health effects. In stress research generally, we expect stressful life events to result in distress. For example, we study various long-term outcomes of child abuse, including depression, anxiety, problems with intimacy, and feelings of helplessness (Derogatis 1982; Browne and Finkelhor 1986).

However, findings from stress research are mixed. Little variation in health outcomes is explained by simple introduction of measures of stressful life events (Perkins 1982; Cohen and Hoberman 1983). The pathway from distressful life events to various health outcomes is not a direct one. Consequently, researchers have begun to examine a number of potential moderating factors, including the presence and strength of supportive social relationships.

Social support is broadly understood as the resources provided to a person by others. It is used most often in two models in stress research. The first model assumes that people "buffer" the effects of stressful life events for one another through supportive action after the events occur. An alternative model, termed the *direct-effects hypothesis,* assumes that a person embedded in a supportive network of friends and family members is more resistant to distress than the person who is isolated or unsupported. Within these conceptual frames, researchers enumerate social support in a number of ways, for example, by assessing the number of people in a social network, or by evaluating individuals' satisfaction with received, perceived, or available support.

Researchers also study the functions of social support. Typically, functional measures of social support address such dimensions as:

- material or tangible aid,
- instrumental support,
- a sense of friendship and belonging with others,
- attachments to people who respect others and treat them with esteem,
- informational support, and
- help in appraising and making sense of circumstances

(Thoits 1982; Bruhn and Philips 1984; House and Kahn 1985; Cohen and Syme 1985; Pearlin and Aneshensel 1986; Sarason et al. 1987.).

The notion that people help one another through difficult times is intuitively valid and powerful. Unfortunately, hypotheses regarding social support do not always hold under empirical analysis, and results in many quantitative examinations have been inconclusive. These findings have led some reviewers to note the inadequate conceptualization and operationalization of social support (Bruhn and Philips 1984).

III. The Field Research

In 1986–87, I conducted field research with a group of women who identified themselves as having been abused by family members when they were children. This research stemmed from my interests in the processes of healing and adaptation after trauma, and in the ways people help one another in recovery. The question asked of the women in this project was, How have your relationships with others affected your ability to deal with difficult times in your life?

The results reported here are drawn from group interviews, and include responses to open-ended questions and spontaneous storytelling.

Interviews were taped and transcribed, and data from the transcriptions organized using Glaser and Strauss techniques (Glaser 1978; Glaser and Strauss 1967).

The women described a variety of experiences in their relationships with others. Their stories tell how social support can moderate the long-term consequences of stressful life events. Themes from their stories, however, differ remarkably from intuitive conceptions of supportive interactions. These accounts show how relationships moderate distress, but also obstruct healing after trauma.

A. Respondent Sample

The sample for this study was purposively selected and theoretically derived. I sought participants who had experienced battery or sexual violence as children. I elected to interview adult women only. I was concerned that participants identify themselves as having been abused. It was important to this study that themes not be determined in advance by the researcher, but emerge from the data. Instead of creating a list of the characteristics of abuse and fitting participants to that list, I sought women who thought they had been abused, asked them about their experiences, and observed the themes arising from their descriptions.

I was concerned that there was potential to do harm by conducting an open-ended study about the intimate details of violence in women's lives. Thus, I thought it advisable to meet with potential respondents who had been through counseling, or who were actively involved with a support group.

To gain entry to the field, I first approached counselors of groups of adult survivors of child abuse. After a series of meetings, I found one counselor who was willing to ask members of two groups if they would be interested in participating in the study. I prepared a letter that introduced the nature of the project and described how it would be conducted. The letter included information on confidentiality and my credentials as a researcher. It was given to the counselor to distribute to all members of the groups. In addition, I asked the counselor to request permission from the groups for me to meet with them, so that I could describe the project in more detail. One group rejected the project. The second agreed to an introductory meeting, in which all of my assurances were audiotaped by them. Members of this group subsequently agreed to participate in the study.

The sample included six women. All of the participants were white and well educated, and they ranged in age from mid-twenties to mid-thirties. At the time of the interviews, all were unmarried and without children. All had sought, received, and paid for psychological counseling. Despite this homogeneity, participants represented a wide range of experiences they considered abusive. Three of the women had been repeatedly beaten by a parent or stepparent, a fourth was repeatedly beaten by a spouse, and a fifth experienced childhood "accidents" such as being pushed down a flight of stairs by a parent. Three had been sexually assaulted by a parent or stepparent. One reported an alcoholic parent. Three had impaired memory of childhood events, but experienced nightmares of trauma and intrusive thoughts. Two had run away from home as minors in order to escape repeated physical harm by a parent or stepparent. Two were substantially physically handicapped, and experienced emotional abuse and neglect by parents when they were particularly vulnerable.

B. Data Collection

Data were collected in group interviews, using open-ended questions. The group met on six occasions and agreed to be audiotaped in four extensive group interviews. Consistent with inductive techniques, hypotheses were developed and shaped as the interviews proceeded. Data were collected, transcribed, and analyzed, and the interview schedule was revised after each group meeting. Because of the participants' interest and investment in the study, preliminary written analyses were shared with them twice. The final database consisted of 600 pages of transcripts, with researcher field notes and memos.

Once all the interviews had been conducted, transcripts were combed again for basic concepts. Pertinent information from the transcripts was transferred, with citations, to separate memoranda for each concept. Final analyses of the data were conducted over a two-year period, and consisted of defining each theme and identifying key codes that linked several concepts.

IV. Findings

The three primary findings of this field study may be summarized as follows:

1. Intimate relationships are not limited to supportive behaviors. While they may function to support a healing process after trauma, they may also obstruct recovery.

2. Supportive and obstructive behaviors coexist in intimate relationships, and can operate quite independently of one another.

3. The obstructive qualities of relationships, accounted for independently of physical violence, shed light on the ways the emotional content of physically violent experiences can recur and be reinforced in later, nonviolent experiences.

A. The Meaning of Social Obstruction and Support

Social support can be understood as the extent to which one's basic social needs—for affection, esteem, belonging, identity, and security—are gratified through interaction with others (Thoits 1982). Each of the women in this study described resources that had been offered to her, and upon which she had drawn: membership, friendship, protection, tangible aid, information, guidance, validation of her experience, respect, forgiveness, and mercy.

However, it is abundantly clear among survivors of child abuse that relationships are not limited to supportive behaviors. Relationships can be harmful as well as helpful; they can hinder as well as support. And they can serve to eradicate one's resources as well as expand them.

The women in this study all believed that they were undergoing a process of recovery from trauma. Each woman felt that she had expended great effort to accomplish some degree of healing, and each considered that she had been upheld in this process by various forms of social support. Each woman also believed that her recovery had been obstructed by behaviors that stripped her of the natural resources of confidence, assurance, clarity, and faith in her own experiences. Social obstruction can therefore be seen as the inverse of social support. It is the degree to which basic social needs are violated through interaction with others. It may also be broadly understood as behaviors that impede, block, or delay normal progress through life, and by which people take away from a person those resources the person needs to proceed on a chosen course of action.

The themes of support arising from this study reiterate many concepts in social-support research, but themes of social obstruction seem to counteract them. Juxtaposed, this study's key findings of obstruction and support appear to form a pattern:

Themes of obstruction	Themes of support
Isolation	Membership
Stigmatization	Befriending
Disconfirmation Deceit Betrayal	Validation
Confusion	Sorting out (appraisal)
Threatening acts	Protection Tangible support Teaching self-sufficiency
Retribution	Mercy
Humiliation	Respectful acts

The counteracting pattern can be seen when themes of support and obstruction are examined closely. For example, an important support theme emerging from the interviews is validation, i.e., the behaviors by others that confirm or authenticate one's experience. Validation provides external evidence that one's internal experience is true. Two accounts by a woman called Barbara shed light on the importance of the validation theme, especially taken in the context of disconfirmation.

As an adolescent, Barbara was repeatedly raped and beaten by her stepfather. Her reports of these experiences to other family members did not bring her any assistance. She alternately ran away from home and became suicidal when returned to her family. She said:

> As a child my parents took me to a therapist who never talked to me except to tell me to quit thinking so much. And gave me incredible amounts of [medication]. I lived a good portion of my teenage years in a fog. [Interviewer: This was because you were suicidal?] Suicide attempts, and my parents did not want these things to come out, so I suppose they found someone who had a somewhat similar philosophy and he heavily sedated me.

Even in the intimate stronghold of a relationship with a caregiver, relationships can disconfirm as well as confirm one's value and the validity of one's experience. The intimate relationship can obstruct healing rather than encourage it.

At a later time, Barbara had this experience with another counselor:

> I had just tried to commit suicide and this psychologist that I didn't even know put his arm around me and said, "I know there is a lot wrong with your family and there's not a lot of love there, but you have to believe that you can be better than that, and you have to stay there for a while. But you'll be able to get out and you'll be able to do good things because there's good things in you." And just to this day, that's something inside of me that I carry with me. That I just pull out like a little prayer book. Just that one man's faith. And I never saw him again after that. It's almost like, to me, like God saying, "Come on!"

Sometimes interactions with others do indeed validate one's experience. Validation was important to these women, not only to verify that certain events had occurred (allowing them to participate in consensual reality), but also to reassure them that they were, indeed, valuable.

Barbara's accounts raise the question whether supportive action may take on a special meaning when it follows harmful experience of a particular kind, but hers are not the only stories that suggest this notion.

Another illustration of the conjunction of obstruction and support is particularly interesting in the context of current ideas about appraisal: Elizabeth was battered by her father, and her memory of childhood events was impaired. When she began to have problems with intrusive thoughts, she asked her nonbattering mother for clarification.

> I kept hearing this voice in my head that [said] "Don't kill the baby, please don't kill the baby, oh my God you're going to kill the baby, stop, don't kill the baby, oh please God don't kill the baby. . . ." So I called my mother and I asked in kind of an oblique way, "I was wondering, when I was a kid, maybe when I was real young, did I ever, did you ever know me to hurt another child?" And she was real quiet for a long time, and she said, "Don't borrow trouble." And I thought, I've for sure done something really bad and it has to do with a baby.

In fact, she thought she had killed a baby. At the time of this talk with her mother, Elizabeth was seeing a counselor.

> I told my counselor that I was thoroughly disgusted with people who killed other people. I thought it was disgusting and awful, and there was no excuse for it, and I didn't ever want to have anything to do with people who ever killed anyone. And I did not want to remember this thing, so I wasn't going to. And she looked me straight in the eye. She doesn't even remember she said this. This is one of the most important things anyone ever said to me. She looked me straight in the eye and she said, "People can be driven to that." And I knew then that no matter what I had done it could not be so terrible that she would not be willing to sit there with me and talk about it. And that was my idea of what it is to be loved. And then I remembered.

What Elizabeth remembered was that she had seen someone else attack a baby, and that she had jumped the man in order to (successfully) stop the attack. The intrusive cry she had heard was the memory of her own voice.

In addition to helping others evaluate their situations and sort them out, intimates can confuse issues. Acts to confuse others can be more than acts of omission, such as ignoring a call for help. At times, people actively and intentionally confuse one another. All of these women reported that they had been mixed up by the behavior of many people they knew. They reported lies, deceits, double entendres, erratic conditions, and people who acted one way in public and another way in private.

B. The Independent Operation of Obstruction and Support

Preliminary analysis suggests that the themes of obstruction and support cluster along specific, polar dimensions. If the list of themes is read across, certain obstructive acts might be seen as polarities to certain acts of support. For example, disconfirmation may be seen as a polarity to validation.

However, further analysis shows that the themes can be interpreted by reading down the columns—not as polarities of independent dimensions, but as indicators of two large, underlying factors: support and obstruction. The data suggest there may be important reasons to consider these two clusters against one another. Among them is the clear indication that love and cruelty coexist in time, and sometimes within a single relationship.

If it is indeed true that intimate relationships at any given time are concomitantly harmful and helpful, we need to consider harmfulness and helpfulness as independent concepts. Until then, we cannot evaluate whether and how they offset one another. A critical finding from this study is that social obstruction and support may operate independently of one another and, further, that they may interact in important ways.

C. Separating Social Obstruction from Physical Violence

The third major finding from this study is that, even in the absence of battery or sexual assault, the emotional context of abuse can be reiterated in relational exchanges. In order to assess the level at which obstruction exacerbates the trauma of abuse, it must be accounted for separately and treated independently within research models.

Transcripts from this research show clearly that the psychological context in which physically abusive events occur were repeated and reinforced in other social contexts by people who were not physically abusive to the participants.

Emily was beaten by her mother until late adolescence, when she developed a degenerative and disfiguring (but not contagious) disease. At that time, both of her parents stopped touching her. They also stopped touching anything that belonged to her—her clothes, bedding, and furniture. This created a problem for Emily, who was unable to feed or clothe herself:

> I however do think of myself as totally disgusting. And that is because my parents still to this day will not touch my clothing. . . . Everything about me to them is gross. You know, it's dirty. And that has real, real far-

reaching implications for me. I'm still blown away if people touch me. I, I think that they don't know better.

Emily is now in her thirties, and her parents still do not touch her.

Barbara carries the same theme into relationships with people outside the family, "I remember telling my girlfriend. The horror. You know, just like I was a leper."

Alice, who was born with a physical handicap but who is not at all diseased, described isolation and stigmatization by nonbatterers within a close group, but went on to explain how that isolation can resound through other relationships:

> There is a big part of me that has always thought of myself as being disgusting and filthy. . . . To avoid contaminating other people with my disgusting disease, [I was always] holding back, staying out of things where I might get close to somebody because I knew that awful things would happen if I did.

Most of the participants in the study identified themselves as diseased, malformed, disgusting, contagious, and ugly—descriptions incorporated thematically under obstruction as stigmatization. In acts of physical violence, the women were demeaned and their status as human beings was called into question. They were told, either by actions or in words, that they were substandard. They came to believe that they were marked in a physically obvious way with a sign of shame. Their shame was reinforced when they were rejected by others outside the immediately violent relationships of their lives. They bore the stigma of abuse. They were isolated by others, but they also removed themselves from social contacts as a consequence of their interpretation of the reasons for their abuse.

The physically violent acts we call child abuse occur in conjunction with other elements of human exchange. Often, those exchanges involve humiliation, betrayal, deceit, or vengeance. These psychological components of interaction can reverberate throughout life and through many other relationships. The echo may be especially strong when events in other relationships mimic the psychological components of a violent event, whether or not the new events are physically violent.

In order to disentangle the effects of initial physical trauma and the consequences of repeating the emotional components of abuse, social obstruction and violence must be treated independently in research models. Until that is done, we will not be able to see how social obstruction and physical violence covary. Nor will we understand how trauma from physical violence is exacerbated, reinforced, and recreated by social obstruction.

V. Summary

Research on posttraumatic stress disorder shows that in the long process of recovery from multiple, severe losses, individuals often reexperience traumatic events (Horowitz 1986; American Psychiatric Association 1987).

This appears to be a natural aspect of grief. Literature on bereavement (Hofer 1984) suggests that losses are multiple; when one loses a beloved other, one also sustains a loss of anticipations and expectations, of fantasy and hopes for the future. Multiple losses may be experienced as representational units of grief, occurring again and again over time, each as a new pain, each experienced afresh.

From a social perspective, relational obstruction is a way in which some components of the losses sustained in physically violent events may be re-created in other social settings, in other relationships, at other times. If that is true, it suggests that physical trauma with psychological overtones may require more than one recovery, if it is followed by harmful later interactions that repeat the quality and tone in which the violence initially occurred. If there is one rape, and there are one hundred humiliations, one hundred recoveries may be necessary.

*   *   *   *   *

I began this study with the idea that things can happen in relationships that aid recovery from child abuse. I continue to hold that idea. The participants described their commitments to service, their love for others, their pleasure in life. Of the six women in the group, five elected to go into helping and teaching and guidance professions. Some of them decided to focus their work on recovery from abuse. By doing these things, they enter into a kind of group membership that is extremely important to them.

In retrospect, they seem to have arrived at the places they happened to be by moving through substantial impediments set for them by other people important in their lives. These women described a long struggle. The stories about meaningful help they received as they attempted to overcome their humiliation and loneliness suggest that it may be fruitful to study the nature of those impediments.

To understand how relationships mediate the long-term consequences of abuse, we must expand the range of our conceptions of human interaction. Intimates are sometimes supportive, and sometimes cruel. When harmfulness and helpfulness coexist in one's group of relationships, it is natural to expect that they would interact with one another, although in ways that are as yet unknown to us. In order to understand how harm and help offset one another, we need to study them as independent dimensions. In order to understand the extent of harm, we must assess the ways psychologically obstructive behaviors compound the ramifications of violence.

To understand the multiplicity of losses incurred in abuse, we must examine social relationships in their complexity. To understand the process of recovery, we must become knowledgeable about what is to be healed.

Chapter 8

The Admissibility of Expert Testimony on the Battered-Woman Syndrome

Debra F. Kromsky and Brian L. Cutler

I. Introduction

Expert psychological testimony is, with increasing frequency, admitted into criminal and civil trials. Grisso (1987) notes that clinical psychologists testify about such matters as insanity and competency to stand trial, understanding one's rights, parenting, the management of one's estate and financial transactions, and consent to treatment. In death penalty cases, psychologists are called upon to testify about competency for execution (Radelet 1988). Clinical psychologists also testify about a variety of psychological syndromes, including rape trauma syndrome (Frazier and Borgida 1985) and the battered woman syndrome (Walker 1979). Expert psychological testimony has not been limited to clinical testimony. Social and cognitive psychologists have testified about matters such as eyewitness memory (Loftus 1986) and pretrial publicity (Fulero 1986).

Considerable scholarly debate exists over the appropriateness of expert psychological testimony (see, for example, Rogers 1989; Saks 1986). Among the issues addressed are the need for expert testimony, the morals and ethics of expert testimony, and the effects of expert testimony on both jury decision making and the reputation of the field of psychology. In this chapter we address the justification for expert testimony on the battered-woman syndrome by examining the extant research on the lay person's knowledge for the syndrome, including our own survey.

A. Use of Expert Testimony

Expert psychological testimony is sometimes used to establish that a victim suffers from the battered-woman syndrome. The purpose of the testimony is to educate the jury about the pattern of the characteristics and behavioral reactions of women involved in abusive relationships. The expert attempts to parallel those characteristics of battered women drawn from psychological research to those characteristics of the (alleged) battered woman involved in the trial. Attorneys attempt to encourage the jury to conclude that the woman involved suffers from the battered-woman syndrome. Generally, prosecuting attorneys use the expert testimony to convict a batterer by establishing that a victim has been assaulted repeatedly. Defense attorneys use expert testimony on the battered-woman syndrome in cases involving women who kill their abusers.

B. The Admissibility of Expert Testimony on Battered-Woman Syndrome

There are two prerequisites for testimony to be admitted at trial: it must be material, and it must be relevant (McCormick 1972). With respect to expert testimony, a court will usually require that the testimony meet either the three criteria set forth in recent case law (Dyas v. U.S., 1977) or Rule 702 of the Federal Rules of Evidence. A tripartite test for admissibility of expert testimony states:

> (1) The subject matter must be so distinctly related to some science, profession, business or occupation as to be beyond the ken of the average layman; (2) The witness must have sufficient skill, knowledge or experience in that field or calling as to make it appear that (her) opinion or inference will probably aid the trier in (her) search for truth; and (3) Expert testimony is inadmissible if the state of the pertinent art or scientific knowledge does not permit a reasonable opinion to be asserted even by an expert.

Federal Rule 702 states:

> If scientific, technical or other specialized knowledge will assist the trier of fact to understand the evidence or to determine a fact in issue, a witness qualified as an expert by knowledge, skill, experience, training or education, may testify thereto in the form of an opinion or otherwise.

Expert testimony on the battered-woman syndrome has received a mixed reception, with some jurisdictions holding it admissible and other jurisdictions ruling it inadmissible. When an expert's testimony is based on a novel subject, the state requires that the science or pertinent art be sufficiently developed to permit a reasonable opinion to be asserted (*Tonkovich v. Department of Labor and Industry*, 195 P.2d 638, Wash., 1948). It is often argued that the battered-woman syndrome is a novel subject, i.e., a new finding, and thus not yet fully accepted in the courtroom. This is despite the considerable study it has received, and the well-established symptomology of the syndrome (e.g., Martin 1976; Moore 1979; Walker 1979).

Seven states have unconditionally admitted the battered-woman syndrome expert testimony: Georgia, Kansas, Maine, New Hampshire, New York, Pennsylvania, and Washington (Coffee 1986–87). Courts in these states have concluded that the testimony was relevant, that the expert was qualified to testify, that the defendant established herself as a battered woman, and that the state's standard for admissibility was fully satisfied.

Expert testimony has been deemed conditionally admissible by the District of Columbia and five states: Florida, Illinois, New Jersey, North Dakota, and South Carolina (Coffee, 1986–87). In these states admissibility is not admitted until the expert demonstrates sufficient skill or expertise and/or the state of the art would support an expert opinion.

Four states hold expert testimony on the battered-woman syndrome inadmissible: Louisiana, Ohio, Texas, and Wyoming (Coffee 1986–87). Among the various reasons for excluding the testimony are that such testimony could only apply to a claim of mental disease or defect and that expert testimony for prior battering incidents in the absence of an overt act is not admissible.

Arguments against the admissibility of battered-woman syndrome evidence are sometimes based upon the contention that the expert's testimony is already within the ken of the jury. Judges have often assumed that jurors are aware of the factors that influence the battered woman and can understand her fears. This issue is a reflection of concerns for eyewitness testimony. Experts on eyewitness memory have been routinely prohibited from testifying on the assumption that the testimony is within the common knowledge of the juror (Walters 1985). This assumption has been tested in a number of surveys (see Wells 1984, for a review) that uniformly demonstrate jurors are indeed uninformed about how a substantial number of factors reliably influence eyewitness memory. Further, studies of lay knowledge have revealed that certain groups of professionals who should be well-informed—including juries, judges, police officers, and attorneys—appear to be uninformed (e.g., Brigham 1980). Although there are several studies of juror understanding for eyewitness behavior as well as a study on lay knowledge for rape trauma syndrome (Frazier and Borgida 1985), the examination of lay knowledge for the battered-woman syndrome remains largely unexplored.

The Battered-Woman Syndrome

The battered-woman syndrome is presumably a result of a cycle of violence that is perpetuated by socialization (e.g., Dobash and Dobash 1977; Gelles 1974; Martin 1976; Straus et al 1980; Walker 1979). The feminist orientation (Walker 1979) analyzes the battering in the social, political, and economic context of sexism, whereas the general social orientation (Gelles 1974) places the crime in the context of general societal violence. Children who witness violence in their homes or who are themselves the victims of abuse are more likely than others to believe that violence is an acceptable and legitimate way to solve problems. They will therefore be more likely than those who do not witness or experience abuse to have violent adult relationships (Fleming 1979; Gelles 1974; Ganley 1980; Hilberman and Munson 1978; Straus 1977).

The battered-woman syndrome pertains to a set of particular symptoms, characteristics, and problems experienced by a woman engaged in an ongoing abusive relationship with a man. Walker, the pioneer in this field, contends:

> Any woman can find herself in a violent relationship with a man once. If it occurs a second time and she remains in the relationship, she is defined as a battered woman. A battered woman is one who is repeatedly subjected to any forceful physical or psychological behavior by a man in order to coerce her to do something he wants her to do without any concern for her rights. Battered women include wives or women in any form of intimate relationships with men. Furthermore, in order to be classified as a battered woman, the couple must go through the battering cycle at least twice. (1979:xv)

The following is a hypothetical description of a battered woman. The abuse occurs in a cycle that consists of three distinct and predictable phases, rather than in a random or constant pattern.

1.   The first phase is the tension-building phase, during which physical violence may or may not be present, but when it is present it is regarded as minor. The victim works hard during this phase to keep her mate calm and to keep peace. She gives in to his demands, no matter how unreasonable, and tries to keep things under control. During this phase she is able to maintain some control, but with each minor incident (verbal, psychological, physical, and/or even sexual abuse) the tension builds. The man becomes more possessive, accusing, and irrational. The minor incidents become more frequent and more severe. She continues to try to appease him and to satisfy his demands. She develops anger and resentment but denies it while internalizing the blame for the abuse

(Walker 1979). She withdraws in order to avoid any outburst, but no matter what she does, he views her actions as negative and provocative. Once the tension becomes unbearable, the couple enters the second phase of the cycle.

2. The severe battering incident occurs during the second phase. It generally lasts from 2 to 24 hours and can be triggered by any outside event or any behavior by the victim. It can also be triggered just on sight of the victim, as many women relate incidents beginning when they were asleep. This severe battering usually happens in private or with only the children present. The destructiveness in this phase is regarded as serious, even by the victim. The man is perceived as being out of control and in a rage. No matter what she does or says, the batterer becomes more angry. If the victim is passive, she gets beaten. If she tries to defend herself, she is beaten even worse. After the event, both parties agree that he was "out of control" although they recall the events differently. She tends to recall vivid details, while he remembers very little and has no understanding of what happened. He may attempt to justify his behavior by blaming her or other external factors, such as drugs or alcohol. The violence in this phase ends only when the couple is separated for a substantial period of time or he is simply tires himself out. After the battering ends, both the man and his victim react with disbelief, shock, and denial at the seriousness of the violence (Walker 1979:xv).

It has often been argued—erroneously—that women provoke the violence that occurs in the second phase. This phenomenon can be explained by the woman's desire to maintain control over when and where the incident will occur. It also ensures a speedier retreat to the third phase of the cycle (Walker 1979).

3. In the third phase, the batterer appears to be his loving, warm, and affectionate self. He is generous and consumed by grief and remorse. He is full of apologies and promises. He begs her not to leave and convinces her that it will never happen again. Even if there is no affection or remorse in this phase, the absence of violence and tension is the reward that so often keeps the woman in the relationship. This is the phase that cements the victim to her batterer. It is known as the "honeymoon phase."

Battered women develop constellations of particular psychological characteristics that constitute the battered-woman syndrome (Walker 1983). These characteristics include fear, shame, isolation, guilt, depression, passivity, learned helplessness, traditional sex role attitudes, low self-esteem, and dependency (Dobash and Dobash 1979; Hilberman 1980; Moore 1979; Walker 1979).

Learned helplessness is a term coined by Seligman (1975) and applied by Lenore Walker to explain a battered woman's inability to take control of her situation. A battered woman suffers from learned helplessness when she believes that her reinforcements or punishments are not contingent upon her performance. In other words, the battered woman perceives that the battering will occur regardless of her behavior. Many of the characteristics are adopted as survival techniques in a violent situation and preclude the development of other skills that would enable the battered woman to escape by ending the relationship (Walker 1983).

II. Empirical Assessments of Lay Knowledge for the Battered-Woman Syndrome

A. Research Methods

Studies of lay knowledge regarding eyewitness behavior of rape trauma show that it is often at odds with psychological findings. Consequently, we predict that lay knowledge for the battered-woman syndrome is inconsistent with findings from psychological research on battered women. The study we discuss below empirically examines the arguments against the admissibility of the battered-woman syndrome by assessing lay and professional opinion. Its purpose is to compare these opinions to psychological knowledge about the battered-woman syndrome, and to use these data to determine whether or not expert guidance is needed in cases involving battered women.

We constructed a lay-knowledge questionnaire containing 11 multiple-choice items. Each question elicits opinions about a different aspect of the battered-woman syndrome. The questionnaire was distributed to samples of prospective jurors, police officers, and attorneys. While data from the prospective jurors are relevant to the debate over the admissibility of expert testimony on the battered-woman syndrome, data from the legal practitioners can be used to ascertain the need for educating professionals about the battered-woman syndrome.

The questionnaire is designed to determine the proportion of respondents who know that:

1. The majority of battered women file charges in order to get protection.
2. Most battered women drop the charges after they are filed.
3. The majority of battered women stay in the relationship because they are afraid that their abusers will harm them should they leave.

4. Only a very small percentage of battered women report the battering to the police.
5. A primary factor leading to an abuser's behavior is exposure to violence as a child.
6. Domestic violence occurs in a predictable cycle.
7. Battered women suffer from guilt, learned helplessness, fear, shame and isolation.
8. Police typically respond to domestic-dispute calls by attempting to mediate the dispute.
9. The most effective way to decrease recidivist wife assault is to arrest the offender.
10. Only a small percentage of batterers are arrested.
11. The battered woman suffers most from the psychological abuse experienced.

The prospective-juror sample consists of 91 registered voters interviewed at the Miami International Airport. Ninety-four officers from Miami, Florida, were polled. Fifty attorneys from the Metro-Dade Justice Building in Miami were interviewed, i.e., 27 public defenders (from the Public Defender's Office) and 23 state attorneys (from the State Attorney's Office).

The questionnaire was administered individually or in some instances to small groups of three or four people. Respondents were instructed not to talk about the questionnaire items. The first page of the questionnaire gathered demographic information including age, race, sex, extent of work with domestic violence, number of children, and education.

B. Findings

1. Prospective Jurors. Our findings indicate that prospective jurors are knowledgeable about some issues but quite unaware of others. More than 75% of the prospective jurors indicated correctly that a battered woman files charges primarily to get protection, and that she typically drops the charges, suffers from guilt, learned helplessness, fear, shame and isolation, and is most affected by the psychological abuse. On the other hand, only 41% were aware that only a small percentage of battered women report the battering to the police. Only 38% knew that the spouse abuse follows a predictable cycle, whereas 68% were aware that fear of harm keeps the battered woman in the relationship. Most—59%—knew that batterers typically experienced violence in their homes as children. Although 61% were aware that the typical police response to domestic-dispute calls is to attempt to mediate, only 24% knew that arrest is the most effective method of reducing recidivist wife assault. More than 67% knew that only a small percentage of batterers are arrested. In summary, 7 out of 11 questions were answered correctly by less than 70% of the sample. Thus, we conclude that while prospective jurors are somewhat knowledgeable about the battered-woman syndrome, there is certainly a need for additional education.

2. Police Officers.   Perhaps the knowledge that is most in need of dissemination among police officers is that arresting the offender is currently thought to be the most effective method for reducing recidivist battering (Berk and Newton 1985; Jaffe et al. 1986; Sherman and Berk 1984). Only 24% of the police officers we surveyed answered this question correctly.

Overall, the police knowledge of the battered-woman syndrome is comparable to that of the prospective jurors. On average, the police answered 70% of the items correctly. The police performed poorly on items explaining why battered women stay in the relationship, the percentage of battered women who report the battering to the police, the cycle of violence, and the most effective way to reduce recidivist spouse assault. Their responses to some items are likely to be affected, quite understandably, by their personal experiences with domestic-violence cases. To illustrate, although battered women come from all races and socioeconomic groups, police tend to see a disproportionate number of poor victims, and blacks or other minority group members. Other women who experience domestic violence problems are less likely to call the police, and more likely to seek help from family members or private attorneys.

3. Attorneys.   The attorneys, on average, show more knowledge of the battered woman syndrome than the prospective jurors and police. They are most likely to answer correctly items explaining why the battered woman files charges, the likelihood of dropping charges, the characteristics of battered women, and the police procedure for handling domestic disputes. The attorneys are least knowledgeable about the percentage of battered women who report the battering to the police, the cycle of domestic violence, and the most effective way of reducing recidivist battering.

The defense attorneys and state attorneys differ significantly on only two items. The defense attorneys are more likely than the state attorneys to know why battered women stay in the abusive relationship. They are also more likely to know about the common police strategies for handling domestic-dispute calls.

III. Conclusions and Implications

The surveys we conducted show that prospective jurors are not sufficiently knowledgeable about critical aspects of the battered-woman syndrome that would help them judge a case. Schuller's experiment (1988) on the effects of expert testimony on the battered-woman syndrome and related research on the effects of other forms of expert testimony show that expert testimony can have beneficial effects without prejudicing the jury. Consequently, our conclusions, although based on the first known empirical inquiry of this question, are instructive:

1.   The lay and professional populations lack knowledge about some of the important aspects of the battered-woman syndrome.

2.   Expert testimony on the battered-woman syndrome can assist the jury.

Part III

Social Responses to Family Violence: Batterers and Their Victims

To what extent should social services or counseling be available to batterers? Should the courts mandate therapy? What should social-service agencies do in response to a substantiated case of child sexual abuse: remove the perpetrator? Place the victim in a foster home? These and other difficult questions are raised by researchers who examine social-service intervention strategies.

Richard M. Tolman and Gauri Bhosley provide the results of an evaluation of a shelter-sponsored group intervention program for men who batter their female partners. Fifty-three women agreed to telephone interviews one year after their partners participated in the batterers' program. Indices of direct physical aggression, indirect physical aggression, and psychological abuse are the outcomes researchers measured. Also, women rated their current intimate relationships in the areas believed by the researchers to be affected by the abuse. Results of the study, summarized in "The Outcome of Participation in a Shelter-Sponsored Program for Men Who Batter," show that 58.5% of the men were not directly violent after participation in the therapy program. Most women reported a decreased fearfulness of their partners and an increased comfort in expressing anger to their partners. Tolman and Bhosley conducted research that convincingly indicates victim benefits from a batterers program.

Patricia Ryan, Bruce L. Warren, and Peggy Weincek are researchers at the Institute for the Study of Child and Family. Their study, "Removal of the Perpetrator versus Removal of the Victim in Cases of Intrafamilial Child Sexual Abuse," highlights the critical shortage of empirical study on the effects that different social-service agency interventions can have on the victims of abuse and on the victim's family. They examine 133 cases of child sexual abuse in which social-service agencies intervened. Their analysis shows that the social-service agency's decision to remove the victim of sexual abuse from her or his home is indeed one that reflects numerous factors, such as the seriousness of the offense and the

111

mother's ability to protect the child against subsequent acts of abuse. These researchers elicit the troubling question, What should we do?

In "Perceptions of Verbal Aggression in Interspousal Violence," Teresa Chandler Sabourin discusses her research, which focuses upon the relationship between verbal aggression and the severity of spouse abuse. Chandler also summarizes the advantages and drawbacks associated with using a retrospective research method to gather information from women once battered by their spouses. She shows us the necessity of analyzing specific communication patterns and the more global interactional patterns among partners who batter. Chandler's research is praiseworthy for several reasons. Most importantly, she shows us how to bring observations and recollections from victims into the research agenda without blaming the victim, a problem heretofore ignored or dismissed by those studying interpersonal violence.

Chapter 9

The Outcome of Participation in a Shelter-Sponsored Program for Men Who Batter

Richard M. Tolman and Gauri Bhosley

I. Introduction

This chapter presents the results of a project evaluating the efficacy of a shelter-sponsored intervention program for men who batter. The program is a 26-week, structured group intervention based on cognitive–behavioral and feminist principles. The pilot study of the program indicated that approximately one-half of the men were not directly aggressive toward their partners following intervention (Tolman et al. 1987). Most women also reported decreases in emotional abuse and improvements in their relationships.

The current study assesses whether men stop their threats of violence and their direct physical aggression following involvement in the program. Men who batter often display high levels of nonphysical or psychological abuse of their partners. Psychological abuse alone may cause harm; when it occurs in combination with physical abuse, it may be devastating. Gondolf (1986) suggests that men who batter may give up their physical abuse as a result of intervention, but may continue or intensify their use of other forms. In this chapter, we examine the relative psychological impact of physical abuse, threats of physical abuse, and psychological abuse on the women.

Measurement tools developed in the first phase of the study were refined and used. A follow-up telephone survey was used to ensure a high survey response rate. For this phase of the study, we contacted program participants and their partners approximately one year following participation.

II. Methods

A. Subjects

We included in the study all male clients who completed their program participation between February 1986 and February 1988, if they had attended at least one group session after intake. The initial pool of clients included 99 men and their partners at the time of entry to the program. In all, we interviewed 53 women. We failed to reach 32 women, either because telephones were disconnected, they had moved, or no one answered (up to 30 attempts were made to contact them). Fourteen of the women declined to participate.

The average age of the women interviewed is 35.8 years (S.D. = 7.6). They are predominantly white, with an average education of 12.9 years (S.D. = 1.9). Thirty-nine of the women worked outside the home, 21 full-time. Forty of the women still live with the men who had abused them.

The average age of the partners of the women interviewed is 37.2 years (S.D. = 8.0). Forty-eight are white. The men completed an average of 12.1 years (S.D. = 2.1) of school. The men participated in an average of 12 sessions (S.D. = 9.2).

B. Intervention Procedures

The Crisis Center for South Suburbia (CCSS), founded both as a crisis line and shelter for battered women, also provides nonresident services such as legal advocacy, support groups, and job and housing support to battered women and their children. In 1982, in response to numerous requests from shelter residents, and a desire to address woman abuse in a comprehensive manner, the agency founded a program for both court-ordered and voluntary-client batterers.

The groups for men are co-led by a woman and a man at various locations in the community. The agency, consistent with its philosophy, places the sole responsibility for violence on the abuser. The program does not advocate conjoint therapy for abusers and victims until the abuser has taken responsibility for his abusive behavior, stopped his physical aggression for several months, and both the victim and abuser indicate willingness to begin conjoint work.

Men must first learn to stop their abusive behavior and learn alternative skills for coping with emotional arousal and conflict resolution. The group also confronts the perceived entitlement of men to be violent, and explicitly focuses on male sex role socialization as it relates to men's abuse of women. The group setting as well as the dual focus on cognitive–behavioral skills and issues of sexism make the program fairly representative of "mainstream" treatment for men who batter (Gondolf 1986).

Men learn of the program from their partners who are clients of CCSS, police or court contact, other social-service agencies, public-service announcements, or previous participants. Once a man has learned of the program, he must call the program to initiate treatment. Two individual intake sessions follow, which focus on obtaining demographic material and clinical information, and engage the client in the treatment process. A client with an untreated substance abuse problem or a severe psychiatric problem is not accepted unless he agrees to concurrent treatment for those problems. Men sign a nonviolence pledge, a statement permitting the agency to conduct safety checks by contacting their partners to ascertain the level of violence, and a pledge to remove firearms and other weapons from their possession as requirements for entry into the program.

Following intake, the men attend a pregroup orientation workshop (see Tolman and Bhosley 1988) that introduces the skills to be further addressed in an ongoing group. These skills include self-observation of physical, cognitive, and situational cues that occur prior to abusive behavior, time-outs (leaving a conflict prior to use of abusive behavior), cognitive restructuring (identifying abuse-promoting beliefs or self-statements and replacing them with coping self-talk), relaxation, identification of feelings other than anger or those that underlie anger, and assertive communication and conflict resolution.

Following the intensive workshop, the men join an ongoing group of six to ten men, in which they apply the skills and information presented in the workshop to their current life situations. These ongoing groups provide further development of competence in application of the skills. Further, they serve as a forum to reduce further denial, and foster attitude change supportive of nonviolence by requiring disclosure of abusive behavior, and confronting members who deny or minimize their abusive behavior. The leaders also model confrontation of the sexist attitudes and beliefs that support woman abuse, and encourage group consciousness-raising.

During the time period examined by this study, the program required men to attend 26 ongoing sessions to fulfill their contracts successfully. The program shares attendance data with the men's partners and the court if the men were mandated to treatment. The intensive workshop format minimizes dropping out from the group, but a large percentage of the men (50%) still fail to complete the program.

C. Measures

We developed and used a structured telephone interview questionnaire, which included demographic items, and questions about relationship history, a history of abuse (physical and nonphysical), and current individual and relationship functioning.

1. Abuse. The measure of abuse is a modification of the Conflict Tactics Scale (CTS) (Straus 1979). The CTS was expanded to include types of physical and nonphysical abuse commonly reported by battered women. Women were asked if each act had occurred at all since their partner had completed participation in the program, and to rate the frequency of occurrence on a scale of 1 (not at all) to 7 (once a day). Because men who batter tend to underreport their abusive behavior (Edleson and Brygger 1986), women's perceptions provide a more valid program outcome measure. Three scales—direct physical aggression, indirect physical aggression, and psychological abuse—were created from the modified CTS items.

2. Personal Problems. A 20-item psychosocial problem checklist (Hudson 1982) measures the number and degree of intrapersonal and interpersonal problems the women experience. Additional items asking about women's problems with finances, health, and substance use were added. Women rated the occurrence of each problem on a five-point scale (1, rarely or never; 5, very frequently). We hypothesized that women who were continuing to experience abuse would report more personal problems than women for whom the abuse had ceased. Reports of high numbers of personal problems or high intensity of several problems by women who did not report overt aggression may indicate that those men have stopped overt aggressive behavior, but continue to dominate and control their partners through more subtle types of abusive behavior.

3. Relationship Change. Relationship change was measured by using a series of scale items including closeness, comfort in expressing anger and other feelings, fear of partner, power, decision making, division of household tasks, and conflict. The relationship areas probed were hypothesized to be related to the depth and sincerity of a man's change. Thus, a man who gave up physical abuse but continued to dominate decision making would have only been successful in terms of one dimension of the program. A woman's continued fear, or her inability to express anger to her partner, even if the physical aggression ceased, could be a function of ongoing dominating and controlling behaviors.

III. Findings

A. Direct Physical Aggression

Table 1 presents the incidence of men's direct physical aggression and the average (mean) frequencies of these acts in the past six months.

Table 1. Women's Reports of Program Participants' Aggression

	After program (%)	In past 6 mos. (%)	Mean number of incidents in past 6 mos. (S.D.)	
Psychological maltreatment				
Screamed or insulted	81.1	75.4	2.1	(1.3)
Belittled	58.5	71.7	4.0	(1.9)
Sulked or withdrew	58.5	71.7	2.0	(2.4)
Interrupted eating or sleeping	43.4	41.5	1.8	(2.4)
Kept her from leaving or seeing certain people	26.4	22.6	0.8	(1.8)
Verbally pressured for sex	20.8	15.1	0.7	(1.9)
Threatened to leave or have an affair	45.3	43.4	1.1	(1.6)
Psychological abuse index	92.5	86.8	12.8	(11.0)
Indirect physical aggression				
Threatened to hit her	30.2	24.1	0.8	(1.5)
Threw, hit, or kicked an object	49.1	41.5	1.0	(1.6)
Destroyed property	22.6	18.9	0.4	(0.9)
Drove recklessly	28.3	22.6	0.6	(1.4)
Threatened life	26.4	20.7	0.5	(1.2)
Threatened with weapon	5.7	3.8	0.1	(0.3)
Indirect aggression index	73.6	64.2	3.4	(3.9)
Direct physical aggression				
Burned	0.0	0.0	0.0	(0.0)
Pushed, shoved, or grabbed	37.7	32.1	0.9	(1.5)
Slapped or spanked	15.1	11.3	0.3	(1.0)
Bit or scratched	1.9	1.9	0.02	(0.1)
Hit with object	7.5	1.9	0.5	(0.3)
Hit her	28.3	18.9	0.5	(1.1)
Punched repeatedly	22.6	15.1	0.3	(0.8)
Threw her bodily	18.9	9.4	0.1	(0.4)
Beat unconscious	0.0	0.0	0.0	(0.0)
Choked or strangled	11.3	9.4	0.1	(0.4)
Physically forced her to have sex	11.3	7.5	0.2	(0.7)
Used weapon	0.0	0.0	0.0	(0.0)
Direct aggression index	41.5	35.8	2.8	(5.0)

These ratings for the occurrence of each act were summed to create an index of direct aggression ($\alpha = .78$).

In all, 41.5% of the men were physically aggressive at some point following participation in the program; in the past six months, 35.8% of the women were victims of direct aggression. In the six months prior to the program, all the men were physically aggressive toward their part-

ners. The types most prevalent subsequent to the program were pushing, shoving, or grabbing; hitting; punching; and slapping or spanking.

B. *Indirect Physical Aggression*

Indirect aggression consists of acts that threaten the use of physical
aggression but stop short of direct physical contact. Table 1 shows that
73.6% of the men used some form of indirect aggression at some point
following program participation; within the past six months, the figure
is 64.2%. The most widely used acts of indirect aggression following the
program were throwing, hitting, or kicking objects; threatening to hit;
driving recklessly; and threatening her life. Analysis revealed margin-
ally acceptable reliability of the index of indirect physical aggression (α
= .62).

C. *Psychological Abuse*

We define psychological abuse as those behaviors that do not constitute physical aggression or the threat of physical aggression, but
nonetheless may harm the victim. Table 1 shows the number of women
who report that a particular type of psychological abuse occurred, and
the mean scores for an index of psychological maltreatment (α = .82).
Psychological abuse was more prevalent than the other forms of abuse.
Only 7.5% of the women reported that no occurrences of any type of
psychological maltreatment had occurred since her partner completed
the program.

D. *Relationship Change*

Women's ratings of the current status of their relationship compared
to the past are presented in Table 2. Women rated the most improvement
in the following areas: reduction in fear of her partner, reduction in
conflict in the relationship, increase in her power relative to her partner's, and comfort in expressing anger to her partner. A high percentage
of women (59%) report that their closeness to their partners increased,
but many women (22%) also reported a decrease in perceived closeness.
Forty-five percent of the women report an increase in their comfort in
expressing feelings other than anger. Thirty percent report an increase
in the partner's sharing of household tasks. We assume that some of
these items represent a deep level of change in a relationship.

E. *Women's Problems*

Table 3 presents the average (mean) ratings of women's reported problems, a total problem index (α = .90), and indices of intrapersonal prob-

Table 2. Women's Evaluation of Current Relationship with Abuser[a]

	Mean problem rating (S.D.)		Increase (%)	Same (%)	Decrease (%)
Closeness with partner	3.3	(1.4)	59	18	22
Comfortable in expressing anger to partner	3.1	(1.4)	57	36	7
Comfortable in expressing feelings other than anger	3.2	(1.3)	45	45	10
Fearful of partner	2.1	(1.0)	6	17	77
Power relative to partner	3.0	(1.3)	63	32	5
Have a say in important decisions	2.9	(1.0)	47	53	0
How fairly household tasks are divided	2.8	(1.4)	30	52	19
How conflictual relationship is	3.0	(1.1)	9	18	72

[a] N = 40; excludes women who say they have no significant ongoing relationship with abuser.

Table 3. Women's Reports of Psychosocial Problems

	Mean problem rating (S.D.)		Those with problem (%)
Feels depressed	2.6	(1.4)	64
Low self-esteem	2.1	(1.5)	30
Feels unhappy	2.8	(1.3)	52
Feels afraid	2.4	(1.5)	47
Feels anxious	2.7	(1.5)	56
Feels nervous	2.8	(1.4)	62
Has disturbing thoughts	1.9	(1.2)	32
Problems with anger	2.3	(1.1)	38
Has nightmares	1.6	(1.1)	17
Problems with identity	2.0	(1.4)	36
Problems with sex life	1.9	(1.4)	30
Poor work quality	1.9	(1.4)	30
Problems with relationships with friends	1.3	(0.7)	11
Problems in family relationshps	2.0	(1.3)	34
Problems with children	2.2	(1.5)	36
Problems with mother	1.5	(0.9)	13
Problems with father	1.4	(0.9)	13
Problems with finances	2.9	(1.4)	64
Problems with health	2.1	(1.4)	33
Problems with substance use	1.2	(0.6)	7
Total problems index	43.4	(16.4)	
Intrapersonal problems index	24.4	(10.3)	
Interpersonal problem index	13.1	(6.2)	

Table 4. Hierarchical Regression: Women's Total
Problem Index

	Beta	Change in R^2
Direct aggression	−.30*	.03
Indirect aggression	.12	.27**
Psychological abuse	.46**	.19**
Fear of partner	.28**	.07**
Conflict in relationship	.28*	.04**

R^2 (adjusted) = .55.   *p = <.05.   **p = <.01.

lems (α = .91) and interpersonal problems (α = .72). The range of scores is wide, indicating that some women report relatively high numbers of intense problems, while others report that their current lives are relatively problem free.

F. Abuse and Womens' Problems

The relationship between women's current functioning and the level of abuse they experienced during the follow-up period was examined using a regression analysis. The independent variables are the women's ratings of how fearful they were of their partners, and the conflict in their relationships. The psychosocial problem index is the dependent variable. We entered the physical, indirect, and psychological abuse indices, in that order, to assess their relative contributions to women's problems. Because physical abuse almost always occurs concurrently with some level of psychological abuse, it was entered first in order to allow physical abuse to account for any variance shared with indirect and psychological abuse. The same assumption dictated entry of indirect aggression prior to psychological maltreatment, and then the variables fear of partner and conflict in relationship were added to assess any additional explanatory power. Table 4 shows the results of this analysis. Psychological abuse is the most powerful predictor of women's problems. In the presence of the other predictors, indirect aggression does not significantly predict women's problems. Both relationship variables significantly add to the explained variance. Overall, the model accounts for 55% (adjusted R^2) of the explained variance in the psychosocial problem index.

IV. Discussion

The results of this study indicate that a majority of men did not use direct physical aggression toward their partners after participation in a program for men who batter. The rates of direct and indirect aggression in the past six months are comparable to those previously reported (Edleson and Grusznski 1988; Edleson and Syers 1990).

In addition to documenting the favorable changes in physical aggression for a substantial number of participants, this study provides empirical evidence for the belief that psychological abuse is in itself harmful. A highly significant predictor of women's personal problems is the amount of psychological abuse to which they are subjected by their partners. This supports the contention that intervention for men who batter must focus on the entire spectrum of their abusive behaviors.

The reader is reminded that all the women interviewed are victims of physical aggression. Therefore, the impact of ongoing psychological abuse must be considered in light of the women's previous experience of the very real potential of physical violence by their partners. It is quite possible that men's psychological abuse keeps the threat of physical aggression salient, but unnecessary for maintaining control over their partners.

Only a small percentage of the women interviewed reported deterioration in their relationships with the abuser following treatment. Many report an increase in ability to share anger and other feelings with their partners, an increase in power, and equal division of tasks in their households—important evidence that the changes men made in their abusive behavior were clinically significant.

The evidence suggests that some men involved in an intervention program are able to refrain from direct aggression following their participation in the program, and they reduce other abusive behaviors. While these results provide grounds for some tentative optimism regarding the effectiveness of the batterers' program, a number of limitations of the study must be considered. Without a control group, the improvement in men's behavior cannot be attributed to participation in the program; other factors may have contributed to the men's improvement. However, the use of quasi-experimental comparisons to assess relative contribution of program participation and other factors can be illuminating. The prediction of program outcome using program and nonprogram variables is addressed in an earlier paper (Tolman and Bhosley 1988).

Finally, we must acknowledge that a substantial proportion of program participants continued physical aggression toward their partners, and most of the men continue some forms of indirect aggression and psychological abuse. To the extent that participation in the program can inadvertently keep women in a abusive relationship that they might otherwise leave, intervention with men who batter may be counterproductive (Gondolf 1988). Vigilance to the possibility of the negative effects of men's treatment, as well as vigorous efforts to eliminate those effects, must be ongoing.

Acknowledgment

This study was supported by a grant from the Sophia Fund and by NIMH Grant IT32-MH17152.

Note

1.   Hudson (1982) does not recommend using the total index scores we have computed here. He suggests that if a summative score is desired, one should sum only items scored as 3, 4, or 5 (indicating that the item is a problem at least some of the time) and then divide that sum by the number of such items. When we calculated this index for the total, interpersonal, and intrapersonal items, we found it in each case to be correlated at $>.80$ to the indices we report. Therefore, for ease of interpretation, we used the conceptually simpler summative indices.

Chapter 10

Removal of the Perpetrator versus Removal of the Victim in Cases of Intrafamilial Child Sexual Abuse

Patricia Ryan, Bruce L. Warren, and Peggy Weincek

I. Introduction

Many communities have responded to the dramatic rise in intrafamilial child sexual abuse by establishing specialized programs for victims and offenders, only to find that the program leads to increased reports of abuse (Barth and Schleske 1985). Growing public and professional education regarding the problem leads to a further rise in reports.

At the present time, there is confusion about the appropriate response to child sexual abuse and about societal intervention. Clearly protection of the child must be the primary consideration, but whenever possible, continuity of the family is also an important concern. In most states, there are no clear standards for when to remove the victim (Mnookin 1973). There is a growing controversy over the extent to which such treatment further victimizes the child (Bulkley et al. 1982). Altogether, there is relatively little empirical research on the impact of societal intervention.

This chapter reports findings from a research project that studied 278 cases of intrafamilial child sexual abuse. In most of the cases either the victim was removed from the family and placed in foster care, or the perpetrator left or was removed from the home. The focus is on the role of the victim's mother in protecting her child as an intervening factor in the determination of the type of intervention.

II. Background of the Study

During the last decade there has been a rapid increase in the number of reported incidents of child sexual abuse (Kempe 1977; Finkelhor 1979;

Barth and Schleske 1985; Peters et al. 1986). Early studies (cf. DeFrancis 1969) found that a stranger or casual acquaintance was the perpetrator in a preponderance of the cases. Kempe (1977) challenged these findings as he had earlier challenged the assumed rarity of parental battering. With increased public education and increased reporting, it is increasingly evident that the perpetrator is usually a close male relative living in the family, most often the child's father or stepfather, or mother's lover (Finkelhor 1983a). Increased intervention experience with the abused child has called into question both the traditional clinical interpretation of incest and the legal processes that treat the incidents as criminal cases (Mnookin 1973; Stein 1981).

Few acts elicit as strong emotional reactions as does child sexual abuse, and even professionals responding to reports must handle feelings of revulsion and anger. Moreover, the concept of child sexual abuse is not clearly defined. Some states provide no statutory definition, and those that do vary, except for inclusion of sexual intercourse, rape, and oral copulation (Wald 1975; Fraser 1981). There is a widespread perception that the sexual use of children by adults is unnatural and unhealthy at best. Intrafamilial sexual abuse raises the questions of the incest taboo, promulgation of genetic defects, and family disintegration (Justice and Justice 1979; Mrazek 1981a)

Traditionally sexual abuse of children was thought to be extremely rare, limited to pedophiles, the degenerate, the mentally ill or retarded, or to particular ethnic groups. With increased reporting, there is renewed interest in the extent to which such maltreatment is injurious to children. Some observers believe that the harmful effects may be exaggerated due to overreliance on clinical samples (cf. Bernard 1981). As practitioners become more familiar with a variety of families, it becomes apparent that everyone in the family suffers (Justice and Justice 1979; Giarretto 1981). However, the potential for damage is great and justifies immediate intervention to protect and help the child (Freud 1981; Summit and Kryso 1981; Steele and Alexander 1981; Browne and Finkelhor 1986).

A number of clinicians have described the classical incestuous family (cf. Summit, and Kryso 1981; Mayer 1983), but the increased number of families that authorities know of and their characteristics challenges traditional views (Mrazek 1981b). Some families have years of dysfunction while others appear to be able to function fairly effectively until the sexual abuse is uncovered (DeFrancis 1969; Nakashima and Zakus 1980; Mrazek and Bentovim 1981). Especially critical is the role of the mother. Although the myth has been widely held that she is usually aware of the abuse and may contrive in setting it up, this is infrequently the case. If the mother, when confronted with the behavior, chooses to act to protect her child, the prognosis for both the child and the family may be better than for the family that cannot acknowledge the real problem.

Although intrafamilial sexual abuse is a crime, the police are often uncomfortable intervening; they have little understanding of the dynamics of child mistreatment and usually do not know how to interview children (Barth and Schleske 1985). In many states juvenile court judges do not have the authority to remove the perpetrator or to ensure that he will not have access to the child if the mother is not willing to cooperate (Bulkley et al. 1982).

There has been a substantial effort to document the incidence of child sexual abuse and contributing factors, but relatively little study of the effects of various interventions. There are many diverse opinions based on clinical experience and practice wisdom (cf. Kempe 1977; Mayer 1983; Tyler and Brassard 1984; Giarretto 1976, 1981; Paulson 1978). There is, however, a critical need for empirical research to determine the impact that various interventions have on the victim and on the victim's family (Finkelhor 1986).

Disclosure of child sexual abuse focuses attention on the family, and all family members are likely to suffer. Reactions differ from case to case. Noninvolved family members may accept the evidence and act to protect the child. Others may deny the abuse and accuse the child of lying. The family may split, some taking the side of the victim and some that of the perpetrator. Often, keeping the family together seems to be the major concern rather than ensuring the child will no longer suffer maltreatment. If the victim is removed, the child is likely to develop feelings of guilt and unworthiness, especially if he/she was the one to disclose the abuse. If the perpetrator leaves, is incarcerated, is hospitalized, or is ordered out of the home by the court, the child is also likely to feel blame that will be intensified if the family suffers economically or if other family members, especially the child's mother, blame the child.

If the perpetrator is permitted to remain in the home, leaving the victim in the family may put the child in grave jeopardy. This is especially the case if the mother ejects the perpetrator only because she feels such action is necessary to prevent the child's removal. Victims left in the home may also be vulnerable to pressure to change their stories (Topper and Aldridge 1981). Stein (1981) had identified several critical factors regarding the decision to remove the victim or remove the perpetrator: (1) whether the incest was ongoing (2) evidence of parental failure to protect the child (3) the child's desire to stay home (4) the parents' willingness to seek assistance for the problem and (5) the availability of help and, most critically, the availability of an appropriate placement.

Many foster families will not accept or they do not know how to help a child who has been sexually abused (Chiaro et al. 1982; Ryan 1984; McFadden 1986). Foster parents receive very little training and have limited knowledge about the impact of abuse on child behavior. Their attempts at control may lead to rejection or overdiscipline of the child. Sexually acting-out behavior puts children at a greater risk of physical and sexual abuse in family foster homes (McFadden 1984).

The decision to remove a child from the family has serious consequences (cf. Stein 1981; Fernandez 1986) and it causes stress and indecision for social workers. Finkelhor (1986) found that foster care placement occurred more often in cases of sexual abuse than physical abuse, and it was most concentrated among older children who reported their own victimizations. He also found that authorities took criminal action about five times more often in cases of sexual abuse than in cases of physical abuse. Black and poor families did not seem to be the objects of obvious discrimination in the disposition of cases. Ringwalt and Earp (1988) found that when protective-service workers perceive the father to be primarily responsible for the abuse, they are more likely to place the child in foster care. Clearly there is a need to determine the effects of such intervention and to provide an empirical basis for predicting outcomes.

III. Research Methods

This chapter reports on research studying the impact of removing the perpetrator vs. removing the child in cases of intrafamilial child sexual abuse. The data source is case records from three state child welfare agencies, a large metropolitan county agency, and a private agency in another large metropolitan area. A total of 178 cases were studied. Research staff selected cases from those opened by the agencies in selected years between 1981 and 1985. This time frame allowed follow-up of victims and families for a three-year period, or until the case was closed if services were terminated in less than three years. Differences in record keeping limited identification of appropriate cases. None of the agencies had a computerized system that allowed retrieval of appropriate cases for all years in the time frame, necessitating different strategies for each agency. Two agencies were able to identify all cases during 1984 and 1985 and select a random sample from that population. Over 90% of the cases identified were included. In two other agencies, the face sheets used for reports of sexual abuse allowed for identification of cases; however, in one of these agencies staff could only find the complete record for 70% of the cases. In the fifth agency, all cases that agency staff could identify as being reported between 1980 and 1985 were included in the sample. However, it is possible that a number of cases were not identified properly.

Criteria for selection of cases included the age and sex of the victim, and the relationship of the victim to the perpetrator, as well as the date of the report. The victims in all cases were females, between the ages of 3 and 17 at the time the sexual abuse was reported. The perpetrator was typically the child's father or stepfather, or mother's live-in lover. In 12 cases, the perpetrator was an older brother, uncle, or other relative living in the home.

Case readers used a standardized instrument to transfer data from the case records. Five trained readers collected all of the data at four of the sites and agency caseworkers read the records at the fifth site. In addition to structured items, detailed descriptions of the reported abuse, the investigation, and family members' reactions were recorded. This chapter examines the extent to which certain characteristics of the case are related to the nature and to the type of intervention.

The dependent variable for this analysis is type of intervention. Often when a case of intrafamilial child sexual abuse is reported, the victim, and sometimes her siblings, are removed immediately from the home environment and placed either with relatives, in a shelter, or in a family foster home. This may happen even if the perpetrator is jailed, leaves voluntarily, or is forced to leave by the mother.

Once the extent of continued risk to the child is determined, the child may be returned. If the intervening agents do not judge the situation at home or with the other as safe, they will seek relatives with whom to place the child because this is seen as less damaging than placement with strangers. Interventions were coded into one of four categories: victim was never removed from mother, victim was removed from the mother but returned to her in one week or less, victim went to live with relatives either directly from the mother's home or within one week of leaving mother's home, or victim was placed in foster care for more than one week. In seven cases, the child and the perpetrator both remained in the home. In one case, there was no information about the intervention. (That case is not analyzed here.)

The analysis examines the relationship between the nature and extent of the abuse, the relationship of the perpetrator to the victim, selected characteristics of the mother, and her reaction to the abuse and the intervention. Abuse was coded into two categories: (1) penetration or oral–genital contact, and (2) all other forms of sexual abuse. Perpetrators other than the child's natural father or stepfather, or mother's live-in partner, are coded as "other." Other variables are length of time victim lived with the perpetrator, whether mother had been abused, and mother's employment status. Mother's reaction before and after the report are examined separately.

In some cases the reaction of the mother is to oust the perpetrator from the house immediately, or to take her children and leave. She may report the incident to the police or take her daughter for medical help. At no time during the follow-up does she reestablish her relationship with the perpetrator. If married she seeks a legal separation or divorce.

At the other extreme are the mothers who deny the abuse has occurred—even when there is evidence they have witnessed one or more incidents. This type of woman continues to live with the perpetrator, or she lets him return to the home after he is released from jail. She may say openly that, if forced to choose between her man and her daughter, she will choose the man; she often blames her daughter for the sexual behavior or accuses her of lying.

Between these extremes are many different reactions. In some cases a mother was aware of some sexual abuse before anything was reported but thought that it had stopped. When the police or protective services intervene, she then sides with her daughter. In some cases the mother will refuse to believe the abuse occurred until confronted with her daughter's disclosure. When she is convinced, she sides with the daughter. Another mother may believe her daughter, but choose to remain with the perpetrator; or if he leaves the home, she allows him to return despite knowledge that this will lead to the child's removal or retention in care.

Because of the complexity of the patterns of the mother's reactions, two raters independently coded mother's reactions both before and after the report into five categories. If these raters chose different categories, a third rater read the complete instrument. Where all three raters differed, the median category was assigned. Insufficient data prevented coding the mother's reaction before the report for 45 cases, and the coding of mother's reaction after the report for 31 cases.

IV. Findings

Table 1 presents the relationships between selected characteristics of the cases and the type of intervention. Table 2 presents the relationships between selected characteristics of the mother and the type of intervention. Although some of the relationships are interesting, only the ratings of the mother's reactions before and after the report are statistically significant. When the abuse did not involve penetration or oral–genital contact, the victims are likely to remain with the mother. This is also the

Table 1. Relationship between Selected Case Characteristics and Type of Intervention ($N = 277$)

		Type of intervention (%)		
	Not removed (%)	Returned home within one week	Placed with relatives	Placed in foster care
Total	41.2	6.9	17.7	34.3
Age of victim				
Under 12 ($N = 119$)	40.3	9.2	18.5	31.9
12 or older ($N = 158$)	41.8	5.1	17.1	36.1
$\chi^2 = 2.18$, $df = 3$, (n.s.)				
Relationship of perpetrator				
Father ($N = 106$)	45.3	8.5	11.3	34.9
Stepfather ($N = 106$)	34.9	7.5	19.8	37.7
Mother's lover ($N = 53$)	45.3	3.8	24.5	26.4
Other ($N = 12$)	41.7	—	25.0	33.3
$\chi^2 = 9.51$, $df = 9$, (n.s.)				
Nature of abuse: penetration or oral–genital contact				
No ($N = 110$)	44.5	6.4	17.3	31.8
Yes ($N = 167$)	38.9	7.2	18.0	35.9
$\chi^2 = 0.92$, $df = 3$, (n.s.)				
Frequency of abuse[a]				
Once ($N = 28$)	60.7	3.6	10.7	25.0
More than once ($N = 240$)	38.9	7.2	18.0	35.9
$\chi^2 = 4.95$, $df = 3$, (n.s.)				
Duration of abuse[b]				
One year or less ($N = 104$)	40.4	7.7	18.3	33.7
More than one year ($N = 133$)	43.6	6.0	18.0	32.3
$\chi^2 = 0.42$, $df = 3$, (n.s.)				

[a] Missing data, 9 cases.
[b] Missing data, 40 cases.

case when the behavior occurred only once. The data present a clear pattern regarding the mother's reaction before the abuse. When the mother offered any protection whatsoever before the report, foster placement for more than one week was likely to be prevented, and the child would either remain in the home or be returned to the home within one week. The same pattern holds regarding the mother's reaction after the report.

Discriminant analysis, a procedure for identifying relationships between quantitative independent variables and qualitative dependent variables, was used to identify the extent to which these variables predict the various types of intervention. Although the model is based on

Table 2. Relationship between Selected Characteristics of Mother and Type of Intervention ($N = 277$)

	Not removed (%)	Type of intervention (%)		
		Returned home within one week	Placed with relatives	Placed in foster care
Total	41.2	6.9	17.7	34.3
Mother employed[a]				
No ($N = 100$)	36.0	6.0	17.0	41.0
Yes ($N = 131$)	40.5	9.9	19.8	29.8
$\chi^2 = 1.64$, $df = 3$, (n.s.)				
Any indication mother abused as a child				
No ($N = 213$)	43.2	6.6	17.4	32.9
Yes ($N = 64$)	34.4	7.8	18.8	39.1
$\chi^2 = 1.64$, $df = 3$, (n.s.)				
Any indication mother abused as an adult				
No ($N = 181$)	44.2	6.6	18.8	30.4
Yes ($N = 96$)	35.4	7.3	15.6	41.7
$\chi^2 = 3.90$, $df = 3$, (n.s.)				
Length of time victim lived with perpetrator[b]				
Five years or less ($N = 85$)	34.1	7.1	21.2	37.6
Over five years ($N = 148$)	40.5	8.8	14.9	35.8
$\chi^2 = 2.08$, $df = 3$, (n.s.)				
Mother's reaction to abuse before report[c]				
No protection ($N = 74$)	10.8	9.5	17.6	62.2
Little protection ($N = 38$)	52.6	5.3	15.8	26.3
Mostly protective ($N = 36$)	61.1	5.6	19.4	13.9
Very protective ($N = 43$)	72.1	9.3	11.6	7.0
Unaware of abuse ($N = 41$)	56.1	2.4	14.6	16.8
$\chi^2 = 66.99$, $df = 12$, $p = .000$				
Mother's reaction to abuse after report[d]				
No protection ($N = 55$)	—	7.3	18.2	74.5
Little protection ($N = 66$)	27.3	4.5	21.2	47.0
Mostly protective ($N = 62$)	62.9	4.8	16.1	16.1
Very protective ($N = 63$)	69.8	11.1	11.1	8.0
$\chi^2 = 3.14$, $df = 3$, (n.s.)				

[a] Missing data, 46 cases.
[b] Missing data, 44 cases.
[c] Missing data, 45 cases.
[d] Missing data, 31 cases.

Table 3. Classification of Actual Cases of Type of Intervention by Selected Characteristics of Case and Mother[a]

| | | Type of intervention (%) | | |
Actual group membership	Not removed (%)	Returned home within one week	Placed with relatives	Placed in foster care
Not removed (N = 114)	81.6	0.9	2.6	14.9
Returned home (N = 19)	57.9	0.0	0.0	42.1
Placed with relatives (N = 49)	42.9	0.0	6.1	51.0
Placed in foster care (N = 95)	18.9	0.0	4.2	76.8

[a] Percentage of "grouped" cases correctly classified, 61.01%

the assumption of interval-level independent variables, evidence suggests that the linear discriminant function often performs reasonably well for dichotomous variables (Gilbert 1968; Moore 1973).

The 11 variables were entered into the analysis. Using a stepwise procedure and the Wilks lambda as a selection criterion, seven variables were selected: mother's reaction before the report, mother's reaction after the report, victim's age, the relationship of the perpetrator to the victim, how long the victim had lived with the perpetrator, whether the mother had ever been abused as an adult, and how often the abuse occurred.

Table 3 displays the resulting accuracy of the classification table. Using these variables, 61.01% of the cases were accurately classified in the predicted categories. However, the model accurately predicts the intervention in 81.6% of the cases in which the child remained with her mother. It accurately predicts 76.8% of the cases in which the child was placed in foster care for more than a week. In slightly over half (57.9%) of the cases where the child was removed, but returned within one week, the model predicted that the child would not be removed at all; and in 51.0% of the cases where the child was placed with relatives, the model predicted the child would be placed in foster care.

V. Summary and Conclusions

The model specified using seven variables partially predicts the intervention for those children who were not removed, and for those children who spent more than a week in foster care. The model was unsuccessful in predicting return home within a week, or placement with relatives. However, it may be that leaving the child in the home and rapid return, often within hours or a few days, are not really significantly different outcomes. The same may be said for foster care and relative placement. Most agencies attempt to place children with relatives whenever possible. When a child is not returned to the home, relative placement is chosen whenever there are relatives willing to take the child, and if the agency views the relatives as being able to provide an appropriate home.

These data suggest that the decision to place a child is not as arbitrary as the previous research literature has suggested. Altogether, over 40% of the children were left in their home. In some of these cases, the perpetrator had already left the home before the abuse was reported.

Agency staff must decide quickly whether the child can be safely left in the home. They may have little information on which to base the decision. If a number of agencies—law enforcement or medical—are involved along with protective services, there may be pressure to move the child immediately. Once the child is outside the home, there is more time to determine the degree of risk in returning the child to her home.

The two predictors that best explain the pattern of removal are the mother's ability and willingness to protect her child (1) before and (2) after the report of abuse. Victim's age, her relationship with the perpetrator, and how long she has lived with the perpetrator may influence the extent to which her mother might reasonably have been aware of the abuse, or the extent to which protective-service staff believes she was aware. Increases in the number of incidents might be seen as an indicator of the damage already done to the child, and it may cast doubt on the extent to which her mother might have been unaware of the sexual incidents. Whether the mother herself has been abused as an adult may also influence her ability to protect her child.

Those cases where a child was removed and then returned within a few hours or a few days may represent cases in which the agency was overzealous in protecting the child. It is possible that the agency may have caused some harm to the child while attempting to protect her. This might be especially likely when the child disclosed the abuse and was then not allowed to return home. On the other hand, it may be argued that the injury done to a child by removing her from the home for a short time is much less than what she would suffer if left in the home when it is not certain she would be safe. Taking time to ensure that the mother is both willing and able to protect her daughter may be the more prudent course.

When it is unsafe to leave a child in her home, or to return her shortly, another home is needed. Most agencies prefer to place a child with relatives rather than with strangers. However, relatives are not always available and willing to take the child. In some cases the relatives have been victimized by similar abuse situations. Placing a child with them would not be in the child's best interests.

These data suggest that the decision to retain a victim of intrafamilial sexual abuse outside her home is not an arbitrary one. Rather, the decision is made in consideration of the seriousness of the abuse and the mother's ability to protect her child. These findings are provocative. They point to the need for a more detailed analysis of the factors that provide mothers with the necessary resources to protect their daughters. They also highlight the need to verify empirically the extent to which the nature of the reporting process influences the extent to which some children are unnecessarily removed from their homes.

Acknowledgement

This research was funded by the National Center on Child Abuse and Neglect, Project #90CA1308.

Chapter 11

Perceptions of Verbal Aggression in Interspousal Violence

Teresa Chandler Sabourin

I. Introduction

The relationship between verbal communication and physical violence remains unspecified. While some studies suggest the co-occur-
rence of verbal and physical aggression, others suggest that verbal
aggression is a catalyst preceding physical violence (Bagarozzi and Giddings 1983; Chandler et al. 1983; Ponzetti et al. 1982; Purdy and Nickle
1981; Rosenbaum and O'Leary 1981; Steinmetz 1987; Vivian and O'Leary
1987).

A. The Relationship between Verbal and Physical Aggression

Deturck (1987) reports that physical aggression is used as a compliance-gaining strategy when verbal communication fails. Coleman
(1980), in a study of battering males' perceptions, found that 55% of
physically abusive incidents were perceived to have been instigated by
spousal verbal aggression. Insulting behavior (e.g., swearing) or attacking a person's character are two specific acts that may instigate physical
violence.

Physical aggression can follow verbal aggression when the verbal
communication is not accepted as a legitimate form of expression in a
relationship. Moreover, contrary to intuition, Straus (1974) finds that the
venting of aggression verbally sometimes contributes to increased levels
of physical aggression and violence. Walker (1979), in her studies of
women in violent relationships, also finds verbal aggression can provoke battering.

The idea that verbally aggressive language can act as a trigger to
physical violence is supported by the research literature on aggression

(Felson 1984; Gelles 1974). Some studies suggest that verbal aggression leads to physical violence where there are verbal skill deficiencies (Infante et al. 1988). Women are perceived as being more verbally skilled and less physically aggressive than men (Stewart et al. 1986). We would therefore expect to find that *female verbal* aggression and *male physical* aggression would affect varying levels of severity in interspousal violence.

To avoid the implications of a catalyst model (which suggests that verbal aggression causes physical violence), it is useful to consider verbal aggression and physical violence as covariates. This conceptualization can accommodate instances of interspousal violence where physical aggression follows verbal aggression, and instances where verbal and physical aggression occur concomitantly.

B. A Violence Typology

Although some studies of interspousal violence regard all incidents as equally harmful, Steinmetz (1987) shows the utility of examining a variety of violent patterns with different intensity levels. Some couples engage in "mutual combat" where both are equally active in the violence. In other relationships, one spouse is primarily the perpetrator, while the other is the victim, a pattern that Steinmetz (1987) calls the "chronic battering syndrome." Here, the dominant partner is usually the man and the submissive partner is usually the woman. In other cases, the spouses vary in enacting either perpetrator or victim roles; in such "Saturday night brawler" relationships, abuse occurs occasionally, and in relation to some external cue. Finally, in some relationships, violence may be more "habitual" (e.g., Whitchurch 1987).

The research in this chapter elaborates the diverse patterns of interaction that occur among abusive couples by uncovering the relationship between verbal and physical aggression. It is designed to assist the development of couple-appropriate treatment programs.

II. Methods

The following research question is examined: What is the relationship between women's verbal aggression and the severity of men's physical abuse in instances of interspousal violence?

A. Operationalization

In this study, verbal aggression is operationally defined as the *occurrence* and the *intensity* of four specific verbal acts: (1) insulting, (2) accusing, (3) rejecting, and (4) disconfirming. These four acts have been described in the literature as central to verbal aggression (Chandler 1988; Coleman 1980; Infante and Wigley 1986; Straus 1976).

The severity of the male's physical violence is operationalized as the extent of harm incurred by acts of physical aggression (Chandler 1986). In this research, we examine high, moderate, and low severity.

B. Subjects

Data for this study were gathered through face-to-face interviews with battered women residing in protective-shelter houses. Forty-six women from five different shelters volunteered for the study. Their ages range from 18 to 54, with an average (mean) of 30 years. Most of these women (60%) worked in part-time or unskilled positions. Some (40%) are home-makers.

Their spouses are, on average, 34 years old. Fifty-four percent were employed in either part-time or unskilled positions at the time of the study. A minority (6%) were professionally employed, and 40% were unemployed. Demographically, this sample is comparable to those stud-ies in similar inquiries of interspousal violence and to those of shelter populations generally (e.g., Giles-Sims 1983; Walker 1979).

C. Accounts

These shelter women were asked to recall and describe their accounts of acute battering incidents. Each woman was able to recall between one and three episodes of violence which served as the unit of analysis for this study. To maintain the independence of the sample, only one ac-count per woman was coded.

The account is a retrospective data collection method, commonly used to examine interspousal violence (Steinmetz 1987). While this method has some inherent limitations, it also has tremendous value under spec-ifiable research conditions.

Giles-Sims, who used retrospective accounts in her work on systems theory and spouse abuse, provides a rationale for using accounts of relationship violence. She notes:

1. The battered women themselves are the "only ones who can con-vey the complexity of their relationships."
2. Since it is not ethical to instigate violent interactions or practical to observe them over time, "the recorded histories as narrated by the wom-en involved are a special source of data."
3. While the women's stories are admittedly biased, their percep-

tions are "the basis for the women's behavior in their relationship with [the] men who batter them" (1983:2–3).

This last point is especially relevant to the goal of the current study—to explicate the interactive influences between the spouses' behaviors.

There are at least three sources of bias inherent in the accounts method of data collection. First, the point in time at which the retrospective accounts are given can influence the accuracy of the account (Steinmetz 1987). Second, relevant details about a particular incident may be forgotten. Individuals tend to simplify stories to describe complex events in their relationships (Harvey et al. 1982). Third, from living in a shelter, the women may have come to understand their violent relationships differently than they did at the time they were battered. Thus, only women who were new to the shelter, i.e., those residing there for less than three weeks, were asked to participate. This decision is an attempt to maximize the accuracy of their accounts, and standardize the degree to which the women simplify or otherwise distort their recollections of abuse.

The interviewer can influence the account, as it is being recalled by the victim. For this study, the interviewer was also a shelter volunteer for six months prior to the study. Her activity as an interviewer was seen as legitimate by the participants, who were accustomed to being interviewed by shelter staff members. The length of the open-ended interviews (45 minutes on the average) suggests that the respondents felt somewhat comfortable with the interviewer.

Despite the potential problems of retrospective accounts, they provide a crucial source of data for the study of interspousal violence. Larzelere and Klein (1987) maintain that the problem of faulty recall in retrospective research is minimized when information is salient. Because instances of interspousal violence are likely to be salient, they are likely to be recalled with some accuracy. All told, the account is a valid and valuable tool for research.

D. Date Coding

Four verbally aggressive acts are measured:

1.   Insulting is behavior that attacks the other's character, e.g., "if you were more of a man, I wouldn't have to work."
2.   Accusing charges the other with an offense, e.g., "I know you've been cheating on me."
3.   Rejecting shows a refusal to accept the other, declaring the other wrong or evil, e.g., "Don't touch me with those filthy hands."

4.   Disconfirming is negating the other's existence by ignoring, e.g., "I wouldn't talk to him.—I just looked at him, laughing inside."

An examination of the research on verbal aggression indicates that insulting, or attacking the character of the other, is central to the expression of verbal aggression (Coleman 1980; Infante and Wigley 1986; Vivian and O'Leary 1987). Accusing is similar to insulting in that one violates the other's self-esteem, charging the other with an offense or some blame, rather than attacking the other's character directly (Chandler 1986).

When rejecting, one person refuses to accept the other, and declares the other to be wrong, evil, or reprehensible (Chandler 1986). The disconfirming response negates the other's existence through ignoring or through providing only tangential replies to questions (Watzlawick et al. 1967).

To do a content analysis of the behaviors reported in the battered women's accounts, two research assistants were trained to identify the verbally aggressive behaviors and to rate the intensity of the behavior. They read through each of the 46 accounts and identified examples of insults, accusations, rejections, and disconfirmations. They coded only the woman's verbally aggressive behavior.

The research assistants also estimated the intensity of verbal aggression and the significance of the behavior on a 4-point scale, coded in the direction of high intensity. Cohen's (1960) kappa was calculated to assess the reliability of the coders' identification of behaviors.[1] This statistic measures the percentage of actual agreement compared to the potential for agreement between independent coders.

The severity of the man's physical violence, as reported in the woman's accounts, was measured using a Q-sort procedure. Research assistants placed each of the 46 accounts into three predetermined categories (from least to most severe) as suggested by Brooks (1970). No attempt was made to analyze specific behaviors.

As a result of this procedure, the accounts of physical violence were distributed in three groups of low ($n = 13$), moderate ($n = 14$), and high ($n = 19$) severity. To estimate the extent of agreement between the coders on their placement of accounts into these categories, Pearson correlation coefficients were calculated.[2]

III. Findings

To examine the relationship between verbal aggression and the severity of physical violence in accounts of interspousal conflict, a stepwise

Table 1. Discriminant Analysis of Interspousal Aggression—
Stepwise Summary Table

Step variable entered	R^2	Partial F	$p < .05$	Wilks' λ	Prob. λ
1. Insulting	.133	3.31	.04	.86	.04
2. Accusing	.091	2.16	.12	—	—
3. Rejecting	.030	.67	.51	—	—
4. Disconfirming	.079	1.86	.16	—	—

discriminant analysis was performed. The four verbally aggressive behaviors (insulting, accusing, rejecting, disconfirming) were treated as
the independent variables to predict the level (low, moderate, high) of
severity in physical violence. The summary statistics for the stepwise
entry are given in Table 1.

Only one type of verbal aggression (insulting, $p > .04$) is significant in
discriminating between levels of physical severity. Insulting accounted
for 13% of the variance among levels of severity. A post hoc Scheffe test
indicated that the significant difference was between groups 1 (low) and
3 (high). The other three verbal aggression variables (accusing, rejecting,
disconfirming) were not significant in discriminatory power.

In Table 2 we show the average verbal aggression scores that are
associated with low, moderate, and high levels of physical aggression.
These data show clearly that verbal aggression decreased as the severity
in physical aggression increased. Said differently, we find an inverse
relationship between female verbal aggression and male physical violence. In battered women's accounts that are rated lowest in severity of
physical violence, the most intense and most frequent acts of verbal
aggression are found. Verbal aggression in these incidents is not met
with intense physical violence, suggesting perhaps that the verbal aggression does not violate relationship norms (Straus 1974). In accounts

Table 2. Average Verbal Aggression Scores
and Levels of Physical Violence

Type of verbal aggression	Severity of physical violence		
	Low	Moderate	High
1. Insulting	.654	.392	.052
2. Accusing	1.346	.714	.657
3. Rejecting	.346	.250	.105
4. Disconfirming	.346	.107	.000

describing moderately severe attacks of physical violence, moderate amounts of verbal aggression are also found. In accounts describing high levels of physical abuse, verbal aggression by women is infrequent. Here, the male's physical violence appears to dominate the episodes completely. The observed differences are not statistically significant (except in the case of insulting behavior). However, the consistency in the direction of these findings indicates that there is a pattern of association between verbal aggression and the severity of physical abuse.

IV. Discussion

The empirical picture presented here suggests a complex relationship between verbal aggression and the severity of physical violence. According to Steinmetz (1987) and Whitchurch (1987), abusive couples can be characterized in various ways, including their style of interaction. The various patterns linking levels of verbal aggression and physical violence uncovered here suggest a typology for distinguishing types of aggressive couples.

In cases of low severity of physical violence, where the woman is more verbally active and her partner relatively less active, the couple may be classified as the "mutual-combat" type (Steinmetz 1987). Both partners contribute actively to the aggressive interaction that takes place. Verbal behavior dominates episodes of mutual aggression.

Relationships characterized by moderate verbal and physical aggression may be classified as the "Saturday night brawler" type. Both partners are somewhat aggressive, but the physical aggression tends to dominate. These couples may be flexible in their expression of violence; in one instance the woman may be dominant, and in another the man. Due to the relative infrequency of the violence, the patterns may not be as stable as in other types of violent relationships.

Relationships characterized by male-dominated physical aggression may be classified as the "chronic battering type." Here the differences between the spouses are great. The man's physical violence dominates, while the women's level of verbal aggression is low. The lack of verbal aggression by the woman indicates passivity, and the extreme male physical violence indicates dominance. Violent episodes in this type of relationship represent unilateral violence, in which one spouse (usually the man) is consistently the perpetrator, while the other (usually the woman) is consistently the victim.

The typology of aggression sketched here is at odds with a linear approach that assumes that (1) abuse increases over time, and (2) verbal and physical aggression increase or decrease together. In some relationships, as verbal aggression increases, physical violence escalates. In other relationships, however, verbal aggression and physical violence combine to form different patterns that may remain stable or change over time. Not all interpersonal violence will necessarily worsen over time (e.g., the "Saturday night brawler" type). Constructing a typology of relationships for examining aggression is helpful. It can incorporate the "catalyst" function of verbal aggression to explain physical violence. It can also explain the complex interactive patterns in abusive relationship.

V. Conclusions

This empirical study and its resulting typology can inform practitioners and researchers who need to explicate the role of communication in interspousal violence. It can help practitioners develop and adopt couple-appropriate communication training programs for violent clients. For example, some partners can be trained to express their emotions more assertively, while others who are more passive can be trained to identify their needs. While a number of possibilities exist, a general prescription simply for "more communication" may not serve this heterogeneous group of clients trying to change their interactions to reduce violence. Rather than looking for a linear pattern of interaction that leads to violence, researchers must develop models that can incorporate various patterns of interaction.

This study invites the construction of new strategies for stopping the violence.

Endnotes

1.   k = .77 indicates an adequate level of reliability for the coders' ratings. We note that the coders showed less agreement on their rating of intensity than on the occurrence of the behavior; however, the rate of agreement (r = .50) was considered sufficient to proceed with the analysis.

2.   The average correlation was .72, suggesting an adequate level of agreement among coders.

Part IV

Legal Responses to Family Violence

In response to public outcry, in anticipation of an increase in the incidence and the prevalence of family or intimate assault cases, the legal system has acted and reacted in recent years in abrupt and sweeping fashion. Legislators draft new statutes to prohibit the rape of a spouse or the assault of a child. Lawmakers instruct the courts to recommend therapy for victims and to mandate treatment for perpetrators. Police are required to arrest abusive spouses. District attorneys are instructed on how to prosecute child sexual-abuse and spouse-battering cases.

Noble intentions notwithstanding, the legal system can inadvertently generate a set of problems, and it can be affected by unanticipated problems that stem from uncommon legal-program implementations.

The legal responses to the crisis of family violence are the focus of Part IV, which contains studies on the role of police, the courts, the prosecutors, and victim advocates in the struggle to minimize the trauma of family violence.

Richard K. Caputo, in his study "Police Classification of Domestic-Violence Calls: An Assessment of Program Impact," assesses the effects of a demonstration program pertaining to police emergency calls in Chicago. The program was designed to help police officers distinguish between true domestic-violence calls and general-disturbance calls. Police were expected to make referrals to service providers for domestic-violence incidents. This research suggests that police are reluctant to respond to emergency domestic-violence calls. Moreover, this research addresses the indispensable function of police in the legal response to family violence.

The Massachusetts District Attorney Reporting Law is the subject of inquiry for Bruce K. Mac Murray's study, "Legal Responses of Prosecutors to Child Sexual Abuse: A Case Comparison of Two Counties." Mac Murray obtained a random sample of documentary data on sexual-abuse cases collected from the prosecutor's files in two metropolitan counties. He finds that prosecutors approach implementation of the reporting law in different ways. His analysis suggests that one county serving a particular metropolitan area uses a "modified system efficiency policy," emphasizing the use of the guilty plea, admissions to sufficient facts, and pretrial probation. A second county developed what Mac Murray calls a "trial sufficiency approach," emphasizing case screening based on evidentiary aspects to prosecute sexual-abuse cases. He concludes his study with a discussion on the implications of the various prosecutorial responses to child sexual-abuse cases.

The Connecticut Legislature passed the Family Violence Prevention and Response Act of 1986. This is among the most comprehensive laws in the nation that are designed to respond adequately to the tragedy of family violence. An intervention unit—a team of family relations staff and family violence victim advocates—was created to work in the lower courts in Connecticut to implement the 1986 law. Eleanor Lyon and Patricia Goth Mace focus on the victim advocate's perspective in their unique study, "Family Violence and the Courts: Implementing a Comprehensive New Law."

Based on interviews with victim advocates throughout the state and on comparisons of courts situated throughout Connecticut, Lyon and Mace illustrate the problems and conflicts associated with the implementation of the family violence law. They conclude their analysis with an assessment of needed research on the impact of laws designed to control offenders and treat victims.

Debra Whitcomb is project director for the Child Victim as Witness Project conducted by the Education Development Center. As project director, she evaluated seven prosecutors' offices funded by the Bureau of Justice Assistance to create special units for the prosecution of child physical- and sexual-abuse cases. The special units are designed to assist in the successful prosecution of crimes against children. They are also designed to help prevent the revictimization of children within the judicial system—children who are both victims of heinous crime and the state's key witnesses.

Whitcomb summarizes the major findings from the evaluation studies. She also describes findings from a three-year study funded by the Office of Juvenile Justice and Delinquency Prevention that was designed to examine empirically the effectiveness of different evidentiary and procedure techniques used in the prosecution of child sexual-abuse cases.

David A. Ford concludes this volume. He examines data from the Indianapolis Prosecution Project, a field experiment designed to show the effects of alternative prosecution programs for wife batterers. His study considers the possibility that criminal sanctions meted out to individuals convicted of conjugal violence misdemeanors are as likely to elicit anger as they are to have a deterrent effect. He explores whether the batterer's anger in response to a punitive sanction has the effect of dampening the deterrent effect of criminal sanctions.

Essentially Ford finds that sanctions per se work to deter subsequent acts of conjugal violence. More severe sanctions are more likely than less severe sanctions to provoke anger and resentment among batterers. However, the severely sanctioned batterers are no more likely than others to be recidivists. Ford cautions against drawing any firm conclusions regarding the appropriate punishment for spouse abusers. He notes that prosecution outcomes do not necessarily reflect the actual policy that guides the prosecution process.

David Ford invites continuing research designed to center on the preventive effects of alternative prosecution programs and policies. Like his colleagues whose work is contained in this volume, he invites us to continue searching for efficacious means to stop the abuse, to heal the injury, to help the family.

Chapter 12

Police Classification of Domestic-Violence Calls: An Assessment of Program Impact

Richard K. Caputo

I. Introduction

This chapter presents findings from a domestic-violence demonstration program, sponsored by a family service agency in Chicago. The project initially operated in two police districts between July 1, 1983, and June 30, 1986. On July 1, 1986, it expanded to include two more police districts. The program provided a variety of social, legal, and advocacy services to victims. Social services were offered to batterers as well. A full description of the project can be found elsewhere (Caputo and Moynihan 1986). In this chapter, we focus on the program's efforts, as a strategy of social change (Rein and Miller 1967), to encourage police to report accurately incidents of domestic violence.

II. The Background

In general, police response to domestic violence is controversial (Sherman and Berk 1984; Fain 1981; Parnas 1972). Police are reluctant to become involved in family disputes and, when they do, victims sometimes accuse them of siding with male batterers. Moreover, Ruben (1984) finds that police underreport incidents of domestic violence and often classify them as miscellaneous, noncriminal incidents. The Illinois Domestic Violence Act of 1982 (Public Act 82-621; IDVA) was enacted to remedy these situations. The program assessed in this chapter was designed to encourage police to comply with the provisions of IDVA. The program staff consisted of a team of social workers, lawyers, and client advocates who combined case management, social support, and legal services. Program staff provided direct services to police referrals whom they were able to contact and who wanted assistance as a consequence of a family violence incident.

Upon receipt of police referrals, IDVA program staff are required to reach battered victims by phone or, if that fails, by letter. When contact is made, a social worker assesses the situation and initiates intervention reflecting the need for safety and the family's concerns. The attorney advises the battered victims of their options in civil and criminal courts, so that they can make informed decisions about possible actions they might pursue—exclusive possession, orders of protection, divorce, and child custody. The attorney represents the client in civil court. The community advocates assist the state's attorney in criminal court. They support the victims through numerous court delays, postponements, and, at times, change of venue.

The director of the IDVA program attended roll call in each of the participating police districts and educated the police on the program's services. Most police officers reported to the program director that they had few positive experiences in dealing with domestic violence. Police officers complained about recidivism, expressed their beliefs that social agencies fail to follow through, and expressed a fear that violence might be directed at the officer.

III. A Program Assessment

A. Design

The Chicago police collected data on more than 149,000 calls regarding domestic violence that were made to the two police districts in which the program initially operated (hereafter called Districts 13 and 23) from January 1, 1983, through October 31, 1986. Districts 8 and 16 were added later and had an additional 52,000 reports from January 1, 1986, through October 31, 1986. The calls were classified into three major categories: domestic-violence calls, "other" calls, and those for which no determination could be made, hereafter referred to as miscellaneous 19P calls.

Referrals to the IDVA program were aggregated on a monthly basis. A *referral ratio* (number of referrals/number of domestic-violence calls) was calculated. It was intended to monitor the success of the program's efforts to maximize referrals, and to monitor the accuracy in the police classifications of emergency calls. We expected that the referral ratio would approach 1.0 over time, indicating that for every emergency call the police classified as domestic violence, there would be a corresponding referral to the IDVA program.

A. Findings

1. Demographics of Police Districts. According to census data, the four police districts included in the study varied by size and racial composition. District 13 has a total population of 80,945 and is primarily Hispanic (40.3%) and black (30.4%). District 23 has a total population of 74,915 and is primarily white (70.6%). Districts 8 and 16 have populations of 206,266 and 193,089, respectively, and they are primarily white (83.2 and 98.2%, respectively). Black victims and batterers are disproportionately represented in all districts.

The population in District 13 is the least educated, most densely populated, and the poorest of the four districts. Sixty-four percent of its population over age 18 had a maximum of three years of high school; for the other districts, the comparable figures are less than 40%. Slightly more than half (50.6%) of District 13 households have three or more persons living in them, and the mean household income is $13,204, with a median of $10,129. More than 33% of its population fell below the poverty line, over twice the figure for District 23, and over six times as high as Districts 8 and 16.

2. District Variations. During any given month, District 13 police refer fewer clients to the IDVA program ($\bar{X} = 29.4$ referrals) than do District 23 police ($\bar{X} = 54.1$ referrals). District 23 police actually made more referrals to the program than they classified as domestic violence, exceeding a referral ratio of 2.0 in 6 of the 19 months under investigation in this program assessment. In District 23, 19P or miscellaneous calls also increased. In District 13, on the other hand, the referral ratio fell well below 1.0 (from .16 to .32) throughout the entire study period.

District 8 police made an average of 60 referrals to the program monthly, while District 16 police made 46.5 referrals in an average month. In both of these districts, the referral ratio remained below 1.0. In District 8 the referral ratio averaged .24, while in District 16 it averaged .43.

The IDVA program obviously influenced police districts differentially. The number of referrals was greatest in District 23. Program staff frequently claimed that District 23 police were cooperative, indicated by enthusiasm during roll call, questions about the progress of specific referrals, and the relatively large number of referrals made to the program. The referral ratio, originally conceptualized as a measure of program success, proved fruitful as a way to monitor program involvement. It also enabled administrative staff to specify a given goal for subsequent months. An anomaly, however, appears in District 23. A referral ratio that exceeds 1.0 went beyond the logic of the design. As the ratio approached, and then exceeded 2, it became clear that District 23 police made more frequent use of the 19P category of emergency calls than did those in other districts.

There are three apparent explanations for why District 23 police referred more clients to the program than they classified as domestic-violence calls. First, the district 23 commander worked directly with IDVA program director in an attempt to encourage police officers to overcome any reluctance to involve themselves in family disputes.

Second, special reports were required on every emergency call verified as domestic violence, but not for the 19P category. Thus, District 23 police maintained higher levels of referrals, but they avoided the paperwork associated with the domestic-violence classification by greater use of the 19P category.

Third, informal agreements between dispatching and beat officers in District 23 appear to have reduced the number of emergency calls initially dispatched as family violence; when the 19P classification was verified by beat officers, both groups of officers avoided paperwork. District 13 officers were dispatched from District 23 but the lack of regular, personal contact due to the physical distances involved prevented the development of such informal collusive actions.

IV. Conclusions

In general, police respond to emergency domestic-violence calls reluctantly, and with a sense of futility. Further, police are often fearful that the violence occurring in an incident of spouse abuse may be redirected toward them. Police reluctance is difficult to overcome. In light of the increased attention given to domestic violence, many states have passed legislation that gives police specific remedies and options regarding their response to family violence incidents. Invariably these laws seek appropriate classification of calls to police in order to understand better the nature and scope of the problem.

This chapter assesses the impact of a Chicago project designed to improve police response to domestic violence and police classification of emergency or 911 calls. It examines how more than 201,000 disturbance calls were classified. It also examines the relationship between calls verified as true domestic-violence incidents and the nearly 3,300 referrals police made to the IDVA program over a 40-month period.

Several conclusions can be drawn. First, a formal relationship between the police department and a domestic-violence program is essential. Police need to know the results of their efforts. They need to learn that what they do makes a difference for the better in some instances. A formal mechanism of information exchange is necessary to ensure that appropriate police response is encouraged.

Second, like many professionals who work with people, beat officers attempt to avoid paperwork as much as possible. Given an opportunity, they will follow the path of least resistance. Nonetheless, in light of the importance of accurate information, verified classification of domestic-violence calls should be monitored more closely than is normally the case. The IDVA program strategy provides a mechanism to do so.

Third, the implementation of intervention strategies takes time. Police attitudes about domestic violence and their responses to it do not change overnight, regardless of statutes that may dictate otherwise. A police department that wants its officers to respond more appropriately to domestic violence must implement a long-range strategy that also makes provisions for some immediate changes on a trial basis. The overall strategy, however, should cover a three- to five-year period. It should institutionalize what works over time, and modify what falls short of expectations.

Finally, police departments should take advantage of social and legal services in the community. These services are essential for victims of domestic violence. Agencies can also provide a range of distinct services to the police officers themselves, as the IDVA program director's involvement indicated in this program assessment.

Chapter 13

Legal Responses of Prosecutors to Child Sexual Abuse: A Case Comparison of Two Counties

Bruce K. Mac Murray

I. Introduction

American society has witnessed a tremendous shift in the public exposure to issues involving domestic and family violence recently; indeed, family violence has become a significant and growing research area in its own right. Social-service agencies have seen both enlarged caseloads and increasing political attention to abuse in the domestic arena. Public policy also has focused on changes in the law and the way the criminal justice system handles cases involving abuse allegations (see Langan and Innes 1986; Lerman 1981; Mac Murray and Carson 1990; Sherman and Berk 1984). The most visible direction for this new approach is a "get tough" posture that emphasizes the *criminal* act and the appropriate *punishment* following a criminal conviction (U.S. Department of Justice 1984).

New legislation that directs the criminal-justice system's response is accompanied in many jurisdictions by alterations in policies and practices for the processing of domestic- and family-violence cases. Nevertheless, there is reason for concern about the consequences of these changes. How is increased criminalization toward family violence implemented by criminal-justice agencies in the processing of cases? What are the implications of this approach for treatment and/or punishment of perpetrators and victims? And even more fundamentally for social policy, what are the resulting consequences from these dispositions for future abuse, violence, and crime among these individuals?

This chapter examines criminal decision making for cases involving child sexual abuse. Specifically, two country prosecutors' offices are studied and compared regarding (1) the office's official position on the criminalization of child sexual abuse, (2) the office's policy for handling abuse cases, (3) the means by which the cases are processed through the criminal court, and (4) the dispositional consequences for the cases.

A. *The Critical Role of Prosecutors in Criminal-Justice Policy*

The office of the prosecutor (called the district attorney in Massachusetts) was chosen as the focal point for this research for several reasons. First, the prosecutor occupies a central position within the criminal-justice system. The prosecutor works with police and various agents of the criminal court, such as judges, defense attorneys, victims, witnesses, and jurors. In addition, the prosecutor makes sentencing recommendations to the judge upon conviction.

The prosecutor also serves as the gatekeeper for the criminal-justice system whose decisions have implications with respect to (1) who is or is not charged and formally prosecuted for a crime, (2) which cases go to trial vs. which receive negotiated plea agreements, and (3) which convictions are followed by a recommended sentence of jail time vs. community probation. In this respect, prosecutors serve at least implicitly as public policymakers, who interpret and evaluate the law by deciding which crime problems to emphasize.

B. *Prosecutorial Policy and Action*

The prosecutor plays a pivotal role in transforming legislation or public sentiment into action within the criminal-justice system. She or he is also relatively free to interpret changes in the law and the wishes of the public into policy (see Jacoby 1979; McDonald 1979). Discretion is converted into action for prosecutors, primarily via the related mechanisms of (1) establishing written office policies and guidelines for such important issues as plea bargaining or sentencing diversion, (2) establishing a hierarchical system for supervision and monitoring the deputy or assistant prosecutors, and (3) increasing the computerization of case file information and records, which facilitates court scheduling and allows prosecutors to assess the performance of assistant prosecutors (see American Bar Association 1973; Mac Murray 1988b).

The most informative work on prosecutorial policies (Jacoby 1979) formulates a typology of four ideal and relatively pure models: (1) legal sufficiency, (2) system efficiency, (3) defendant rehabilitation, and (4) trial sufficiency. Each emphasizes a different goal and primary concern. Two of these are crucial for this research: First, the system efficiency approach aims for the early and timely disposition of cases by whatever means are possible, often through plea bargaining. Second, the trial sufficiency approach stresses rigorous case screening so that weak cases can be rejected, with the remaining cases fully prosecuted through the criminal-trial process. This approach tends to discourage plea bargaining and diversion of cases.

This research examines prosecutorial policies regarding child sexual abuse both as stated by district attorneys and as carried out through the actions of their office staffs.

C. *Massachusetts and the District Attorney Reporting Bill*

The passage and implementation of Massachusetts legislation in 1983 regarding the handling of child abuse cases required an interface between the Department of Social Services (DSS) and the jurisdictional district attorneys' offices. The District Attorney Reporting Law (Chapter 288) was enacted in large measure because of media attention to incidents involving serious injury and death resulting from physical child abuse. In these publicized cases, the DSS failed to coordinate with law enforcement agencies, despite prior identification that the parent had caused severe physical injury to the child (Wilber 1985; see also Blose 1979).

As a result of this new legislation, a number of key changes took place. First, the new law provided clear momentum and a strong mandate for the criminalization of child abuse. The law specifically targeted the prosecutor as the appropriate criminal-justice agent responsible for the handling of these cases. Second, the new law mandated timely referral of cases from the DSS to the prosecutor's office. The legislation left to the discretion of the individual district attorneys whether criminal charges and prosecution were appropriate. The new legislation took effect on October 12, 1983. The two major requirements in the law concern (1) the mandatory referral of serious cases from DSS to the appropriate district attorney within five working days after investigation, and (2) the convening of a multidisciplinary team for each case.[1]

This mandate from the legislature encouraged local prosecutors to establish policies on child abuse cases and to implement these policies through the actions of their staffs. These actions involved the development of policy statements and guidelines, the creation and hiring of new staff positions, and the careful monitoring and assigning of prosecutors and staff.

II. Method

A. *Research Sites*

This research examines two metropolitan Boston county district attorneys' offices, referred to by the pseudonyms South County and North County, which are not representative of their true geographical locations.[2]

B. Data Collection and Sampling

The data collection procedure required several techniques, producing different types of information. First, in both counties, case file data were obtained for samples of the child abuse cases referred to the prosecutor's office under the first two years of the Chapter 288 legislative mandate (October 12, 1983–October 11, 1985). This scheme employed a random-sampling design (see Williamson et al. 1982) but differences in the total number of referred cases for the two counties over the period of study required differing sampling frames. In South County, the first of every three referred cases was chosen for inclusion, yielding 87 cases from the total universe of 259 cases. In North County, the fourth of every five cases was chosen, yielding a sample of 91 cases out of a total of 446 cases.

All the available information in the sampled case files as well as additional logbook notes were collected, and most contained the following types of data: information regarding the initial referral of the case, including a cover letter from DSS to the prosecutor describing the abuse, the victim, and the alleged perpetrator; agency forms describing the original abuse report, and subsequent investigation and substantiation decisions and rationale; internal memoranda, notes, and correspondence related to either the investigation of a case or prosecution actions; and documents covering the proceedings in a case within the court system. In addition, some cases contained police reports where investigations had been conducted; records or letters by physicians, hospitals, counselors, therapists, and psychiatrists; newspaper clippings; and related correspondence between the prosecutor's office and outside persons or agencies.

Other data were also gathered over the study period, primarily observational field notes collected by the researcher while in the two prosecutors' offices. These include notes taken from unstructured interviews with prosecutorial office personnel, and notes on meetings attended and informal conversations with prosecutors, child abuse investigators, police officers, and victim/witness advocates. Office memoranda, policy guidelines, and newspaper articles that related to the topic of sexual abuse prosecutions for the specific counties studied were also collected.

III. Findings

A. Prosecutor Policies toward Child Sexual Abuse

The office policies of the two prosecutors are quite similar. Both of the prosecutors' offices expressed satisfaction that the Chapter 288 legislation had passed, both perceived it as an important step in the public recognition of sexual-abuse cases, and both hoped that the criminal-justice system could be helpful in remedying the problem.

A letter by the North County District Attorney commenting on the prosecution of child sexual-abuse cases was published in the office's periodic newsletter:

> I start with this perspective: any individual who physically abuses a child, or sexually assaults or rapes a child, has committed a serious crime which must be considered as such, regardless of the relationship of the victim to the offender. The perpetrator should be subject to public identification, prosecution and sanctions. There is absolutely no moral justification for ignoring cases where the acts of physical or sexual abuse are committed by a family member, while strangers are treated as criminals for committing similar acts of violence. (March 1986:1)

This prosecutor went on to add,

> In the interest of the powerless, vulnerable child victims and the public, these cases must be prosecuted as the serious crimes which they are. Treatment, prevention, education and therapy may be added as parallel measures and are certainly to be encouraged as supplemental disposition-al tools. To date, when they have stood alone and without the threat of criminal prosecution and sanctions, they have utterly failed as effective responses to the problem. (March 1986:2)

To outline his position further, the prosecutor indicates that several steps are necessary in order to demythologize child abuse and sexual abuse cases:

1. Prosecutorial review does not necessarily mean that the child victim will be forced to testify at trial, or that the offender will necessarily go to jail.

2. The investigation of child abuse cases is conducted in an inter-disciplinary manner, involving police, social-service, medical, and legal personnel who are specially trained in a swift and coordinated approach.

3. A serious effort is made to minimize any possible negative traumatic effects on the child.

4. These serious and complex cases are reviewed differently when the "family" is involved.

5. Once convictions are obtained, criminal sanctions are presumed to be the appropriate response, with treatment utilized in addition to punishment, not instead of it.

6. The district attorney must take the lead in informing, educating,

and training other professionals about the criminal-justice process and the nature of the procedures in these cases.

7.   Most mental-health professionals agree that the leverage of pending court proceedings is crucial for effective treatment, that prosecution validates the value of the child by making it clear that the abuser's behavior is unacceptable and not to be tolerated, and that prosecution helps to remove the social stigma of victimization.

The South County district attorney has no regular newsletter, but unstructured interviews provided several comments that are quite similar to those expressed by the North County district attorney. For example, the South County prosecutor emphasized the role of the Chapter 288 legislation in helping to change the reputation of child abuse cases among the police and DSS. This prosecutor noted that, at first, the police wanted nothing to do with these types of cases as a result of both a lack of training about what to do in investigating them and because of their low status among the police. The South County district attorney perceived that Chapter 288 has helped to redefine child abuse offenses as crimes, and to train and hire specialized personnel to handle these cases.

The South County prosecutor observed that before Chapter 288 he never saw these cases, because DSS provided a sympathetic ear and did the investigatory work needed to provide a social-service solution. Such actions served to "cool out" many complainants. In other cases, probate options were used—restraining orders, or care and protection petitions. Most of these cases were never directed to the prosecutor. Only the rare exceptions—when someone contacted the police rather than DSS—resulted in a case being brought to the prosecutor.

The South County prosecutor feels that sexual abuse is nondeterrable. Incapacitation (through incarceration) is a major approach that must be utilized. As long as the perpetrators are off the streets, "the public is safe from their actions." From his perspective, the motivation for the sexual abuse of children:

> may be biological, an intergenerational abuse history, the home situation that the offender grew up in, a retarded or undeveloped sex drive—any number of causes. The problem remains with their target—children. . . . Whatever the cause, they have this targeted drive. (Interview, October 1986)

This prosecutor distrusts diversion and treatment programs for these offenders and believes that the average person on the street can predict the treatment potential of offenders as well as any psychiatrist, social worker, or person with a master's or doctor's degree in psychology. Thus, this particular prosecutor adopts a no–plea-bargaining position.

This decision, he claims, is based upon a consideration of the alternatives available and assessing them as no better than prosecution. Even without convictions, with full prosecution the accused are publicly exposed for committing an act of public shame and embarrassment.

The South County district attorney notes that there are some cases where circumstances warrant plea bargaining or alternative action, such as the use of preprobation alternatives if the perpetrator is genuinely interested in therapy and rehabilitation. Similarly, for those cases involving victims who are retarded or children too young to testify in court, or where the prosecutor knows that a case is weak, alternatives to criminal prosecution may be chosen.

In conclusion, the South County prosecutor says he is

> not unaware of the various and complex causes of sexual abuse and related social problems (for example, intergenerational abuse, social learning, the perpetrator's own situation in his family of origin, etc.), but with only a sledgehammer in one hand and a crowbar in the other to deal with this problem, there are difficulties. (Interview, October 1986)

There are several points of similarity and shared policy emphasis for the North County and South County district attorneys. Both seek to treat the physical or sexual abuse of children as criminal behavior. They are pleased that Chapter 288 has provided information about incidents previously not known to them. They have seen large increases in their caseloads as a result of the Chapter 288 legislation's impact, and have hired new personnel to aid in investigating cases and interviewing child victims. Both offices also have arranged for their staffs to receive specialized training in techniques of case investigation, evidence gathering, and prosecution, while also protecting the child victim.

Both have employed special staffs of victim/witness advocates, whose duties include aiding in the investigation and interviewing of child witnesses, comforting and consoling victims and families, explaining the criminal court process to children and families, informing them about the progress and scheduling of testimony, and serving as experts for the prosecutors working on these cases. Both offices have worked on improving their liaison with DSS, and both have established office protocol or guidelines for the systematic and appropriate handling of cases.

A number of points of divergence between these two district attorneys' offices are also apparent. First, the South County prosecutor (the more traditional of the two) is very concerned with treating Chapter 288 cases as criminal, and advocating full prosecution of all relevant charges through trial. This position coincides clearly with the trial sufficiency policy model outlined by Jacoby (1979, 1980).

The North County district attorney also believes that sexual and physical abuse against children should be treated as criminal acts, and that a major responsibility of his office lies in prosecuting offenders. However, the North County district attorney believes that criminal prosecution may not always be in the child's best interest or that of any of the other parties involved in a case. Time and efficiency in the processing of cases, with plea bargaining and alternative dispositions as appropriate options to the formal trial process, make this approach consistent with the system efficiency policy (Jacoby 1979, 1980).

B. Case-Processing Decisions and Actions taken by Prosecutors

The earliest prosecutorial decision is initial screening, in which cases are reviewed for the filing of criminal charges. Screening is crucial for all cases (see McDonald 1979; Boland et al. 1983).

In most instances of criminal events, a report of an alleged incident that includes some follow-up investigation by a law enforcement agency is brought to the prosecutor's office. In the case of the Chapter 288 child abuse cases, however, the prior case screening occurs not by *police* agents, but rather by *social-service* workers. By law, DSS is required to forward to the local prosecutor all cases that meet the stated criteria for child abuse and that have been substantiated by the agency following its own investigation. For this reason, the initial legal screening stage is particularly critical for these Chapter 288 cases (see Mac Murray 1988a,b, 1989).

As the data in Table 1 indicate, at this initial screening point, there are some observable differences in the actions taken by prosecutors in the two counties studied. In North County, fewer than half of the cases sampled (43%) were forwarded for further prosecutorial action, 30% were processed out or rejected, and the remaining 27% of the cases were still open or under investigation at the time these data were collected. For South County, 49% of the cases were forwarded for prosecution

Table 1.   Case-Screening Decisions by County[a]

| | North | | South | |
	%	N	%	N
Forwarded for prosecution	43	39	49	43
Not prosecuted	30	27	40	35
Open	27	24	10	9
Total	100	90	99	87

[a] $\chi^2 = 7.94$, $df = 2$, $p < .02$.

action at screening; however, 40% of the cases were rejected, while 10% remained under active investigation as the data were collected.

These findings could indicate several things. Despite concern with the timeliness of decisions by the North County prosecutor, the investigatorial and decision-making process for screening judgments may be slower than in South County because the caseload is considerably larger in North County—446 vs. 259 cases referred within the first two years. The most straightforward interpretation is that the traditional, trial-sufficient policy of the South County prosecutor rests on a higher standard of evidence to screen a case "in" for court action; thus, cases may be more clear-cut. For North County, the concern with system efficiency, i.e., with documenting that a crime has been committed, and trying to find the most appropriate action to take, may result in delayed screening decisions, perhaps until it is clear that absolutely no formal course of action by the prosecutor's office is possible.

C. Adjudication Mechanisms and Final Dispositions

After case screening, the prosecutor decides how to handle the case via the criminal-court process. Specifically, the prosecutor decides whether to try to obtain convictions by trial or by guilty pleas, or to pursue other nontrial dispositions. Based upon differences in the policy approaches observed in the two offices, we would expect that trials would be more likely in South County, while the North County prosecutor would make greater use of nontrial alternatives.

As Table 2 illustrates, this expectation is supported empirically. Thirty-

Table 2. Convictions by County and Means of Disposition[a]

Means of disposition	North		South	
	%	N	%	N
Trial	33	11	73	11
Guilty plea[b]	67	22	27	4
Total	100	33	100	15

[a] $\chi^2 = 5.13$, $df = 1$, $p < .05$.

[b] Guilty plea includes formal guilty pleas made voluntarily or as a result of plea bargaining, defendant admissions to sufficient facts for guilt (ASF), agreements to continuances without a finding (CWOF), and pretrial probation agreements between the defendant, the prosecutor, and the court.

Table 3. Prison versus Probation Sentence by County
and Means of Disposition

	North		South	
Sentence	%	N	%	N
Prison or jail sentence	36	12	20	3
Probation and or suspended sentence	45	15	40	6
Continued without a finding	9	3	20	3
Not guilty	3	1	20	3
Unknown	6	2	0	0
Total	99	33	100	15

three percent of the cases prosecuted to conviction in North County involved court trials, whereas 73% of South County's convictions resulted from trials. Conversely, North County prosecutors made considerably more use of guilty-plea decisions than did the South County prosecutors.

The greater use of nontrial convictions in North County does not appear to eliminate incarceration for convicted offenders, however. As Table 3 shows, 36% of the offenders convicted in North County were sentenced to prison or jail time, while in South County only 20% of the convicted offenders received a jail sentence.[3]

Approximately two of every five cases resulting in conviction in either county ended with a sentence of probation, usually accompanied by conditions—orders to stay away from the victim, mandated counseling, or a related disposition. The majority of the North County cases and all of the South County cases resulting in incarceration were adjudicated via trial proceedings. In addition, 20% of the cases prosecuted in South County resulted in acquittal, while only 3% did so in North County.

D. Case Processing Time

The data suggest that North County made screening decisions more slowly than South County. The data regarding the processing time between screening and adjudication are summarized in Table 4. The difference between the two counties is greatest in the time for guilty-plea processing. In South County, trials and guilty-plea verdicts kept cases in the system for the same length of time, just under one year. In North County, cases disposed via guilty pleas remained in the system less than 4 months. Cases tried remained in the system for over 15 months.

Table 4. Case-Processing Time
(Months) to Conviction by
County and Means of
Disposition

Means of disposition	North	South
Trial	15.2	10.9
Guilty plea	3.7	10.9
Total	7.5	10.9

[a] $\chi^2 = 2.86$, $df = 1$, $p < .10$.

IV. Conclusions

This study examines how prosecutorial policy for child sexual abuse affects the actions prosecutors take in these cases and the outcomes that result. As these qualitative observations suggest, the district attorneys of North and South counties have approached the implementation of the Chapter 288 legislation in Massachusetts in somewhat different ways. While both welcomed the new law, each adopts a somewhat different posture toward the processing and prosecution of these cases.

For the North County prosecutor, the primary emphasis is upon documenting that a crime has occurred, using whatever means are available to document the incident officially in the legal system. A presumption of prosecution is present, with an emphasis on the speed and timeliness of subsequent court proceedings. The North County prosecutor perceives that trial and incarceration upon conviction do not always provide the most appropriate treatment for a case. With this focus in mind, the North County prosecutor appears to adopt a modified, system efficiency policy that makes considerable use of guilty pleas, admissions to sufficient facts, and pretrial probation. These techniques are used for several related purposes: (1) to get convictions, (2) to demonstrate the seriousness of sexual abuse as criminal behavior, (3) to obtain convictions and admissions of guilt when victims and their families do not wish to prosecute cases, or will potentially suffer severe trauma and related negative consequences if cases are taken to trial, and (4) to force offenders to get treatment under supervision.

In South County, sexual abuse is similarly treated as a serious crime. However, here the prosecutor approaches the cases from a trial sufficiency approach. The initial screening decision is one that emphasizes legal and evidentiary aspects of the case more than a presumption of prosecution. If a case is perceived to be "too weak," it is likely to be screened out and not prosecuted in South County (see Mac Murray 1988a,b).

As this exploratory study suggests, prosecutorial policy affects decision making and case processing for child sexual abuse. The greater reliance upon guilty pleas over trial proceedings in North County did speed up the processing time for cases, without having a major impact upon the likelihood of a sentence of incarceration upon conviction. However, the decision to prosecute presumptively, whenever possible, did appear to slow down the case-screening process in North County, relative to South County.

In South County, the policy directive of utilizing trials rather than plea bargains or other guilty-plea dispositions results in quick and decisive case-screening judgments, with the majority of prosecutions resulting in trial dispositions. At the same time, however, this approach also results in a relatively high acquittal rate in South County. Furthermore, even when conviction did occur, South County prosecutors were no more likely than those in North County to obtain incarceration sanctions for convicted perpetrators.

V. Discussion

The findings from this study clearly show that passage of new legislation does not necessarily result in a singular manifestation of public policy across different state agencies or jurisdictions. Indeed, the prosecutors of North and South counties have interpreted and implemented the District Attorney Reporting Law in Massachusetts with very different emphases. To their credit, both district attorneys seem to have closely and consistently implemented into action their articulated policy for handling child sexual-abuse cases. At the same time, the differences between the two policies suggest very different actions regarding how cases should be handled. Because of the different fact patterns, case characteristics, and nature of the particular incidents involved in each unique case, it is difficult to infer accurate generalizations regarding the most just or appropriate prosecutorial policy for child sexual-abuse cases overall. However, the present research clearly suggests the potential advantages of the modified system efficiency approach—subscribed to by the North County district attorney—in terms of timeliness, conviction rates, and resulting sentences for convicted offenders. The North County prosecutor's policy approach may indeed prove useful in family violence cases in other jurisdictions. Nonetheless, the broader and ultimately more important questions of what policy and approach is most appropriate with respect to the consequences for victims, offenders, and the criminal-justice system will require much further research, thought, and examination.

Notes

1. The guidelines in the Chapter 288 legislation specify that substantiated cases must be referred to the district attorney if they fall into one of the following categories: (1) death of a child, (2) rape of a child, (3) brain damage, impairment, or loss of bodily functions or organs or substantial disfigurement suffered by a child, (4) sexual exploitation of a child, and (5) serious bodily injury resulting from a pattern of repeated actions. At the time of this study, DSS could also refer cases involving allegations of indecent assault (involving, for example, the fondling of a child) to the prosecutor on a discretionary basis. Despite the breadth of these criteria, roughly nine of every ten referrals concern substantiated allegations of sexual abuse in Massachusetts as well as for the two counties studied (data extracted from DSS monthly reports on Chapter 288, for the period 1983–86).

2. Crucial to carrying out the data collection for this research was access to personal and confidential information regarding the sensitive details of child sexual-abuse cases. For South County, access was granted following a set of discussions about the research between myself, the director of the Victim/Witness Advocacy Program, and the chief of the Sexual Abuse Investigation Unit and the final approval of the district attorney. In North County, similar discussions took place between myself and the chief deputy district attorney of the Criminal Division, the director of the Victim Services Bureau, and the chief of child abuse prosecutions in the office, again with the final permission of the district attorney. Contact and clearance for the research also included the Massachusetts Criminal Systems History Board. This entire access and entrée process took a total of six months before permission was granted and data collection actually began.

The collection of both the qualitative and the quantitative data for this research was conducted over an 18-month period from October 1986 through April 1987. Data from the prosecutor case files was summarized in field notes, with additional information coded for the social characteristics of the victim(s) and alleged perpetrator(s), the nature of the abusive incidents involved, and related information concerning the reporting and processing of the cases by DSS, the prosecutor's office and the criminal court.

3. Because of the small expected frequencies for this table (less than five for over 20% of the cells), a χ^2 test could not be performed.

Chapter 14

Family Violence and the Courts: Implementing a Comprehensive New Law

Eleanor Lyon and Patricia Goth Mace

I. Introduction

In the past 15 years, increased awareness of domestic violence has spawned widespread debate over the most effective ways to respond (Ferraro 1989; Williams and Hawkins 1989; Caringella-MacDonald 1988; Fagan 1988; Horton et al. 1987; Lerman 1986; Saunders and Size 1986; Wermuth 1983). Some have argued that "compassionate" therapeutic and educational interventions are most likely to be successful, whereas others have maintained that it is imperative to use "control" approaches that involve the criminal-justice system (cf. Mederer and Gelles 1989; Newberger and Bourne 1978).

Many state and local jurisdictions have passed new laws that clearly define domestic violence as a crime. These laws are a response, first, to concerns raised by workers in shelters for battered women, and by the women's movement more generally, that violence against women has not been taken as seriously as other criminal behavior. Second, the laws received impetus from the Minneapolis Police Experiment (Sherman and Berk 1984), which found that arrest was associated with fewer subsequent reports of violence than separating the parties or providing mediation and advice.

Some laws reflect an effort to combine the compassionate and the control responses by including provisions for pretrial therapeutic or educational diversions for offenders. Many of these programs have been evaluated by social scientists, with mixed results (see Eisikovits and Edleson 1989, for a review). Finally, many state and local jurisdictions adopted mandatory arrest policies, and some have developed programs to coordinate responses among the police, the courts, and social-service agencies (Gamache et al. 1988).

In Connecticut, a successful civil suit filed by Tracy Thurman against her town and 29 of its police officers for failure to protect her civil rights provided an immediate impetus for policy change. Consequently, the state legislature passed the Family Violence Prevention and Response Act of 1986. The new law represented a comprehensive combination of compassion and control approaches. The control provisions included:

1. mandatory arrest with probable cause,
2. increased accessibility and use of protective orders,
3. arraignment on the next court day following the arrest.

The law's compassionate responses included:

1. victim assistance and notification of rights by the police,
2. training in the law and family violence dynamics for all law enforcement and court personnel,
3. a six-week pretrial offender education program, and
4. the creation of an intervention unit in court to provide information and assessment services to victims and offenders.

The intervention units consist of family relations staff and specialized family violence victim advocates. The advocates are hired under contract to the local shelter projects, in part because the law's creators felt that they would be able to perform their often critical function within the court system more effectively if they were independent of it. In addition, the advocates' link to the shelters was intended to facilitate referrals and increase cooperation and mutual understanding between the two systems.

The family violence victim advocate position was created by the law. It is the only advocate position for any kind of crime victim operating exclusively in the state's lower courts, where arraignments are held. Family violence charges adjudicated in the lower courts are primarily the least serious assault, breach of peace, and disorderly conduct.

Research was supported by a contract from the Connecticut Commission on Victim Services to investigate gaps and problems in the services provided by the advocates across the state. The commission receives an allocation from the legislature to contract for advocate services. The advocates are hired and supervised by local private, nonprofit domestic-violence shelter programs. Data collected for the project included statistical analysis of case and service records for 6,487 victims referred to advocates during three months spanning 1988 and 1989. Also, interviews were conducted with all but one of the advocates, a random sample of nearly half of the family relations staff, and other court and law enforcement personnel who affect their work. The views presented here are not necessarily shared by the commission.

II. Family Violence Case Processing

Criminal processing in family violence cases under the new Connecticut law generally begins with a call to the police, most commonly by one of the parties involved, but frequently also by someone not directly involved, such as a neighbor. When the police arrive, they decide whether or not there is probable cause to believe that a family violence crime, as defined in the statute, was committed and by whom.[1] If there is probable cause, the officer arrests the suspect. If the police believe that both (or all) parties have committed family violence crimes, the law requires them to arrest both (or all) people involved in the incident (termed "dual arrest"). When this occurs, there are two or more victims and two or more defendants in a single case; all parties involved may be both "victim" and "defendant." Use of dual arrest varies from one police department to another across the state.

At the time the police make this determination, they are also required to complete a report containing information about the parties and the incident, assist victims to obtain medical help, tell victims of their right to pursue an arrest, and provide information about available services, including potential compensation. Most departments have cards that contain service information and can be distributed; their use has increased, but varies from one police department and officer to another.

If an arrest is made, the defendant may be taken into custody or given a summons or citation to appear in court on the next day it is in session. If a custodial arrest is made, the defendants may be released on bail or held overnight. On the next day the court is in session, the defendants appear for arraignment, either from "lock up" or from the community.

To begin court proceedings, police reports are sent to the prosecutor's office in the morning. The office staff review the reports and refer family violence cases (except the most serious felonies, which are transferred to a higher court for trial) to the family relations office (the "family violence intervention unit") for assessment and recommendations about immediate action or interventions, including protective orders. This unit in court formally consists of family relations counselors and family violence victim advocates.

Family relations counselors try to gain an understanding of violent incidents by speaking to defendants (and victims, if possible) so that a recommendation can be communicated to the state's attorney for immediate action in court (dismissal, nolle,[2] changes in charges or bond, or continuance, in combination with orders). The family violence victim advocates may receive automatic referrals from family relations staff to contact victims, determine their safety concerns and desires for a protective order, and provide other immediate counseling or information and

referral services. Victims may appear in court or be contacted by telephone before the case is called, or by telephone or letter following the
arraignment.

Unit organization varies greatly from one court location to another.
Generally, advocates speak to at least some victims on the day of arraignment, and make the information they obtain available to the family
relations staff for consideration in their recommendations to the state's
attorney. In most cases a continuance date is set, by which time family
relations staff will attempt to interview both victim and defendant. In
addition, the advocates will have provided a written report with information about the victim's perspective and desires for case outcome. In
some courts, advocates have contact with victims—for the first time or
as follow-up—between the arraignment and the continuance date. Further recommendations for the case, such as the pretrial education program, counseling, drug or alcohol treatment, or prosecution, are subsequently provided to the state's attorney by the family relations
staff.

In most of the courts, family relations staff refuse to accept referrals
from the state's attorneys after the same defendant has been arrested
repeatedly and the available pretrial options have been pursued. These
cases are sent back to the prosecutors for action, often after the advocate
has assessed the need for a protective order.

Prosecutors sometimes involve the family violence victim advocates in
those cases which proceed to trial. Advocates provide information and
support to victims, and help them prepare for oral or written statements
to the court during the trial or at sentencing. Such cases occur infrequently, however, and use of the advocates in this way varies across the
state.

The Connecticut law created intervention units to operate in the 21
lower courts across the state. The units consist of experienced family
relations staff who serve in multiple capacities in both civil and criminal
cases,[3] as well as the advocates, who are specialized and serving in a
role that is new to the entire system. In these units, at the time of the
study, a total of 27 advocates filled 20 full-time equivalent positions in
the 21 courts. Their job was to serve over 26,000 victims of domestic
violence in a state with a population of 3,326,420. The variability in case
processing described above can be attributed in part to case volume,
which doubled in the law's first year and has continued to increase, and
in part to local variations in the population and legal personnel. Connecticut is a highly diverse state. It has, simultaneously, the highest per
capita income in the nation and three of its poorest cities. The courts
reflect this variation.

III. Family Violence Incidents

According to the Connecticut State Police (Family Violence Reporting Program 1989), the family violence arrests in 1988 stemmed from incidents in which nearly 84% of the victims were women, whereas over 89% of the offenders were men. In over 75% of the cases, the parties were involved in current or former romantic relationships. Alcohol or drugs were factors in 48.4% of the incidents, and children were present in 45% of the cases. In addition, physical injury occurred in 68% of the incidents. In 13% of the cases, court orders had been issued previously. Finally, all parties were arrested ("dual arrest") in just under 20% of the cases.

IV. Issues

The advocate study documented a number of issues of which administrators had become aware from working in the system; these interrelated issues affected the advocates' work in various ways.

A. Case Volume

Although an increase in the number of arrests was anticipated, the magnitude of the increase—more than double—was not. More court personnel have been hired, but not in proportion to the increase in cases. Case volume alone has created pressure to process all cases as quickly as possible. Moreover, because family violence cases must by statute be arraigned on the next court day, court personnel are able to exercise control over their workload only in the way they respond to cases. The largest urban courts, in particular, have experienced difficulty "moving the cases" every day—especially on Mondays, since over one-third of all arrests have been made on weekends. The court days following holidays—and Super Bowl Sunday—have proved to be the most crowded.

At times, moving cases has become a goal in itself. Instead of responding to the needs presented by individual victims and offenders, prosecutors at times argue for dismissal or decide to nolle cases following only limited consultation with the intervention unit staff.

The sheer number of cases also affects the advocates' work directly. The average number of victims to be contacted by advocates in a given month varies from one court to another, and ranged from 66 to 206 for an advocate working full-time during the study period. Contacting the victims before arraignment so that their wishes can be considered in the recommendations and orders granted that day is often difficult, particularly when referral information is inaccurate or incomplete.

The resulting lack of time to contact all victims and adequately convey the available options is lamented by many advocates, who note that it is impossible to try to build up a victim's sense of self-worth or to communicate that there is a better way to live in "just a few minutes." Nevertheless, advocates contacted almost 60% of all referred victims in person or by telephone during the research period. The remainder received letters describing available services. The direct contact rate has continued to increase since that time.

Advocates and other staff also recognize that it is important to contact victims immediately after the incident when the details of the recent violence are readily recalled, and victims are also more receptive to intervention. Family relations staff recognized that many victims minimize the significance of the violence over time; the description of the incident they hear 6 to 12 weeks after the arrest may be quite different from what is told to advocates within a day or two of the violence.

B. Resources

Limited resources compound the difficulties experienced in responding to expanding case volume in a number of ways. First, available allocations at the time of the study were sufficient for only 20 full-time equivalent (FTE) positions, yet there are 21 court locations. In addition, the largest urban courts experience such large case volumes that more than one FTE advocate is imperative. As a result, many advocates are hired part-time, and some full-time advocates cover more than one court. Both arrangements mean that some advocates are not available in court throughout the day, every day, when victims and other court staff might need their services. The advocates' absences mean that they are systematically not exposed to particular types or stages of case processing in court, and their first-hand knowledge is reduced. Limited resources undermine the team effort, the advocates' credibility, and the program's ability to provide full coverage for victims.

Second, limited resources and the advocates' contractual status keep their salaries low. Their annual pay when the law was first implemented averaged about half of that received by the family relations staff with whom they worked. Low pay contributed to high rates of turnover, especially when the law was first implemented. High turnover is perceived by advocates to undermine their credibility with other court personnel, and reduce their effectiveness in courts. One advocate speaks for several when commenting on the meaning of low salaries:

> We need to be paid more. We do more than [other court] staff and their pay is much higher. That's bad because it's a way of valuing our work. There should be more seriousness attached to victims' and women's issues. . . . I also think we'd get more respect in court if we were paid more.[4] (Interview with female advocate, Connecticut, 4/28 1989)

Finally, space and other resources in court buildings are significantly limited. The family violence law was first implemented just after additional court personnel had been hired for other specialized programs and to respond to increasing drug arrests. Thus, the advocates represented a new and undefined position in an already clogged system. In many courthouses, the most basic resources required to conduct work are unavailable—telephones, for example. This makes victim contact on the morning of arraignment difficult, at best. Many advocates described conducting their "confidential" interviews with victims in hallways and stairwells, where they are justifiably concerned about potential intimidation from nearby defendants. One advocate described talking to victims outside the courthouse in a snowstorm. Despite ingenious solutions, such as the use of credit cards for pay telephones in some locations, limited resources in court make difficult work more difficult for all concerned.

C. Information Flow

Processing family violence cases through the criminal-justice system involves many different groups: victim advocates, family relations counselors, prosecutors, bail commissioners, and judges. These cases contain complex and crucial information, and family situations or dynamics continue to change after an arrest is first made. Thus, the flow of information among the groups working on these cases is often a source of difficulty.

At the time of an arrest, it is the police officer's responsibility to inform the victim of services available at the court, and to encourage the victim to come to the arraignment the next day. The police also are responsible for getting complete and accurate information on how victims can be contacted. However, many victim advocates complain that inaccurate information often permits them from reaching victims who do not come to court.

Each court has a different protocol for responding to cases. This affects the timing of case processing and the staff who have access to information regarding victim contact and the details of the incident. Advocates who have access to information from police and prosecutors' files report that the information is helpful for their conversations with victims, allowing them to probe into areas they might otherwise not pursue as diligently. For example, some advocates observed that victims had "neglected" to mention that the offender had a gun during the incident—important information for a safety assessment.

The way that advocates relay to family relations staff the information they obtain from victims on the day of arraignment is inconsistent across the state. In many courts, effective systems for exchanging information have been established between advocates and family relations personnel. However, when advocates do not have access to information about cases, and are also unable to convey information that they have attained, their effectiveness is seriously compromised.

Finally, both advocates and family relations personnel lamented their lack of knowledge of case disposition. In no court is there a systematic mechanism for informing the intervention units of the outcome of their services and recommendations. Consequently, the staff remain uncertain of their effectiveness.

D. Decision Making

Significant issues have also been identified in connection with the different points in case processing where decisions have to be made, starting from the first call to police. These are decisions made by victims, police, the intervention unit, prosecutors, and judges.

1. Victims. Victims who are not familiar with the law often do not realize that they are essentially giving up their ability to make a decision about arrest and initial court appearances once they call the police. They may want the violence to stop, but prefer that an arrest not be made. They also face the risk that they will be arrested. Since the statute refers to physical injury or bodily harm, any damage inflicted by victims—even in self-defense—makes them potentially eligible for arrest. Police are sometimes said to be reluctant to make decisions regarding culpability and will arrest both parties, leaving it to the judge to sort out the details. Nearly all advocates reported hearing victims (primarily those who had been arrested) assert they would never call the police again.

2. Police. Although the law states that police must make an arrest when they have probable cause, the individual police officer still decides what charges to apply in each case, and whether or not to arrest both parties. Some of the advocates contended that police in some districts are biased toward making dual arrests when there is doubt about the circumstances, thus revictimizing the victims.

3. Intervention Units. In some courts, the family relations counselors try to speak to both victim and defendant on the day of arraignment. They may also refer victims to the advocates. In other courts, they speak primarily with defendants and refer the victims to the advocates. In either case, the potential for conflict among intervention unit staff is clear: family relations counselors hear either the defendant's story or the stories of both parties (the "balanced view"), while advocates hear only the version presented by the victim. On the day of arraignment family relations staff have the authority to make decisions related to the day's recommendations to prosecutors. These involve trying to ascertain whether there is a "real" victim in dual-arrest cases, decisions about protective orders, and referrals to the pretrial education program, all made more difficult by the speed with which they must be made.

In dual-arrest cases, both parties are legally considered "victims" and "defendants." Advocates in some locations reported in interviews that they speak to both parties in these cases, while others talk only to the woman. Many advocates have developed language to separate the two "victims." For some there is a "victim" and a "complainant," while others distinguish between the "real victims" and the "paper victims." Advocates maintain that the real victim is nearly always the woman, who frequently has been arrested because she was defending herself or because her partner is manipulating the law, as the following illustrates:

> I think I'm objective. There are nearly always conflicting stories. Men know the law now, and will tell the police she did something so that they'll both be arrested. When both people were actively involved in the violence the stories are more consistent. It's most often (but not always) true when the woman says she did nothing or was defending herself. (Interview with fe adv, Connecticut, June 5, 1989)

Advocates express concern that some prosecutors and family relations staff do not believe women when they claim self-defense. From their perspective, this demonstrates a lack of understanding of the woman's position. Some family relations staff, however, express the parallel concern that advocates "automatically" believe the women's stories because they are biased.

Family relations staff have the authority to make recommendations to the prosecutors about protective orders, usually after conferring with the advocates. These orders are basically of two types: those prohibiting further violence (*partial orders*), and those requiring the defendant to leave the residence and forbidding further contact (*full orders*). In a majority of the courts, advocates and family relations staff agree about orders most of the time.

Advocates maintain that when there are disagreements, they are one of two types. In some courts, when the advocates hear from victims about repeated violence and threats with weapons, they recommend full protective orders. This is sometimes met with resistance by family relations counselors. When this occurs, the counselors may argue that the defendant has no place to go. The counselors sometimes assert that there are shelters for women and none for men, so if someone needs to leave the house, it should be the woman (i.e., the victim).

More frequently, advocates report that disagreements arise when they convey the victim's preference for a partial order, but the family relations staff insist that the danger involved warrants a full order. Advocates comment that they share the counselors' concerns for the victim's safety, but believe that the victim knows her situation best, and what will most ensure her safety. Some victims claim that they feel safer knowing where the offender is, rather than wondering if and when he might appear, and in what condition.

From the advocate's point of view, both differences are indications that the family relations staff do not fully understand the dynamics of family violence, or support victims as much as they should. Some of the family relations counselors have found the advocates' recommendations for full orders to be unfair and indicators of their bias against men.

Family relations counselors also make recommendations about pretrial referrals of defendants to the six-week education program. Most intervention unit staff questioned whether six weeks is enough to change fundamental patterns of relational violence and control. The primary issues that have emerged are whether the education program is appropriate for both parties in dual-arrest cases, and whether educational groups for both men and women are as effective as same-sex groups.

4. Prosecutors.   Prosecutors clearly play a significant role in disposing of the family violence cases. Advocates and family relations counselors expressed concern about prosecutors' decisions to pursue cases and the attitudes some displayed toward victims. On the average, about 75% of the cases are nolled, while charges are dismissed in other cases. Most intervention unit staff believe that more cases should be prosecuted actively, particularly those involving defendants with prior arrest histories. Unit staff also reported that some prosecutors, despite their support for the law, have been insensitive to victims. They expressed anger at those prosecutors who allow the offender to return home after a full protective order has been entered.

5. Judges.   Judges are the ultimate (and most visible) court authorities, and as such exercise great influence in diverse ways. Advocates and family relations counselors report concern regarding some judges who "lecture" women about how they should leave an abusive relationship. Inattention to educational opportunities in court was cited as a sign that family violence is not taken seriously enough by the system, as the following indicates:

> I think [the new judge in the rotation] doesn't understand yet. He thinks we're here to mediate. He may ask family relations to work something out. . . . He refers to a protective order as something the woman has applied for. The other day he referred to a case where the woman was choked as a "tiff." (June 14, 1989)
>
> [The judges] treat cases nonchalantly. They should convey to the defendant that what they've done is wrong. They should be firm. In court you're not just talking to the defendant, you have an audience of others. You could give them an education, too. It would be good prevention. (April 1989)

E. Sanctions

The limited sanctions available in these cases are a major source of frustration for all involved. High volume and serious overcrowding in the state's prisons make incarceration a realistic option in only the most serious cases. Many advocates and family relations counselors perceive that limited sanctions directly affect their ability to work with victims, thus undermining their own morale. The following excerpts from interviews are illustrative:

> The court just hands out too many slaps on the wrist. That's demoralizing for victims, and for us, too. It teaches the guys that they can beat the charges, and that spreads fast . . . . [When no longer referred for alternative interventions] they learn that you can beat your wife for $100—you just have to do it more than once. (June 30, 1989)
>
> The system can be an obstacle. The defendants know that jail is very unlikely. It's easier to get into an elite university than into jail in this state! Other sanctions are unlikely, too. (May 9, 1989)

V. Impact of the Law

Despite the concerns reflected in the issues described above, the overwhelming majority of intervention unit staff report that the law has had a positive impact on victims. Most have said in interviews that the law is a "good first step" in part because it connects victims with the system, so that they obtain information about available alternatives and resources, and learn that they are not alone. Many have commented that the law makes it clear to victims that family violence is wrong and a crime, and they do not have to tolerate it. Unit staff have also noted that ready access to protective orders has enhanced victim safety. One advocate was particularly clear about two types of victim responses she has seen:

> Some of them really expect something stronger will happen to the defendant than a referral to family relations, and it's very upsetting to some of them. . . . For some, it's a real positive experience, because it's empowering to them, at least short-term. When they realize they can do something, they take steps. . . . The law helps them realize that this is not the way a relationship should be. It gives them more chutzpa to help themselves. And for some it's like coming out of the closet after a long time. I've seen a few who have made big changes after 60 years of [a violent] marriage! (June 15, 1989)

Most intervention unit staff reported in interviews that they have observed two primary responses among offenders:

> I think [the law] helps with first-time offenders. They're being more careful now. The others have gotten courtwise and don't give a hoot. It's a slap on the wrist. They know there's no space in the jails for them. (June 23, 1989)
>
> It seems there are two categories of abusers: the bad and the mad. The mad don't know how to respond appropriately to stress. It's a role they've observed all their lives, and they can be helped. They can learn to behave differently. The bad are evil, and seem to enjoy abuse. They're very unlikely to change; I think most of them are beyond help. (January 24, 1989)
>
> I think we have a chance with the people where it's the first time, there's no history of violence, they're young, and it's early in the relationship. They're scared and open to change. They'll listen. (June 15, 1989)

VI. Discussion

The Connecticut legislature passed one of the most comprehensive domestic violence laws in the country. As in any major new undertaking, the law's implementation has been a process. Changes in responses at all stages of the criminal-justice process have been adopted as needs have been identified (cf. Lyon et al. 1989). The law's designers and frontline staff, however, generally remain convinced that it has been the right policy to adopt.

The major difficulties encountered are related to the massive numbers of cases. The problems associated with limited resources and the inability to impose punitive sanctions would be significantly reduced if case volume were lower. Other issues can be addressed through staff training. Provisions for such education were written into the law. Another important feature of the legislation was a record-keeping requirement for all agencies involved and the creation of an interagency monitoring committee responsible for annual reports to the legislature.

This group has contributed to cooperative approaches to problems and encouraged coordination of policy modification efforts.

The law combines both compassion and control elements, but has not synthesized them. The tension between the two is perhaps inevitable. Based on experience with the implementation of this law, other jurisdictions contemplating similar statutes would be well-advised, first, to anticipate the volume of cases likely to appear in court and to provide the resources—staff, space, and equipment—necessary to handle them. Second, if new positions are created (such as specialized advocates), their roles and authority should be clearly delineated. Third, the resources for substantial alternatives for both compassion and control elements should be provided. In particular, support for more extensive education and therapeutic responses, and an array of punitive sanctions, including alternatives to incarceration, seem especially important. Family violence is more pervasive than many policymakers believe; it will not be reduced without more concerted efforts at prevention and response.

Acknowledgement

The authors wish to acknowledge Julia Hunt's substantial contributions to this research.

Notes

1. As defined in the statute, family violence is an incident that results in physical harm, bodily injury, or assault, or an act of threatened violence that causes fear of imminent physical harm, bodily injury, or assault, which occurs between or among family or household members. Verbal abuse or argument does not constitute family violence unless there is present danger and the likelihood that physical violence will occur (Family Violence Reporting Program 1989).

2. A nolle prosequi is an interim disposition wherein prosecution is deferred for 13 months. If no further infractions occur during this period, the case is formally dismissed. In theory, if additional crimes are committed during the 13 months, the prosecution will activate the original case, and proceed with the new charges as well. This commonly does not occur in practice.

3. Family relations staff have rotating responsibilities for mediating or making disposition recommendations in minor nonfamily criminal cases, and mediations and custody and visitation studies in divorce cases.

4. To protect the anonymity of respondents the city in which they were interviewed is not disclosed.

Chapter 15

Improving the Investigation and Prosecution of Child Sexual-Abuse Cases: Research Findings, Questions, and Implications for Public Policy

Debra Whitcomb

I. Introduction

National outrage over child sexual abuse has encouraged criminal prosecution of offenders. Intrafamilial cases, which have traditionally been handled by the protective-service and juvenile-justice systems, are finding their way into the criminal-justice system. One recent study suggests that the criminal-justice system is even more likely than the child welfare system to take action in child sexual-abuse cases (Chapman and Smith 1987).

Controversy continues over the value of prosecuting child sexual-abuse cases. Proponents of prosecution argue that criminal intervention clearly establishes the child as the innocent victim and the perpetrator as criminally and solely responsible for wrongful behavior. Punishment validates the victims' and society's sense of fairness that an adult cannot violate or exploit the relative weakness of children. Those favoring prosecution contend further that, on the one hand, successful prosecutions and public identification of offenders can deter others in the general population who are tempted to commit similar crimes. Additionally, the court can order convicted offenders into treatment programs in order to modify abusive behavior and reduce the likelihood of recidivism. Finally, criminal prosecution gives the offender a criminal record that will follow him or her from state to state (Peters et al. 1988).

Opponents of prosecution believe that criminal prosecution can only exacerbate the trauma that child sexual-abuse victims already experience as a result of their victimization. They argue that civil abuse and neglect proceedings are sufficient, especially for intrafamilial cases. They contend that formal prosecution can cause undue interference with the child's developmental process. Opponents also charge that prosecutors' offices and the courts are ill-prepared for these cases, especially when young child victims are required to be witnesses for the state (Sandberg 1987; Newberger 1987).

Those aspects of the criminal-justice process that are thought to be most stressful for child victims are repetition of the story, confronting the defendant, repeated continuances, hostile cross-examination, the physical environment of the courtroom, identification in the media, fear of retaliation, and the presence of spectators, judge, and jury (Whitcomb 1985).

Empirical studies designed to determine the extent of harm experienced by child victims in their role as court witnesses generate somewhat inconsistent findings. Tedesco and Schnell (1987) report that although the interview and litigation process in general is not harmful to children, repeated interviews and requiring the child to testify in court induce increased stress. A study by Runyan et al. (1988) indicates that the protracted proceedings of criminal court may be detrimental to the child's well-being, but testifying in juvenile court may actually be beneficial. Runyan et al. corroborate Melton's review (1984) of several studies, in which he suggests that court testimony can be empowering for the child victims who need to regain a sense of control over their lives. Goodman et al. (1989), however, report that child victims are adversely affected by the act of testifying in criminal court and, further, that delays and continuances can contribute to the children's recovery. All told, the empirical research highlights the complexity of child sexual abuse and the criminal-justice system, as well as the multifaceted dynamics that influence the child victim's capacity to withstand and endure stress.

II. The Call for Reform

Responding to increased public outrage over child sexual abuse and the concerns voiced by child advocates, legislators and child-serving professionals seek to reform the process of investigating and adjudicating reports of child sexual abuse in ways that are thought to accommodate the perceived special needs of child victims. The presumption is that efforts to alleviate the trauma experienced by child victims will benefit not only the children, but the prosecution as well.

Table 1 shows five goals that underlie the movement to modify existing procedures for investigating and adjudicating child sexual-abuse cases. For each goal, Table 1 displays the interventions that have been proposed and/or implemented in various jurisdictions throughout the

Table 1. Goals of Proposed Interventions on Behalf of Child Victims[a]

	Orientation of activity	
Goal	*System*	*Child*
Expedite case	Faster setup of case-processing points Strict continuance policy Active case monitoring Use of fast-track system for charges Prompt delivery of results of medical tests on child	Earliest contact with child by police, social agencies, prosecutor
Provide people support to victim	Early identification of child advocate/guardian ad litem Coordination of case management with multidisciplinary team Early referrals for treatment/services for child and child's family	Continuous contact between child and child advocate, social-service agencies
Reduce unnecessary contact of child with system	Waiver of discretionary contact points between child and system Reduction in number of interviews with child through coordination in case management	Use of videotape in place of live appearance by child at subsequent stages in proceedings, where original testimony would be recited
Institute child-friendly procedures	Use of anatomical dolls, artwork, etc., to help elicit child's testimony Use of screens, one-way mirrors, and appropriate furniture placement to reduce visual contact between victim and defendant in court Use of closed-circuit TV Modifications to courtroom environment, (e.g., use of scale furniture and appropriate colors), frequent breaks during child testimony Limitations on movement and voice levels by attorneys	Explanation to child of purpose of proceeding and development Debriefing after testimony and disposition of case, including delivery of victim impact statement Limitation on media coverage of proceedings and other public identification of victim Preparation and delivery of "certificate of participation/cooperation/truthfulness" (for example) as indication of appreciation of child's assistance to authorities

(continued)

Table 1. (*Continued*)

Goal	Orientation of activity	
	System	Child
Enhance case development	Use of exceptions to hearsay rule	Modification of oath for child witnesses
	Use of expert witnesses to strengthen child's testimony	
	Improved methods of establishing competency of child witnesses	
	Vigorous use of general and case-specific medical tests and research with involvement by local medical community	

a Prepared by Education Development Center, Inc., under Grant No. 87-MC-CX-0026 from the Office of Juvenile Justice and Delinquency Prevention, Office of Justice Programs, U.S. Department of Justice.

United States. Some are directed to the criminal-justice system; others are focused upon the child. Some require legislation before they can be implemented. Others depend solely on the discretion of the individuals or agencies involved.

Proposed reforms on behalf of child victims address every point in the process of investigating and adjudicating reports that are filed with the mandated authorities. For example, many states require the cross-reporting of sexual-abuse cases between child protection and law enforcement agencies. The intent is to ensure that children are protected and that cases are reviewed for possible criminal-justice intervention.

In some jurisdictions, joint interviews and/or multidisciplinary case review teams are adopted in efforts to streamline the investigation process. In other jurisdictions, prosecutors routinely assign a victim advocate or guardian ad litem to assist child victims through the criminal-justice system.

Prosecutors' offices and law enforcement agencies in some of our larger communities have designated specialized units or personnel for cases involving child victims. To minimize the number of people and interviews imposed upon the child, these units typically emphasize vertical case management. This policy enables a single prosecutor or investigator to maintain responsibility for the case from the time a file is opened until final disposition.

Another popular investigation technique is videotaping the child's first full statement to guard against subsequent retractions or memory loss and to reduce the need for additional interviews.

Perhaps the most controversial reforms are those that attempt to ameliorate the presumed trauma of testifying at trial. The American Prosecutors Research Institute reports that, as of December 31, 1988, 36 states permit videotaped testimony to substitute for in-court testimony by child sexual-abuse victims. In 29 states, child victims are permitted to testify via live, closed-circuit television. A total of 26 states have created special hearsay exceptions to allow into evidence certain out-of-court statements made by the child sexual-abuse victims. In 20 states, child sexual-abuse cases are given special priority on the courts' trial calendars. In addition, in 12 states trial courts are permitted to exclude spectators from the courtroom during the child victim's testimony.

Because their implementations may threaten defendants' constitutional rights to varying degrees, these reforms are subject to judicial interpretation (*Coy v. Iowa* 1988; *Globe Newspaper Co. v. Superior Court* 1982). Less radical courtroom reforms include establishing ground rules to guide the attorneys' behavior when questioning the child; permitting the child to use anatomical dolls or artwork as demonstrative aids; alternative seating arrangements (e.g., directing the child's attention away from the defendant or jury); allowing judges to wear informal attire; and providing smaller witness chairs (Whitcomb 1985).

In fact, there are many possibilities for modifying current procedures on behalf of child victims. Yet little is known about whether innovative techniques actually achieve their dual goals of (1) reducing the trauma experienced by child victims in the criminal-justice system and (2) improving the outcome of prosecution.

III. Evaluation of Programs for the Effective Prosecution of Child Physical and Sexual Abuse

In 1985, the Bureau of Justice Assistance (BJA), U.S. Department of Justice, initiated a large-scale demonstration program in the area of child abuse. The stated goal of the program was to prosecute effectively individuals accused of physically or sexually abusing children, and at the same time to reduce the trauma to the child victims and their families.

Prosecutors' offices throughout the country applied for 18-month demonstration grants. The principal requirements were to (1) establish a dedicated child abuse prosecution unit and to (2) institute a multidisciplinary approach to case management. Grants were awarded to prosecutors' offices in the following jurisdictions:

- Bexar County (San Antonio), Texas
- Dade County (Miami), Florida

- Hampden County (Springfield), Massachusetts
- Madison County (Huntsville), Alabama
- Snohomish County (Everett), Washington
- Trumbull County (Warren), Ohio

A grant was also awarded to the American Indian Law Center in Albuquerque, New Mexico, to support prosecution of child abuse cases in the Eight Northern Pueblos. These grants started up over the first three months of 1986. In addition, the Hennepin County Attorney's Office (in Minneapolis, Minnesota) was invited to participate in the demonstration as an unfunded site.

An evaluation grant was awarded (Whitcomb 1985), and the essential findings from the evaluation are highlighted and discussed below.

A. Research Design

A quasi-experimental design was used to compare case management and case outcome for specified periods, before and after the demonstration grants were awarded. Both quantitative and qualitative measures were employed.

1. Quantitative Measures.   Researchers drew two samples of physical- and sexual-abuse cases that were referred for prosecution in each jurisdiction participating in the study during identical intervals, before and after the demonstration grants were awarded. These cases were tracked through final disposition or for a one-year data collection period.

A systematic sampling procedure was used to select the cases. Each site provided an estimate of the total number of cases that would be referred for prosecution over a six-month period, and the sampling procedure was designed accordingly, to yield one hundred cases for the study. The jurisdiction with the heaviest caseload selected every fourth case referred. The smaller jurisdictions simply captured the universe of cases referred.

The data collection instrument was designed to gather (1) background data on characteristics of the victim, the perpetrator, and the case; (2) procedural data on interviews conducted with child victims and any innovative techniques that were employed; and (3) basic case-tracking through the criminal-justice and child protection systems. These data were to be drawn from existing case files maintained by the respective agencies.

2. Qualitative Measures.   Qualitative data collected for the evaluation study include relevant statutes and court rules, training materials, task force reports, statistical reports, and existing protocols and policies guiding the investigation and prosecution of child abuse cases.

Each site participating in the research program was visited. Two conferences were held for all participating sites. The site visits and the conferences generated information used in the evaluation study.

B. Findings

BJA evaluation researchers find that special prosecution units dedicated to child abuse cases may not be equally feasible everywhere. Burnout is a major cause of turnover in units dedicated to child abuse cases. One method to counteract burnout is to allow the prosecutors some mix in their caseloads, either within a more broadly defined special unit (e.g., for sexual assaults or family violence) or from the general criminal caseload.

This comprehensive evaluation also finds that there are several ways to achieve a coordinated, multidisciplinary approach to case management. Ideally, teams comprising representatives of all the involved agencies meet regularly to receive new reports and to monitor the progress of ongoing cases. However, where agencies are overburdened by soaring caseloads or where there is a history of either poor communication or "turf" conflicts in the community, achieving a coordinated team can be an enormous challenge. Some successful approaches were observed among the demonstration projects. Our researchers observe that in some jurisdictions, changing the people who are involved in case management can result in personalities more amenable to coordinated efforts. In other communities, enacting a law requiring some form of interagency communication provides an important incentive to overcome conflicts.

Centralizing the decision-making process—specifically in a "children's center" as in the well-known program in Huntsville, Alabama—provides a convenient forum for cross-agency communication and team case review. Strengthening the role of the prosecutor instills the leadership that may be necessary to motivate cooperation.

This evaluation observes that vertical prosecution is commendable as a means of reducing the number of prosecutors who interview child victims, but its positive effect is essentially nullified if the child has already encountered numerous law enforcement officers, child protection workers, and medical and mental-health personnel. Where investigations are conducted insensitively or in a fragmented or duplicative fashion, child victims and their families will become less cooperative, and the potential for successful case outcome will decline.

Finally, this study finds that videotaping can substantially reduce the required number of interviews with child victims, provided that interviewers are thoroughly trained and skilled in techniques of interviewing and operating the equipment. Joint interviews involving two or more agency representatives can achieve the same goal, but such interviews are exceedingly difficult to arrange.

IV. The Child Victim as a Witness: Research and Development Program

The Office of Juvenile Justice and Delinquency Prevention (OJJDP) established The Child Victim As a Witness Research and Development Program (U.S. Department of Justice 1984) in an effort to address the question, How can prosecutors most effectively prosecute child sexual-abuse cases without imposing additional trauma on the children?

In numerous ways, the OJJDP project picks up where the BJA project left off. This three-year study, funded in September 1987, represents a collaborative effort involving Education Development Center, Inc., of Newton, Massachusetts, the University of North Carolina, and the American Prosecutors Research Institute. The project will explore five specific research questions:

1.   What characteristics of the child, the family, the incident, the community, and the legal environment influence the decision to prosecute child sexual-abuse cases?

2.   How do these same characteristics influence the decision to use certain evidentiary or procedural techniques when prosecuting child sexual-abuse cases?

3.   How does the availability of innovative techniques influence the decision to prosecute child sexual-abuse cases?

4.   What impact does the use of innovative techniques have on the outcome of case prosecution and on the child's emotional trauma?

5.   Are there additional factors that influence the decision to prosecute, the use of innovative techniques, and ultimately case outcome and child trauma?

The project examines case processing and its effects on children in four jurisdictions:

- Erie County (Buffalo), New York
- Polk County (Des Moines), Iowa
- San Diego County, California
- Ramsey County (St. Paul), Minnesota

Each participating site designated a program team consisting of top officials from all the agencies that deal with child abuse cases. These program teams work with the research team to identify and implement promising strategies for alleviating the child's trauma in the criminal-justice system.

A. Research Design

In the first phase of the research program, researchers and program teams engaged in a period of assessment and program development. Current policies and practices were assessed, areas needing improvement were identified, and prosecutorial strategies were selected for study.

Following the assessment and development was a period of operation and evaluation. Baseline and prospective samples of up to 200 cases in each of the 4 sites were drawn from reports of child sexual abuse that were substantiated by law enforcement and social-service agencies and referred for criminal prosecution. Each sample includes cases that are accepted for prosecution, as well as cases that are not prosecuted.

For each case, detailed information about the child, the case, and the systems' response is collected. Local law students were trained to track cases through the criminal- and juvenile-justice systems, using a structured case records form. Also, local mental-health professionals were specially trained to conduct a direct assessment of the psychological well-being of children in the prospective sample only. Each child selected for the study whose parent or guardian consented to participate is tested at two points: shortly after the case is referred for prosecution, and again after nine months.

B. Progress to Date

Program teams in the participating sites are continuing to refine and improve their management of child sexual-abuse cases.

In Erie County, prosecutors from the Comprehensive Assault, Abuse, and Rape (CAAR) Unit have instructed officers in the major law enforcement agencies to consult the CAAR Unit before making arrests in child sexual-abuse cases. This change in procedure should result in fewer children having to swear out arrest complaints and testify at preliminary hearings, since prosecutors have the option of initiating cases via the grand jury.

In San Diego, all child victims attend a "court school" to prepare them for their role as witnesses. This new program is designed to strengthen the child's testimony at preliminary hearings (which are required in California), ideally encouraging guilty pleas and obviating the need for trials.

In Polk County, a Child Victim Review Team was created to provide multidisciplinary case review for nonfamilial cases. This new team complements the Intrafamilial Sexual Abuse Program Team, which has been active for nearly 10 years. Nonfamilial cases should benefit from the more focused review, and more child victims of nonfamilial offenders should receive counseling through the efforts of the new team.

With a similar goal in mind, the Ramsey County Attorney's Office expanded its Juvenile/Family Offenses Division to include responsibility for cases involving child victims of nonfamilial perpetrators.

The research team continues to work with the program teams through periodic visits and ongoing technical assistance provided by the American Prosecutors Research Institute. Impact analyses will be conducted on more than 200 child victims who completed both of the psychological interviews.

This project will contribute to the continuing development of empirically based guidelines for determining the need for special interventions on behalf of child sexual-abuse victims. Judges, prosecutors, investigators, and child-serving professionals in a wide range of disciplines who seek to improve the plight of sexually victimized children will benefit from the study findings in designing prosecution programs to help child victims heal while improving prosecution.

Chapter 16

Preventing and Provoking Wife Battery through Criminal Sanctioning: A Look at the Risks

David A. Ford

I. Introduction

Current advocacy for battered women is unwavering in its insistence on rigorous criminal-justice intervention to prevent continuing violence. Perceived certainty that criminal sanctioning will deter wife batterers derives from convergent research findings and ideologies (Mederer and Gelles 1989). The Sherman and Berk (1984) Minneapolis Police Experiment demonstrated that arrest had specific deterrent impacts on wife batterers, making it the most effective police response for protecting victims from repeat violence. By extension, and with support from both feminists and advocates of a control approach to crime, the Attorney General's Task Force on Family Violence Final Report (U.S. Department of Justice 1984) called for rigorous prosecution of wife batterers. Nevertheless, many recognize that criminal sanctions may arouse resentment and anger leading to retaliatory violence (e.g., Field and Field 1973; Finesmith 1983; Gayford 1977; Lerman 1982; Truninger 1971). Indeed, many victims are known to fear retaliation (Ford 1983; Lerman 1981).

Concern over violent reprisal is voiced by victim advocates and police alike. Some police officers express their concern as justification for their inaction (Ford 1987; Jaffe et al. 1986), whereas arrest advocates find the risk of retaliation cause *for* arrest (Fromson 1977; Walker 1979). Parallel concerns over prosecuting wife batterers are also articulated (Gayford 1977).

To minimize the risk of retaliation, policy must be sensitive to individual victim vulnerability (Elliott et al. 1985; Ford 1983; Goolkasian 1986; Lerman 1980; also, review by Elliott 1989) and attentive to relevant theory and research (Mederer and Gelles 1989). But what are the trade-

191

offs? Are the risks of retaliatory violence outweighed by the preventive impacts of punishment through criminal sanctioning?

Based on data from interviews with batterers and victims, this chapter first examines the issue of whether prosecution initiated by an on-scene warrantless arrest by police is more risky than prosecution following a victim complaint to the prosecutor. In the event of a victim-initiated complaint, the differential effects of bringing the batterer to court either by summons or by warrant are also considered. Finally, we analyze differences in reactions stemming from four court outcomes: case dismissal, pretrial diversion to counseling, sentencing to counseling as a condition of probation, and sentencing to other sanctions.

II. Conceptual Background

Competing conceptual orientations give rise to contradictory expectations for the effects of criminal-justice intervention. One theory suggests that repetition of violence is prevented through deterrence and/or reformation; another suggests provocation to violence through anger with aggression–arousal.

A. Deterrence

Deterrence, stated in its classical form, is the preventive effect of swift, certain, and severe punishment (Beccaria 1963; Bentham 1962). Specific deterrence is the impact that punishing an individual for a proscribed behavior has on reducing the likelihood that he or she will repeat that behavior. For law enforcement, deterrence is associated with any one of its basic elements, but most commonly with punishment severity and certainty. For wife battery and criminal justice, specific deterrence predicts that a man who batters his partner and is punished by harsh criminal sanctions, or even by arrest only, will be *less likely* to batter again than if he experienced milder sanctions or no arrest. The Minneapolis Police Experiment (Sherman and Berk 1984) found that arrest— a relatively harsh sanction—had a specific deterrent impact on wife batterers.

B. Reformation

Reformation is the preventive impact that results from a punishment teaching an individual that his or her behavior is wrong. For some offenders, punishment provides a "moral jolt" causing them not only to learn that their behaviors are inappropriate, but also to lose all capacity for even contemplating engaging in the behavior again (Andenaes 1968;

Gibbs 1975). Dutton (1988) calls this the "didactic function" of criminal-justice intervention.

C. Arousal

Arousal, in contrast, predicts a promotive impact for criminal sanctioning. Arousal is an agitated psychophysical state manifested in aggressive behavior that is less susceptible to normative controls (Zimbardo 1969). Resentment, and especially anger, are common manifestations of arousal. Indeed, it is a truism in clinical explanations of wife battering that anger is a primary determinant of violence. Most batterer treatment programs are premised on the notion that "anger control" is essential to violence reduction (see Dutton 1988). The effect of arousal on violence is indicated by reports of anger and resentment toward the victim.

III. Methodology

A. Case Samples

For this study, a subsample of cases from a major field experiment on the specific preventive impacts of alternative prosecution policies on wife batterers was drawn from a larger study designed to evaluate two sets of punishments/treatments presumed to influence an accused batterer's future violence toward his partner (Ford 1985). The first set is *mode of entry*, and includes (1) summoning to court following a victim complaint, (2) arrest on a warrant following a victim complaint, and (3) on-scene warrantless arrest. The second set is *prosecution outcomes* and includes (1) having a case dismissed (nolle prosequi), (2) pretrial diversion to counseling, (3) adjudication to conviction with sentencing to counseling as a condition of probation, and (4) conviction with sentencing to any other—presumably harsher—sanction. The various punishments/treatments are ranked within each set according to severity, consistent with a previous analysis of defendant perceptions of severity.

Data were collected for cases of misdemeanor conjugal violence brought to the attention of the Marion County, Indiana, Prosecutor's Office over 13 months, beginning in late June 1986. Each case was first identified following either a victim-initiated complaint to the prosecutor or a warrantless, on-scene battery arrest by a police officer responding to a violent domestic disturbance. Each case was tracked through the prosecution process and six months beyond the date it was settled, for evidence of recidivism.

The present study examines victim reports of any violent episode occurring after the case is filed, and within the six-month follow-up period. Three separate measures for the different time frames are used: (1) presettlement—after filing until the case is settled in court, (2) 30 days postsettlement—immediately following the court settlement, and (3) six months postsettlement.

B. Interviews

1. Victim Interviews.   Victims were interviewed soon after their cases were approved for prosecution, typically within one month of filing. The initial interview provided information on the couple at the time of the violent incident that brought the case to the attention of the prosecutor. The first follow-up interview was conducted by telephone at least 30 days following the case being settled. It is the source of data on presettlement and 30-day follow-up violence. The principal follow-up interview was conducted in person six months after the case had been settled, and provides data on violent episodes in the postsettlement period.

2. Defendant Interviews.   Defendants were interviewed immediately following case settlement. The defendant interview focused on the individual's reactions to his criminal-justice experience, including his anger over the way he was brought into the prosecution process and his case outcome. Defendant reactions to prosecution outcomes do not necessarily indicate a reaction to an outcome actually "experienced" by defendants at the time they were interviewed. For example, a man sentenced to counseling as a condition of probation would typically not have completed the mandated counseling; the questionnaire tapped his reaction to perceived anticipated punishments.

The defendant interview asked how well the statement "I felt angry" described his reaction to being summoned or arrested. Response categories are "Not at all," "Somewhat," or "Definitely." Later he was asked the same question to describe how he felt about the outcome of his case.

This study examines a sample of 512 cases consisting of all cases that had been settled for at least six months. A subsample of 346 cases includes those with victim six-month follow-up interviews.

Table 1 describes the sample for each intake set: victim complaints (VC) to the prosecutor or on-scene police arrest (OSA). The majority of all individuals in the samples are white, although nonwhites are overrepresented. The average age of defendants is 30 years, and for victims about 28.

The modal conjugal status of couples is married and living together at the time of the incident, and over 60% had at least one child together. Somewhat surprisingly, only 16% of the couples were separated and/or

Table 1. Characteristics of Victims
and Defendants by Intake Set

	Intake set (%)	
	VC	OSA
Defendant race (%)		
White	54	58
Nonwhite	46	42
N	(366)	(142)
Victim race (%)		
White	56	60
Nonwhite	44	40
N	(368)	(144)
Defendant mean age (years)	30.0	30.3
N	(367)	(143)
Victim mean age (years)	28.0	27.5
N	(367)	(142)
Conjugal status (%)		
Married, cohabiting	30	39
Married, separated	8	7
Divorced	8	3
Unmarried, cohabiting	19	31
Previously cohabited	28	14
Children only	7	6
N	(333)	(114)
Couple has one child or more (%)	61	63
N	(333)	(114)
Defendant non-HS graduate (%)	45	44
N	(312)	(109)
Victim non-HS graduate (%)	40	46
N	(333)	(114)
Defendant unemployed (%)	23	28
N	(320)	(114)
Victim unemployed (%)	42	48
N	(333)	(114)
Defendant criminal history (%)		
No criminal history	25	24
Violent crimes	21	24
Other crimes only	54	52
N	(368)	(144)

divorced just prior to the violent incident, a notable difference from a 1978 study in which 15% of the cases fell under each of these two categories. In contrast, over half of the couples in this study were live-in or previous live-in relationships, much higher than in 1978. These differences reflect an important change in policy over the past ten years. In 1978, battered women found little support for prosecuting (Ford 1983);

today, the prosecutor's office encourages prosecution and offers reasonable support for victims pursuing prosecutorial intervention.

Conjugal status is the only factor on which VC cases are clearly distinguished from those initiated by OSA. The differences reveal a primary criterion in a police officer's decision to make a warrantless battery arrest. Most arrestees were cohabiting under marital or live-in arrangements. In such cases, officers are more likely to find the defendant on the scene and to invoke arrest as the most certain option for removing him.

The samples are very similar in terms of defendant and victim education and employment status. About 45% are high school dropouts, and victim unemployment was about 45%. The samples are similar in defendant criminal histories. Only one out of four defendants had never been arrested before the incident. About one out of five had been arrested for a nonfelonious crime of violence (men previously convicted of felony violence or of violence against the victim in the study case were excluded from the research). Although cases initiated by OSA are arguably more severe (arrest requires a battery with injury), the defendant's criminal histories do not suggest that those arrestees were more severely criminal than those arrested following a VC.

C. Findings

This analysis of preventive and provocative impacts focuses on two aspects: reactions to entry experiences, and reactions to prosecution outcomes. Data are first presented on the indicators of anger-induced provocative effects of alternative criminal-justice treatments. New violence then is evaluated in light of possible treatment-specific preventive effects.

1. Presettlement Violence. What is the impact of alternative entry experiences on the likelihood of subsequent violence? First, based on victim one-month reports, there is a low incidence of what they characterize as "retaliatory violence" by defendants for having been brought into the system for battering. In 13 cases out of 386 on which reports were available, victims claim any form of violence as reprisal for the entry experience. There are no significant differences in such reports by any of the alternative entry experiences. Nor do incidents of retaliatory violence vary by levels of anger over the entry experience.

Defendants who enter the criminal-justice system by OSA are significantly more angered over their entry experience than are those introduced to the system by VC, as shown in Table 2. This is expected, premised on the notion that the more punishing experiences will result in a higher level of anger. Contrary to expectation in VC cases, a warrant

Table 2. Defendant Reports (%) of Anger in Reaction to Their Alternative Criminal-Justice Entry Experiences

| | Mode of entry | | | |
| | VC | | | |
Felt angry	Summons	Warrant	Total	OSA
Definitely	49	48	49	69[a]
Somewhat	23	28	25	20
Not at all	29	23	26	11
N	(177)	(188)	(365)	(144)

[a] $\chi^2 = 19.58$, $df = 2$, $p < .001$ for differences between total VC and OSA cases.

arrest incites no greater anger than does summoning to court. Two factors may account for this finding. First, although a warrant arrest should, in principle, be at least as punishing as OSA, in practice it may differ little from a summons. A man usually knows about a warrant for his arrest and often elects to turn himself in at his convenience, or he is contacted by the warrant service agency and invited to turn himself in. Thus, he may not experience the socially visible punishment of, say, being arrested, handcuffed, and taken away from a workplace. Alternatively, a man who receives a summons for court may choose to ignore it only to be arrested later for failure to appear.

Beyond these explanations, possible selectivity bias associated with the nonrandom assignment of cases to intake sets—determined either by VC or by OSA—may result in unmeasured factors accounting for differences in the defendants' reactions.

What is the effect of anger over the entry experience on repeat violence during the prosecution process? The data displayed in Table 3 show that while "definite" anger over the entry experience is associated with violence rates of at least 20%, regardless of the mode of entry, only in the case of a warrant arrest is there a significant statistical relationship. Defendants who report being "definitely" angered by a warrant arrest are three times more likely than those who feel less anger to commit new acts of violence against their victims. This is a remarkable finding considering that a warrant arrest is no more likely to generate an angry reaction than a summons, and it is less likely to provoke anger than an OSA. Before offering an explanation, it is important to examine the direct impacts of entry experiences.

Table 3 also gives marginal rates indicating the possible direct preventive effects of alternative modes of entry into the prosecution process.

Table 3.   Victim Reports (%) of Violence Prior
to the Settlement of a Case by Defendant
Anger over Entry Experience and Intake Set

	Felt angry		
Intake set	Definitely	Somewhat	Not at all
VC	25	17	19
N	(132)	(75)	(74)
Summons	23	29	26
N	(64)	(35)	(42)
Warrant	26	8	9[a]
N	(68)	(40)	(32)
OSA	20	18	18
N	(70)	(17)	(11)

[a] $\chi^2 = 8.14$, $df = 2$, $p = .017$ for the relationship between anger and violence by warrant.

Overall, about one in five victims reports being subjected to further violence before her case was settled. This likelihood varies little by intake set. However, there is a hint of an immediate deterrent impact insofar as men arrested either on scene or by warrant are less likely to repeat their violence than are those summoned to court, although the differences are not statistically significant.

To understand the differences in anger and violence within the warrant entry category, one must recognize that warrant service can result in vastly different "punishments." Typically, a warrant arrest implies that a suspect is apprehended some time after the criminal incident, usually at some place other than the original crime scene. He may be arrested at home, at work, on the street, in the course of a traffic stop, at any hour of the day or night, or even be tricked by offers of money or jobs. In short, he is rudely inconvenienced at an unexpected time, distant from his offense. Such was the experience of at least half of the men arrested under warrants in this study.

Often men learn of a warrant for their arrest before apprehension and choose to turn themselves in to either the police or the court, as did over 40% of the defendants studied. However, over half of the defendants who did not turn themselves in were angered by the experience—but not significantly more so than those who turned themselves in. In short, the variation in how an arrest is effected can give rise to varying degrees of perceived punishment and treatment-specific anger.

In order to sort out the relative preventive and provocative impacts of alternative entry experiences on the likelihood of at least one new incident of violence prior to settling a case in court, we examine the data

Table 4. Logistic Regression Analysis of the Effects of Entry Experiences on Presettlement Violence

Variable	Initial specification			Reduced model[a]		
	Coeff.	t	p(t)	Coeff.	t	p(t)
OSA	−.36	−.63	.529	−.30	−.94	.350
VCWAR	−1.34	−2.67	.008	−1.23	−2.92	.009
OSAxANG	−.07	−.12	.904			
WARxANG	1.22	2.38	.018	1.23	2.38	.018
SUMxANG	−.24	−.60	.552			
DAYS	.004	3.01	.003	.004	3.00	.003
Intercept	−.162	−4.78	.000	−1.71	−5.81	.000
Log likelihood		−183.615			−183.801	
χ^2		20.78			20.41	
$p(\chi^2)$		.002			.000	

[a] The reduced model includes those regressors which minimize the probability of the model χ^2 statistic.

using a logistic regression model. Table 4 presents the initial analysis of the likelihood of presettlement violence as influenced by indicators of the model of entry (OSA, VCWAR), anger arousal (ANG) in interaction with on-scene arrest (OSAxANG), warrant arrest (WARxANG) or summoning to court (SUMxANG), and the number of days from case intake to settlement (DAYS).[1]

DAYS is an indicator of the opportunity for violence, necessitated by differences in time to settlement among the entry modes. Other things equal, the longer a case is in the system, the more likely is new violence—the extended time frame provides greater opportunity for recidivism. The average number of days to settlement for summons, warrant arrest, and OSA, respectively, are 175, 149, and 148. Men served with summonses spend more time in the system than those arrested, which may account for the slightly higher rate of new violence when summoned. Introducing DAYS into the equation provides a control for such an opportunity effect.

Table 4 presents *t*-values and their probabilities for these variables. The OSA and OSAxANG coefficients are not significantly different from zero, indicating that presettlement violence is unaffected by whether or not a man is brought into the prosecution process by OSA or by VC. Moreover, anger over OSA does not provoke new violence independent of other effects, but this is not to say that anger has no influence. Anger has a significant provocative impact in interaction with a warrant arrest (WARxANG). The analysis in Table 4 confirms that when other factors, including opportunity (DAYS), are controlled, warrant arrest has a significant preventive effect, an effect that is enhanced in the absence of an angry reaction to the experience.

These findings hold in a second logistic regression analysis examining only VC cases, as shown in Table 5, thereby clarifying the apparent effectiveness of a warrant arrest in contrast to a summons in preventing presettlement violence. When analysis is restricted to OSA cases, none of the relevant factors (i.e., ANGRY and DAYS) has a significant impact on new violence.

What can we conclude? First, a defendant arrested on a warrant following a VC to the prosecutor is significantly less likely to batter his victim again before the case is settled in court—warrant arrest has an immediate deterrent impact. Second, although an OSA is more likely to incite anger than is either a summons or a warrant arrest, anger arousal does not result in a greater chance of presettlement violence. However, the absence of anger over a warrant arrest enhances the preventive impact of the warrant. Most important, there is no evidence that presumably harsh entry treatment (i.e., OSA or warrant arrest) places the victim at greater immediate risk than does summoning the defendant to court.

The distinction between VC and OSA cases is maintained as the likelihood of repeat violence following the settlement of cases is examined. The intake-specific findings already seen for presettlement violence reflect unique aspects of the OSA bearing on subsequent prosecution, namely, the presence of a police officer as a witness, and the likelihood of an uncooperative victim-witness.

2. *Postsettlement Violence.*   Criminal-justice systems impose explicit, formal sanctions when cases are settled in court. Defendants may experience punishment during the course of prosecution and prior to case settlement, but it is the criminal sanctions imposed at the end of the process that are both intended and expected to impact future defendant behavior most strongly. In this section we examine the effects of four types of case outcomes. First, jail, fines, and probation are perceived by defendants as the harshest punishments. Second, probation with mandated counseling for anger control, while meant to rehabilitate, is nevertheless experienced as punishing, though less so than the other sanctions. Third, pretrial diversion to counseling frees defendants of the stigma of conviction, providing they successfully complete the rehabilitative treatment; diversion is perceived as less punishing than alternative outcomes following conviction. Fourth, case dismissal is punishing only to the extent that the defendant is still brought to court and forced to stand before a judge to hear charges against him.

What are the impacts of alternative outcomes on the chances of vic-

Table 5. Logistic Regression Analysis of the Effects of Entry Experiences on Presettlement Violence, by Intake Sets

Intake set	Variable	Initial specification			Reduced model[a]		
		Coeff.	t	p(t)	Coeff.	t	p(t)
VC (N = 281)	VCWAR	-1.33	-2.66	.008	-1.23	-2.60	.010
	ANGRY	-.24	-.60	.547			
	WARxANG	1.45	2.23	.026	1.21	2.35	.020
	DAYS	.005	2.75	.006	.004	2.74	.007
	Intercept	-1.68	-4.56	.000	-1.78	-5.38	.000
	Log likelihood	-136.118			-136.301		
	χ^2	19.21			18.84		
	$p(\chi^2)$	.001			.000		
OSA (N = 98)	ANGRY	-.02	-.04	.968			
	DAYS	.003	1.26	.212			
	Intercept	-1.87	-3.25	.002			
	Log likelihood	-47.408					
	χ^2	1.58					
	$p(\chi^2)$	.455					

[a] The reduced model includes those regressors which minimize the probability of the model χ^2 statistic.

tim-reported recidivism within either 30 days or six months of settlement. Within 30 days of settlement 8% of the VC case victims and 10%
of the OSA case victims were battered anew by the defendant. Within
six months, 27% of the VC case victims and nearly 40% of the OSA case
victims were battered again. The 40% stands in marked contrast to the
19% victim-reported recidivism rate for arrest cases in the Minneapolis
Study (Sherman and Berk 1984).

Does the relatively high rate of repeat violence by Indianapolis defendants signify aggression arousal through prosecution treatment? A defendant arrested by the police on the scene of a battery against his
partner is significantly more likely to report being angered by the experience. Nevertheless, after the case is settled, there is no apparent
carryover of that initial reaction. The data in Table 6 show that OSA
defendants as a whole are no more likely to report definite anger over
their case outcomes than are VC defendants. However, Table 6 also
shows that within intake sets, there are differences in levels of anger
under the several prosecution outcomes.

Focusing on the VC cases in Table 6, we see that men who are prosecuted to conviction report significantly greater anger than those with
cases either diverted or dropped. No such relationship exists for men
arrested on scene; but, in general, anger over the outcome of a case does
not arouse subsequent violence, as is apparent in the data shown in
Table 7. Among VC cases, levels of anger and 30-day violence are unrelated. Among OSA cases, the likelihood of 30-day violence diminishes
with higher levels of anger, but the relationship is not statistically significant. After six months, VC case violence continues to be unaffected by
anger, while OSA cases show an elevated likelihood of violence under

Table 6. Defendant Anger (%) over Their Case Outcomes by Alternative
Criminal-Justice Prosecution Outcomes

Intake set	Felt angry	Prosecution outcome				
		Nolle prosequi	Diversion counseling	Probation counseling	Other sanction	Total
VC	Definitely	18	16	40	39[a]	3
	Somewhat	6	17	21	13	1
	Not at all	76	66	39	48	5
N		(66)	(86)	(95)	(100)	(34)
OSA	Definitely	32	21	24	39	2
	Somewhat	5	32	24	32	2
	Not at all	64	47	53	29	4
N		(22)	(34)	(34)	(38)	(12)

[a] $\chi^2 = 33.35$, $df = 6$, $p < .05$.

Table 7. Victim Reports (%) of Violence within 30 Days
and 6 Months Following the Settlement of a Case,
by Defendant Anger and Intake Set

Postsettlement time frame	Entry set	Felt angry		
		Definitely	Somewhat	Not at all
30 days	VC	10	13	5
	N	(82)	(45)	(158)
	OSA	0	4	18
	N	(25)	(27)	(44)
Six months	VC	30	30	26
	N	(78)	(43)	(154)
	OSA	57	29	38
	N	(23)	(24)	(40)

"definitely angry." Although the highest recidivism rate (57%) for any reaction occurs for six-month repeat violence in the OSA/angry cell, it is computed for a small subsample and is not significantly different from the rates under other "angry" categories.

To examine the details of anger-provoked violence by prosecution outcomes we can look at the analysis presented in Table 8 for evidence of marginal preventive impacts. We find no significant differences in either 30-day or six-month recidivism across prosecution outcomes, but one may note that only cases dismissed have a consistent, relatively high recidivism rate. Keeping in mind that these results are based on small subsamples, one cannot say that rates of repeat violence depend on

Table 8. Victim Reports (%) of Violence within 30 Days and 6 Months
Following the Settlement of a Case, by Prosecution Outcome and
Intake Set

Postsettlement time frame	Intake set	Prosecution outcome				
		Nolle prosequi	Diversion counseling	Probation counseling	Other sanction	Total
30 days	VC	11	4	5	12	8
	N	(44)	(74)	(74)	(81)	(274)
	OSA	17	7	18	4	10
	N	(12)	(27)	(22)	(28)	(89)
Six months	VC	37	23	28	28	28
	N	(43)	(73)	(69)	(79)	(264)
	OSA	55	41	50	33	43
	N	(11)	(27)	(20)	(24)	(82)

whether or not cases are adjudicated, dismissed, diverted, or more harshly sanctioned. In short, Table 8 offers no support for a direct preventive effect.

Finally, we consider the simultaneous effects of prosecution outcomes and outcome-specific anger arousal on the likelihood of violence within each of the follow-up time frames. For this analysis, prosecution outcomes are represented by a set of dummy variables—DIVERSION, PROS-COUN, PROS-OTHR—with NOLLE as the reference outcome. ANGRY now refers to prosecution outcomes. A set of dummy interaction variables indicating outcome-specific arousal as the product of ANGRY and each of the prosecution outcomes are created. A final independent variable, PRVIOL, is the predicted probability of violence within the presettlement period. It is derived from the earlier logit analysis of presettlement violence and is included as an indicator of a defendant's propensity to commit violence at the time of settlement, based on his experience with the criminal-justice process up to that point.

Table 9 displays findings from the logistic regression analyses of the likelihood of new violence within 30 days of case settlement. Coefficients for the first set of factors are estimated for the full logit model by intake sets. Among VC cases, only DIVERSION and DIVxANG (anger aroused by being diverted) have effects approaching statistical significance. Those effects are isolated after eliminating nonsignificant factors, in the reduced model. The negative coefficient for DIVERSION means there is a reduced likelihood for immediate violence when men are diverted from trial to an anger control treatment program. But when men are "definitely" angered by the diversion outcome, they are less likely to be affected by the preventive impact of diversion. To clarify, based on contingency tables, the likelihood of new, 30-day violence by VC defendants who are angry over being diverted is .15 (or 1 in 7) in contrast to .02 (or 1 in 50) for those not angered over being diverted.

During the same 30-day follow-up period, defendants who entered the system by OSA are unaffected by prosecution outcomes, as seen in the marginal effects (Table 8) and in the nonsignificant model of effects summarized in Table 9. Also, we see that anger associated with specific prosecution outcomes (the dummy interaction variables) does not arouse violent reprisal in the first 30 days following settlement.

Table 10 shows results of multivariate analyses similarly conducted for six-month postsettlement violence. Findings for the extended follow-up period duplicate the basic results for the 30-day analyses, but with reduced strength of effects. For VC cases, DIVERSION has a slight direct preventive impact; DIVxANG has a continuing promotive impact. However, both of the coefficients for six-month violence are lower than for 30-day violence. This is intuitive for DIVxANG—one would expect a

Table 9. Logistic Regression Analysis of the Effects of Prosecution Outcomes on 30-Day Postsettlement Violence by Intake Sets[a]

Intake set	Variable	Initial specification			Reduced model[b]		
		Coeff.	t	p(t)	Coeff.	t	p(t)
VC (N = 271)	DIVERSION	-2.09	-1.83	.068	-2.14	-2.05	.042
	PROS-COUN	-.96	-1.07	.286	-.89	-1.52	.129
	NOLxANG	.21	.31	.759			
	DIVxANG	.28	.24	.814			
	PRCxANG	2.60	2.03	.043	2.41	1.90	.059
	OTHxANG	.34	.33	.745			
	PRVIOL	-.21	-.29	.776			
		-1.87	-.82	.413			
Intercept		-1.68	-2.40	.017	-1.97	-7.16	.000
Log likelihood		-71.205			-71.869		
χ²		10.24			9.08		
p(χ²)		.249			.028		
OSA (N = 88)	DIVERSION	-1.18	-1.06	.290			
	PROS-COUN	.12	.12	.901			
	PROS-OTHER	-1.40	-1.07	.287	-1.37	-1.26	.209
	NOLxANG						
	DIVxANG						
	PRCxANG						
	OTHxANG						
	PRVIOL	-13.25	-1.04	.300			
Intercept		1.16	.48	.634	-1.89	-4.99	.000
Log likelihood		-23.629			-27.979		
χ²		10.83			2.13		
p(χ²)		.211			.144		

[a] Missing values could not be estimated due to the absence of cases for ANGRY = 1 and VIOL30 = 1.
[b] The reduced model includes those regressors which minimize the probability of the model χ² statistic.

Table 10. Logistic Regression Analysis of the Effects of Prosecution Outcomes on 6-Month Postsettlement Violence, by Intake Sets[a]

Intake set	Variable	Initial specification			Reduced model[b]		
		Coeff.	t	p(t)	Coeff.	t	p(t)
VC (N = 261)	DIVERSION	-.98	-2.02	.045	-.67	-1.83	.069
	PROS-COUN	-.44	-.87	.384			
	PROS-OTHER	-.22	-.48	.629			
	NOLxANG	.24	.28	.774			
	DIVxANG	1.68	2.42	.016	1.51	2.72	.024
	PRCxANG	-.00	-.00	.997			
	OTHxANG	-.56	-1.01	.314			
	PRVIOL	.42	.30	.766			
Intercept		-.62	-1.33	.186	-.84	-5.30	.000
Log likelihood			-150.690			-152.809	
χ^2			9.86			6.29	
$p(\chi^2)$			.275			.043	
OSA (N = 81)	DIVERSION	-.59	-.77	.442			
	PROS-COUN	-.15	-.19	.852			
	PROS-OTHER	-1.40	-1.64	.105	-.96	-1.51	.134
	NOLxANG						
	DIVxANG	.53	.57	.573			
	PRCxANG	-.09	-.09	.927			
	OTHxANG	1.42	1.48	.145	1.39	1.45	.152
	PRVIOL	7.64	1.00	.323			
Intercept		-1.22	-.80	.428	-.14	-.53	.601
Log likelihood			-52.828			-53.842	
χ^2			5.14			3.11	
$p(\chi^2)$			.644			.212	

[a] Missing values could not be estimated due to the absence of cases for NOLxANG = 1 and VIOL6M = 1.
[b] The reduced model includes those regressors which minimize the probability of the model χ^2 statistic.

defendant who is at first angry over having to participate in a treatment program to be less aroused to aggression several months later, especially when the treatment is for anger and violence control. If this occurs, one would also expect enhanced program effects over the longer time frame. Instead, the effect of DIVERSION after six months is at least 50% lower than at 30 days.

Among OSA cases, the prosecution outcome impacts after six months continue to be nonsignificant. There is neither a preventive nor provocative effect associated with prosecution outcomes or anger over those outcomes.

3. Summary of Findings. Analyses of continuing violence against women following their batterers' experiences with alternative criminal-justice interventions demonstrate selective preventive and provocative effects. On-scene police arrest is more likely to anger men than is intake following a VC to the prosecutor's office, regardless of whether the accused men are brought to court by summons or arrested on a warrant. But anger over OSA does not, in turn, result in a higher risk of violence for victims prior to cases being settled in court. There is a uniform preventive impact across entry experiences under a condition of anger arousal. Notably, men subject to warrant arrest are significantly less likely to commit new violence if they do not feel "definitely angry" over the experience, than are angered men. A multivariate analysis of VC cases confirms that there is a trade-off between the preventive and provocative impacts of arrest by warrant vs. summoning to court.

Prosecution to conviction is more likely to anger defendants than is either diversion or case dismissal. Men angered over their convictions are no more likely to commit new violence than men angered by other outcomes. It is only in the case of VC defendants who are diverted that levels of anger predict different probabilities of violence: those who are not angered are less likely to commit postsettlement violence. A multivariate analysis shows that diversion and anger over being diverted have competing influences on follow-up violence. As with warrant arrests, diversion in the absence of anger enhances the preventive effect—rather than anger provoking greater violence beyond that found under other criminal-justice experiences. There is no such relationship for men initially arrested on scene by the police. Indeed, for OSA cases, there is no indication of any significant preventive or provocative impact following prosecution.

IV. Discussion and Conclusion

Findings from this study lend support to advocacy for rigorous criminal intervention against wife batterers, if only to support the notion that seemingly harsher sanctions do not place victims at greater risk of new violence. Criminal-justice processing is likely to anger defendants, and some experiences may be more angering than others. It is the absence of anger that reduces the likelihood of violence, as it enhances whatever preventive impact may follow selected treatments. Such is the case for warrant arrest, and pretrial diversion to anger control counseling.

A concluding caveat is in order regarding policy implications. Overall, there are no significant differences in defendant recidivism under the several modes of criminal-justice treatment. This does not mean that one policy is as effective as another. Instead, it delimits the conclusions that can be drawn from the data presented. To evaluate policy, we must examine the effects of actual policy, rather than policy inferred from defendant experiences. Different prosecutorial policies can give rise to similar court outcomes with very different likelihoods of new violence.

The criminal-justice process is extremely complex. No two defendants will experience exactly the same treatment and consequent punishment, regardless of stated uniformity of policy. Even when policy results in expected prosecution outcomes, events occurring throughout the process may confound the impact of formal sanctions. For example, a unique event, such as being arrested or receiving a harsh sentence, is not the extent of the punishment experienced. It may be at least as punishing to pay a bond, to retain an attorney, to miss work for court, or even to hear a victim's complaint of abuse. In Feeley's (1979) terms, "the process is the punishment." It is not altogether surprising to find that what is actually experienced by defendants reveals few overall differences.

There is a continuing need for an evaluation of the relative preventive impacts of policy meant to track a defendant toward a particular prosecution outcome, regardless of whether the policy objective is attained. At the same time, and based on the findings of this study, we need to learn more about the circumstances of policy implementation—such as procedures that minimize anger arousal—to ensure the greatest protection for battered women.

Acknowledgements

This paper reports work done under grant #86-IJ-CX-0012 from the National Institute of Justice with additional support from the Family Research Laboratory, University of New Hampshire, under a NIMH Post-Doctoral Fellowship, grant #MH15161-13. The views expressed are those of the author and not necessarily those of the funding agencies or of cooperating Marion County criminal justice agencies.

Notes

1.   OSA is coded 1 for OSA and 0 for VC; VCWAR is coded 1 for warrant arrest and 0 otherwise; ANGRY is coded 1 for a report of "definite anger" and 0 otherwise and is used here in interaction with entry experiences; each interaction effect (OSAxANG, WARxANG, SUMxANG) is coded 1 for anger associated with the treatment and 0 otherwise.

References

Abramson, L.Y., Seligman, M.E.P., and Teasdale, J.D. 1978. "Learned Help-lessness in Humans: Critique and Reformulation." *Journal of Abnormal Psychology* 87:49–74.

American Bar Association. 1973. *Standards Relating to Court Organization.* New York: Institute for Judicial Administration.

American Humane Association. 1984. *National Study on Child Neglect and Abuse Reporting.* Denver, CO: American Humane Association.

American Psychiatric Association. 1987. *Diagnostic and Statistical Manual of Mental Disorders,* 3rd ed., rev. Washington, D.C.: American Psychiatric Association.

Andenaes, J. 1968. "Does Punishment Deter Crime?" *Criminal Law Quarterly* 11:76–93.

Arndt, N.Y. 1981. "Domestic Violence: An Investigation of the Psychological Aspects of the Battered Woman." Ph.D. Dissertation, The Fielding Institute, Santa Barbara, CA.

Attorney General's Task Force on Family Violence. 1984. *Final Report.* Washington, D.C.: U.S. Department of Justice.

Bagarozzi, D.A., and Giddings, C.W. 1983. "Conjugal Violence: A Critical Review of Current Research and Clinical Practices." *American Journal of Family Therapy* 11:3–15.

Baron, L., Straus, M.A., and Jaffe, D. 1988. "Legitimate Violence, Violent Attitudes and Rape: A Test of the Cultural Spillover Theory." Pp. 79–110 in *Human Sexual Aggression: Current Perspectives,* edited by R.A. Prentsky and V.L. Quinsey. New York: New York Academy of Sciences.

Barth, R.P., and Schleske, D. 1985. "Comprehensive Sexual Abuse Treatment and Reports on Sexual Abuse." *Children and Youth Services Review* 7:258–98.

Beccaria, C. 1963. *On Crimes and Punishments.* Indianapolis: Bobbs-Merrill.

Bentham, J. 1962. *The Works of Jeremy Bentham,* vol. I (J. Bowring, ed.). New York: Russell and Russell.

Berk, R. A. 1987. "Causal Inference as a Prediction Problem." Pp. 183–200 in *Prediction and Classification,* edited by D.M. Gottfredson and M. Tonry. Chicago: University of Chicago Press.

Berk, R.A. and Newton, P.J. 1985. "Does Arrest Really Deter Wife Battery? An Effort to Replicate the Findings of the Minneapolis Spouse Abuse Experiment." *American Sociological Review* 50:252–62.

Berk, R.A., and Sherman, L.W. 1988. "Police Responses to Family Violence Incidents: An Analysis of an Experimental Design with Incomplete Randomization." *Journal of the American Statistical Association* 83:70–76.

Berk, R.A., Smyth, G.K., and Sherman, L.W. 1988. "When Random Assignment Fails: Some Lessons from the Minneapolis Spouse Abuse Experiment." *Journal of Quantitative Criminology* 4:209–23.

Berman, W.H., and Turk, D.C. 1981. "Adaptation to Divorce: Problems and Coping Strategies." *Journal of Marriage and the Family* 43:179–89.

Bernard, F. 1981. "Pedophilia: Psychological Consequences for the Child. Pp. 189–199 in *Children and Sex: New Findings, New Perspectives*, edited by L.L. Constantine and F.M. Martinson. Boston: Little, Brown.

Besharov, D.J. 1986. "Unfounded Allegations—A New Child Abuse Problem." *Public Interest* 83:18–33.

Blackstone, W. 1778. Commentaries on the Laws of England. (8th edition). Oxford: Clarendon.

Blose, J. 1979. *The Sexual Abuse of Children in Massachusetts: A Preliminary Study of System Response*. Boston: Commission on Criminal Justice Statistical Analysis Center.

Boland, B., Brady, E., Tyson, H., and Bassler, J. 1983. *The Prosecution of Felony Arrests, 1981*. Washington, D.C.: U.S. Department of Justice, Bureau of Justice Statistics.

Borkowski, M., Murch, M., and Walker, V. 1983. *Marital Violence: The Community Response*. London: Tavistock.

Bowker, L.H. 1983. *Beating Wife-Beating*. Lexington, MA: Lexington Books.

Bowlby, J. 1980. *Attachment and Loss*. New York: Basic Books.

Bradburn, Sudman and Associates. 1979. *Improving Interview Method and Questionnaire Design*. San Francisco: Jossey-Bass.

Bradley, J.E., and Lindsay, R.C.L. 1987. "Methodological and Ethical Issues in Child Abuse Research." *Journal of Family Violence* 2:239–56.

Briere, J., and Runtz, M. 1987. "Post Sexual Abuse Trauma: Data and Implications." *Journal of Interpersonal Violence* 2:367–79.

Brigham, J. 1980. "Perceptions on the Impact of Lineup Composition, Race and Witness Confidence on Identification Accuracy." *Law and Human Behavior* 4:315–22.

Brooks, W.D. 1970. "Q-sort Technique." Pp. 165–180 in *Methods of Research in Communication*, edited by P. Emmert and W.D. Brooks. Boston: Houghton Mifflin.

Browne, A., and Finkelhor, D. 1986. "Initial and Long-Term Effects." Pp. 143–179 in *A Sourcebook on Child Sexual Abuse*, edited by D. Finkelhor et al. Beverly Hills, CA: Sage.

Bruhn, J.G., and Philips, B.U. 1984. "Measuring Social Support: A Synthesis of Current Approaches." *Journal of Behavioral Medicine* 7:151–69.

Bulkley, J.J., Ensmenger, J., Fontana, V.J., and Summit, R. 1982. *Dealing with Sexual Child Abuse*. Chicago: National Committee for Prevention of Child Abuse.

Burgess, A.W., and Holmstrum, L.L. 1974. "Rape Trauma Syndrome." *American Journal of Psychiatry* 134:69–72.

Burstein, L., Freeman, H.E., and Rossi, P.H. 1985. *Collecting Evaluation Data: Problems and Solutions*. Beverly Hills, CA: Sage.

Calvert, R. 1974. "Criminal and Civil Liability in Husband–Wife Assaults." Pp.

88–91 in *Violence in the Family,* edited by S.K. Steinmetz and M.A. Straus. New York: Harper and Row.

Campbell, J.C. 1981. "Misogyny and Homicide of Women." *Advances in Nursing Science* 3:67–85.

Campbell, J.C. 1989a. "A Test of Two Explanatory Models of Women's Responses to Battering." *Nursing Research* 38:18–24.

Campbell, J.C. 1989b. "Women's Responses to Sexual Abuse in Intimate Relationships." *Women's Health Care International* 8:335–47.

Caputo, R.K., and Moynihan, F.M. 1986. "Family Options: A Practice/Research Model in Family Violence." *Social Casework* 67:460–65.

Caringella-MacDonald, S. 1988. "Parallels and Pitfalls: The Aftermath of Legal Reform for Sexual Assault, Marital Rape, and Domestic Violence Victims." *Journal of Interpersonal Violence* 3:174–89.

Carson, B.A. 1986. "Parents Who Don't Spank: Deviation in the Legitimation of Physical Force." Ph.D. dissertation, University of New Hampshire, Durham.

Chandler, T. 1986. "A Profile of Interaction in Acute Battering Incidents." Ph.D. dissertation, Purdue University, West Lafayette, IN.

Chandler, T. 1988. "Perceptions of Verbal and Physical Aggression in Interpersonal Violence." Paper presented at the Eastern Communication Association Meeting, Baltimore, MD.

Chandler, T.A., Geist, P.R., and Norton, R.W. 1983. "The Relationship between Marital Violence, Self Esteem and Interaction: An Exploratory Study." Paper presented at the International Communication Association Meeting, Dallas, TX.

Chapman, J.R. and B.E. Smith. 1987. "Child Sexual Abuse: An Analysis of Case Processing." Paper presented at American Bar Association. Washington, D.C.

Chiaro, J., Marden, G.R., Haase, C.C., and Guedes, B. 1982. "Mismatching of the Foster Parents and the Sexually Abused Preschool Child: Critical Factors." Paper presented at the International Congress on Child Abuse and Neglect, Paris.

Claerhout, S.E., Elder, J., and Janes, C. 1982. "Problem-Solving Skills of Rural Battered Women." *American Journal of Community Psychology* 10:605–12.

Coffee, C.L. 1986–87. "A Trend Emerges: A State Survey on the Admissibility of Expert Testimony Concerning the Battered Woman Syndrome." *Journal of Family Law* 25:373–96.

Cohen, J. 1960. "A Coefficient of Agreement for Nominal Scales." *Educational and Psychological Measures* 20:37–46.

Cohen, S., and Hoberman, H.M. 1983. "Positive Events and Social Supports as Buffers of Life Change Stress." *Journal of Applied Social Psychology* 13: 99–125.

Cohen, S., and Syme, S.L. 1985. "Issues in the Study and Application of Social Support." Pp. 3–22 in *Social Support and Health,* edited by S. Cohen and L. Syme. New York: Academic Press.

Coleman, D.H., and Straus, M.A. 1986. "Marital Power, Conflict, and Violence in a Nationally Representative Sample of American Couples." *Violence and Victims* 1:141–57.

Coleman, K.H. 1980. "Conjugal Violence: What 33 Men Report." *Journal of Marital and Family Therapy* 6:207–13.

Conte, J.R. 1985. "The Effects of Sexual Abuse on Children: A Critique and Suggestions for Future Research." *Victimology* 10:110–30.

Conte, J.R., and Schuerman, J.R. 1987. "The Effects of Sexual Abuse of Children: A Multidimensional View." *Journal of Interpersonal Violence* 2:380–90.

Coy v. Iowa, 108 S.Ct. 2798. 1988. [The Supreme Court struck down a state legislature's attempt to recognize a "presumption of trauma" to child abuse victim's in-court testimony.]

Damrosch, S.P. 1981. "How Nursing Students' Reactions to Rape Victims are Affected by a Perceived Act of Carelessness." *Nursing Research* 30:168–70.

Davis, L.V., and Carlson, B.E. 1981. "Attitudes of Service Providers toward Domestic Violence." *Social Work Research and Abstracts* 81:34–39.

DeFrancis, V. 1969. *Protecting the Child Victim of Sex Crimes: Final Report*. Denver: The American Humane Children's Division.

Derogatis, L.R. 1982. "Self-report Measures of Stress." Pp. 270–294 in *Handbook of Stress: Theoretical and Clinical Aspects*, edited by L. Goldberger and S. Breznitz. New York: Free Press.

Deturck, M.A. 1987. "When Communication Fails: Physical Aggression as a Compliance-Gaining Strategy." *Communication Monographs* 54:106–12.

Dietrich, K.N., Starr, R.H., Jr., and Weisfeld, G.E. 1983. "Infant Maltreatment: Caretaker–Infant Interactions and Developmental Consequences at Different Levels of Parenting Failure." *Pediatrics* 72:532–40.

DiPietro, S.B. 1987. "The Effects of Intrafamilial Child Sexual Abuse on the Adjustment and Attitudes of Adolescents." *Violence and Victims* 2:59–76.

Dobash, R.E., and Dobash, R. 1977. "Wives: The Appropriate Victims of Marital Violence." *Victimology* 2:426–42.

Dobash, R.E., and Dobash, R. 1979. *Violence against Wives: A Case against the Patriarchy*. New York: Free Press.

Drake, V.K. 1985. "An Investigation of the Relationships among Locus of Control, Self-Concept, Duration of the Intimate Relationship, and Severity of Physical and Nonphysical Abuse of Battered Women." Ph.D. dissertation, Catholic University of America, Washington, D.C.

Dutton, D.G. 1988. *The Domestic Assault of Women*. Boston: Allyn and Bacon.

Dyas v. United States. 376 A. 2d 827, D.C., 1977.

Edleson, J.L., and Brygger, M.P. 1986. "Gender Differences in Reporting of Battering Incidents." *Family Relations* 35:377–82.

Edleson, J.L., and Grusznski, R. 1988. "Treating Men Who Batter: Four Years of Outcome Data from the Domestic Abuse Project." *Journal of Social Service Research* 12:3–22.

Edleson, J.L., and Syers, M. 1990. "Relative Effectiveness of Group Treatments for Men Who Batter." *Social Work Research and Abstracts* 26:10–17.

Egeland, B., Jacobwitz, D., and Papatola, K. 1987. "Intergenerational Continuity of Abuse." Pp. 255–276 in *Child Abuse and Neglect: Biosocial Dimensions*, edited by R.J. Gelles and J.B. Lancaster. New York: Aldine de Gruyter.

Eisikovits, Z., and Edleson, J. 1989. "Intervening with Men Who Batter: A Critical Review of the Literature." *Social Service Review* 63:384–414.

Elliott, C., Giddings, L., and Jacobson, A. 1985. "Against No-Drop Policies." *Voice* (Summer): 3.

Elliott, D.S. 1989. "Criminal Justice Procedures in Family Violence Crimes." Pp. 427–480 in *Family Violence*, edited by L. Ohlin and M. Tonry. Chicago: University of Chicago Press.

Ellis, D. 1987. "Male Abuse of a Married or Cohabiting Female Partner: The Application of Sociological Theory to Research Findings." *Violence and Victims* 4:235–55.

Fagan, J. 1988. "Contributions of Family Violence Research to Criminal Justice Police on Wife Assault: Paradigms of Science and Social Control." *Violence and Victims* 3:159–186.

Fagan, J., and Wexler, S. 1987. "Crime at Home and in the Streets: The Relationship between Family and Stranger Violence." *Violence and Victims* 2:5–24.

Fain, C.F. 1981. "Conjugal Violence: Legal and Psychological Remedies." *Syracuse Law Review* 32:497–579.

Faller, K.C. 1988. "The Myth of the 'Collusive Mother.'" *Journal of Interpersonal Violence* 3:90–196.

Family Violence Reporting Program. 1989. *Crime in Connecticut, 1988 UCR Annual Report*. Hartford, CT: Department of Public Safety, Division of State Police.

Federal Rules of Evidence for United States Courts and Magistrates. 1975. St. Paul, Mn: West.

Feeley, M.M. 1979. *The Process Is the Punishment*. New York: Russell Sage Foundation.

Felson, R.B. 1984. "Patterns of Aggressive Social Interaction." Pp. 107–126 in *Social Psychology of Aggression: From Individual Behavior to Social Interaction*, edited by A. Mummendey. Berlin: Springer-Verlag.

Fernandez, E. 1986. "Children at Risk of Being Separated from Natural Parents: An Analysis of the Placement Decision." Paper presented at the Sixth International Congress on Child Abuse and Neglect, Sydney, Australia.

Ferraro, K. 1989. "Policing Woman Battering." *Social Problems* 36:61–74.

Ferraro, K.J., and Johnson, J.M. 1983. "How Women Experience Battering: The Process of Victimization." *Social Problems* 30:325–39.

Ferree, M., and Hess, B. 1985. *Controversy and Coalition. The New Feminist Movement*. New York: Twayne.

Field, M.H., and Field, H.F. 1973. "Marital Violence and the Criminal Process. Neither Justice nor Peace." *Social Service Review* 47:221–40.

Finesmith, B.K. 1983. "Police Response to Battered Women. A Critique and Proposals for Reform." *Seton Hall Law Review* (Winter):74–109

Finkelhor, D. 1979. *Sexually Victimized Children*. New York: Free Press.

Finkelhor, D. 1983a. "Removing the Child—Prosecuting the Offender in Cases of Sexual Abuse: Evidence from the National Reporting System for Child Abuse and Neglect." *Child Abuse and Neglect* 7:195–205.

Finkelhor, D. 1983b. "Common Features of Family Abuse." Pp. 17–28 in *The Dark Side of Families*, edited by D. Finkelhor et al. Beverly Hills, CA: Sage.

Finkelhor, D. 1984. *Child Sexual Abuse: New Theory and Research*. New York: Free Press.

Finkelhor, D. 1986. "Designing New Studies." Pp. 199–223 in *A Sourcebook on Child Sexual Abuse*, edited by D. Finkelhor et al. Beverly Hills, CA: Sage Publications.

Finkelhor, D., and Hotaling, G. 1983. "Sexual Abuse in the National Incidence Study of Child Abuse and Neglect." Report to National Center on Child Abuse and Neglect. Durham, NH: Family Research Laboratory, University of New Hampshire.

Finkelhor, D., and Pillemer, K. 1988. "The Prevalence of Elder Abuse: A Random Sample survey." *Gerontological Society of America* 28:51–57.

Finkelhor, D., and Yllo, K. 1982. "Forced Sex in Marriage: A Preliminary Research Report." *Crime and Delinquency* 34:459–78.

Finkelhor, D., and Yllo, K. 1983. "Rape in Marriage: A Sociological View." Pp. 119–131 in *The Dark Side of Families*, edited by D. Finkelhor et al. Beverly Hills, CA: Sage.

Finkelhor, D., and Yllo, K. 1985. *License to Rape: Sexual Abuse of Wives*. New York: Free Press.

Finkelhor, D., Araji, S., Baron, L., Browne, A., Peters, S.D., and Wyatt, G.E. 1986. *A Sourcebook on Child Sexual Abuse*. Beverly Hills, CA: Sage.

Finkelhor, D., Hotaling, G.T., and Yllo, K. 1987. "Stopping Family Violence: A Research Agenda for the Next Decade." Report sponsored by the Conrad N. Hilton Foundation of Los Angeles, California.

Finn, J. 1985. "The Stresses and Coping Behavior of Battered Women." *Social Casework* 86:341–49.

Fleming, J.B. 1979. *Stopping Wife Abuse: A Guide to the Emotional, Psychological and Legal Implications for the Abused Woman and Those Helping Her*. Garden City, NJ: Anchor.

Ford, D.A. 1983. "Wife Battery and Criminal Justice: A Study of Victim Decision-Making." *Family Relations* 32:463–75.

Ford, D.A. 1985. "The Preventive Impacts of Arrest and Prosecution in Case of Wife Battery." Proposal submitted to the National Institute of Justice, Washington, D.C.

Ford, D.A. 1987. "The Impact of Police Officers' Perceptions of Victims on the Disinclination to Arrest Wife Batterers." Paper presented at the National Conference on Family Violence, University of New Hampshire.

Ford, D.A. 1987. "The Impact of Police Officers' Perceptions of Victims on Disinclination to Arrest Wife Batterers." Paper presented at the Annual Meeting of the Law and Society Association, Vail, Colorado.

Forst, B.E., and Hernon, J.C. 1985. "The Criminal Justice Response to Victim Harm." In *National Institute of Justice: Research in Brief*. Washington, D.C.: U.S. Department of Justice.

Fraser, B.G. 1981. "Sexual Child Abuse: The Legislation and the Law in the United States." Pp. 55–74 in *Sexually Abused Children and Their Families*, edited by P.B. Mrazek and C.H. Kempe. Oxford: Pergamon Press.

Frazier, C.E., Bock, E.W., and Henretta, J.C. 1980. "Pretrial Release and Bail Decisions: The Effects of Legal, Community and Personal Variables." *Criminology* 18:162–81.

Frazier, P., and Borgida, E. 1985. "Rape Trauma Syndrome Evidence in Court." *American Psychologist* 40:984–93.

Freud, A. 1981. "A Psychoanalyst's View of Sexual Abuse by Parents." Pp. 33–34 in *Sexually Abused Children and Their Families*, edited by P.B. Mrazek and C.H. Kempe. Oxford: Pergamon.

Frieze, I.H., and Browne, A. 1989. "Violence in Marriage." Pp. 163–218 in *Family Violence*, edited by L. Ohlin and M. Tonry. Chicago: University of Chicago Press.

Frieze, I.H. 1979. "Perceptions of Battered Wives." Pp. 79–108 in *New Approaches to Social Problems*, edited by D.B. Carroll et al. San Francisco: Jossey-Bass.

Fromson, T.L. 1977. "The Case for Legal Remedies for Abused Women." *NYU Review of Law and Social Change* 6:135–74.

Fulero, S.M. 1986. "The Role of Behavioral Research in the Free Press/Fair Trial Controversy: Another View." *Law and Human Behavior* 11:259–64.

Gamache, D., Edleson, J., and Schock, M. 1988. "Coordinated Police, Judicial, and Social Service Response to Woman-Battering: A Multiple Baseline Evaluation across Three Communities." Pp. 193–209 in *Coping with Family Violence*, edited by G. Hotaling et al. Newbury Park, CA: Sage.

Ganley, A. 1980. "Therapeutic Prognosis for Battering Males." Paper presented at Whatcom County Mental Health Center, Washington.

Garbarino, J. 1989. "The Incidence and Prevalence of Child Maltreatment." Pp. 219–261 in *Family Violence*, edited by L. Ohlin and M. Tonry. Chicago: University of Chicago Press.

Garrett, K.A. 1982. "Child Abuse: Problems of Definition." Pp. 177–203 in *Measuring Social Judgments: The Factorial Survey Approach*, P.H. Rossi and S.L. Nock. Beverly Hills, CA: Sage.

Garrett, K.A., and Rossi, P.H. 1978. "Judging the Seriousness of Child Abuse." *Medical Anthropology* 2:1–48.

Gayford, J.J. 1977. "The Plight of the Battered Wife." *International Journal of Environmental Studies* 10:283–86.

Gelles, R.J. 1974. *The Violent Home: A Study of Physical Aggression between Husbands and Wives*. Beverly Hills, CA: Sage.

Gelles, R.J. 1983. "Parental Child Snatching: The Use of Telephone Survey Techniques to Study a Hidden Problem." Paper presented at the National Council on Family Relations Theory Construction and Research Methods Workshop, Minneapolis.

Gelles, R.J., and Straus, M.A. 1979. "Determinants of Violence in the Family: Toward a Theoretical Integration." Pp. 549–581 in *Contemporary Theories about the Family*, vol. 1., edited by W.R. Burr et al. New York: Wiley.

Gelles, R.J., and Straus, M.A. 1988. *Intimate Violence*. New York: Simon and Schuster.

Giarretto, H. 1976. "Humanistic Treatment of Father–Daughter Incest." Pp. 143–158 in *Child Abuse and Neglect: The Family and the Community*, edited by R.E. Helfer and C.H. Kempe. Cambridge, MA: Ballinger.

Giarretto, H. 1981. "A Comprehensive Child Sexual Abuse Treatment Program." Pp. 179–198 in *Sexually Abused Children and Their Families*, edited by P.B. Mrazek and C.H. Kempe. Oxford: Pergamon.

Gibbs, J.P. 1975. *Crime, Punishment and Deterrence*. New York: Elsevier.

Gil, D., and Noble, J.H. 1969. "Public Knowledge, Attitudes, and Opinions about Physical Child Abuse in the U.S." *Child Welfare* 48:395–426.

Gilbert, E.S. 1968. "On Discrimination Using Qualitative Variables." *Journal of the American Sociological Association* 63:1399–1412.

Giles-Sims, J. 1983. *Wife Battering: A Systems Theory Approach*. New York: Guilford Press.

Gilligan, C. 1982. *In a Different Voice*. Cambridge: Harvard University Press.

Giovannoni, J.M., and Becerra, R.M. 1979. *Defining Child Abuse*. New York: Free Press.

Glaser, B.G. 1978. *Theoretical Sensitivity: Advances in the Methodology of Grounded Theory*. Mill Valley, CA: Sociology Press.

Glaser, B.G., and Strauss, A. 1967. *The Discovery of Grounded Theory: Strategies for Qualitative Research*. New York: Aldine.

Glendon, M.A. 1989. *The Transformation of Family Law: State, Law, and Family in the United States and Western Europe*. Chicago: University of Chicago Press.

Glick, I.O., Weiss, R.S., and Parkes, C.M. 1974. *The First Year of Bereavement*. New York: Wiley.

Globe Newspaper Co. v. Superior Court, 457 U.S. 596. 1982. [The Supreme Court ruled that an individualized showing of trauma is required before the courtroom can be closed to the public during a child sexual abuse victim's testimony.]

Goldberg, W.G., and Tomlanovich, M.C. 1984. "Domestic Violence Victims in the Emergency Department." *Journal of the American Medical Association* 251:3259–64.

Goldkamp, J.S. 1979. *Two Classes of Accused*. Cambridge, MA: Ballinger.

Goldkamp, J.S., and Gottfredson, M.R. 1979. "Bail Decision Making and Pretrial Detention: Surfacing Judicial Policy." *Law and Human Behavior* 3:227–49.

Goldstein, D., and Rosenbaum, A. 1985. "An Evaluation of the Self-Esteem of Maritally Violent Men." *Family Relations* 34:425–37.

Gondolf, E. 1986. "Evaluating Programs for Men who Batter: Problems and Perspectives." *Journal of Family Violence* 2:95–108.

Gondolf, E. 1988. "The Effect of Batterer Counseling on Shelter Outcome." *Violence and Victims* 3:275–89.

Gondolf, E.W., and Fisher, E.R. 1988. *Battered Women as Survivors: An Alternative to Treating Learned Helplessness*. Lexington, MA: Lexington.

Goodman, G.S., et al. 1989. "Emotional Effects of Criminal Court Testimony on Child Sexual Abuse Victims." Final Report. National Institute of Justice. Grant No. 85-IJ-CX-0020.

Goolkasian, G.A. 1986. *Confronting Domestic Violence: A Guide for Criminal Justice Agencies. U.S. Department of Justice. National Institute of Justice Issues and Practices*. Washington, D.C.: U.S. Government Printing Office.

Gottfredson, S., and Gottfredson, D.M. 1986. "Accuracy of Prediction Models." Pp. 212–290 in *Criminal Careers and "Career Criminals*, edited by A. Blumstein et al. Washington, D.C.: National Academy Press.

Greenblat, C.S. 1983. "A Hit Is a Hit . . . or Is It? Approval and Tolerance of the Use of Physical Force by Spouses." In *The Dark Side of Families*, edited by D. Finkelhor et al. Beverly Hills, CA: Sage.

Greenhouse, L. 1990. "Child Abuse Trials Can Use Television." *New York Times*. June 28, 1990. A1 and A12.

Grisso, T. 1987. "The Economic and Scientific Future of Forensic Psychological Assessment." *American Psychologist* 42:831–39.

Groves, R.M., and Kohn, R.L. 1979. *Surveys by Telephone: A National Comparison with Personal Interviews.* New York: Academic Press.

Gruzinski, J.R., and Carrillo, T.P. 1988. "Who Completes Batterer's Treatment Groups? An Empirical Investigation." *Journal of Family Violence* 3:141–150.

Hackney, G.R., and Ribordy, S.C. 1980. "An Empirical Investigation of Emotional Reactions to Divorce." *Journal of Clinical Psychology* 36:105–110.

Hamberger, L.K., and Hastings, J.E. 1989. "Counseling Male Spouse Abusers: Characteristics of Treatment Completers and Dropouts." *Violence and Victims* 4:275–86.

Hamen, L.C. 1982. *Separated and Divorced Women.* Westport, CT: Greenwood Press.

Harrenkohl, E.C., Harrenkohl, R.C., and Toedter, L.J. 1983. "Perspectives on the Intergenerational Transmission of Abuse." Pp. 305–316 in *The Dark Side of Families,* edited by D. Finkelhor et al. Beverly Hills, CA: Sage.

Harris and Associates. 1979. *A Survey of Spousal Violence against Women in Kentucky.* New York: Louis Harris and Associates.

Hart, B. 1988. "Beyond the 'Duty to Warn:' A Therapist's 'Duty to Protect' Battered Women and Children." Pp. 234–248 in *Feminist Perspectives on Wife Abuse,* edited by K. Yllo and M. Bograd. Beverly Hills, CA: Sage.

Harvey, J.H., Weber, A.L., Galvin, K.S., Huszti, A.C., and Granick, N.N. 1982. "Attribution in the Termination of Close Relationships: A Special Focus on the Account." Pp. 107–126 in *Personal Relationships,* edited by R. Gilmour and S. Duck. Hillsdale, NJ: Erlbaum.

Helfer, R.E., and Kempe, C.H., eds. 1976. *Child Abuse and Neglect: The Family and the Community.* Cambridge, MA: Ballinger.

Herzberger, S. 1988. "Cultural Obstacles to the Labeling of Abuse by Professionals." Pp. 33–44 in *Professional Responsibilities in Protecting Children: A Public Health Approach to Child Sexual Abuse,* edited by A. Maney and S. Wells. New York: Praeger.

Herzberger, S.D., and Channels, N. 1988. "The Predictors and Consequences of Bail Decision-Making." Paper presented at the American Society of Criminology Conference, Chicago.

Hilberman, E. 1980. "Overview: The 'Wife Beater's Wife' Reconsidered." *American Journal of Psychiatry* 137:1336–47.

Hilberman, E., and Munson, K. 1978. "Sixty Battered Women." *Victimology* 2:460–70.

Hochstim, J.R. 1977. "A Critical Comparison of Three Strategies of Collecting Data from Households." *Journal of the American Statistical Association* 62:976–89.

Hofer, M.A. 1984. "Relationships as Regulators: A Psychobiologic Perspective on Bereavement." *Psychosomatic Medicine* 46:183–98.

Hoffman-Plotkin, D., and Twentyman, C.T. 1984. "A Multimodal Assessment of Behavioral and Cognitive Deficits in Abused and Neglected Preschoolers." *Child Development* 55:794–802.

Hollencamp, M., and Attala, J. 1986. "Meeting Health Needs in a Crisis Shelter: A

Challenge to Nurses in the Community." *Journal of Community Health Nursing* 39:201–9.

Horowitz, M.J. 1986. *Stress Response Syndromes*, 2nd ed. Northvale, NJ: Jason Aronson.

Horton, A., Simonidis, K., and Simonidis, L. 1987. "Legal Remedies for Spousal Abuse: Victim Characteristics, Expectations, and Satisfaction." *Journal of Family Violence* 2:265–79.

Hotaling, G.T., and Straus, M.A. 1980. "Culture, Social Organization and Irony in the Study of Family Violence." Pp. 3–22 in *The social Causes of Husband–Wife Violence*, edited by M.A. Straus and G.T. Hotaling. Minneapolis, MN: University of Minnesota Press.

House, J.S., and Kahn, R.L. 1985. "Measures and Concepts of Social Support." Pp. 83–108 in *Social Support and Health*, edited by S. Cohen and S.L. Syme. New York: Academic Press.

Hudson, W. 1982. *The Clinical Measurement Package*. Homewood, IL: Dorsey.

Hunt, M. 1985. *Profiles of Social Research: The Scientific Study of Human Interactions*. New York: Russell Sage Foundation.

Infante, D.A., and Wigley, C.J. 1986. "Verbal Aggressiveness: An Interpersonal Model and Measure." *Communication Monographs* 53:61–69.

Infante, D.A., Chandler, T.A., and Rudd, J. 1988. "Test of a Model of Interpersonal Violence." Paper presented at Speech Communication Associations Meeting, New Orleans.

Jackson, J.K. 1954. "The Adjustment of the Family to the Crisis of Alcoholism." *Quarterly Journal of Studies on Alcohol* 15:562–86.

Jacoby, J.E. 1979. "The Charging Policies of Prosecutors." Pp. 75–98 in *The Prosecutor*, edited by W.F. McDonald. Beverly Hills, CA: Sage.

Jacoby, J.E. 1980. *The American Prosecutor: A Search for Identity*. Lexington, MA: D.C. Heath.

Jaffe, P., Wolfe, D.A., Telford, A., and Austin, G. 1986. The Impact of Police Charges in Incidents of Wife Abuse. *Journal of Family Violence* 1:37–49.

Janoff-Bulman, R., and Frieze, I.H. 1983. A Theoretical Perspective for Understanding Reactions to Victimization. *Journal of Social Issues* 39:1–17.

Jehu, D. 1989. "Mood Disturbances Among Women Clients Sexually Abused in Childhood." *Journal of Interpersonal Violence* 4:164–84.

Judd, C.M., and Kenny, D.A. 1981. *"Estimating the Effects of Social Interventions."* New York: Cambridge University Press.

Justice, B., and Justice, R. 1979. *The Broken Taboo: Sex in the Family*. New York: Human Science Press.

Karweit, N., and Meyers, E.D., Jr. 1983. "Computers in Research." Pp. 379–414 in *Handbook of Survey Research*, edited by P.H. Rossi, J.D. Wright, and A.B. Anderson. New York: Academic Press.

Kaufman-Kantor, G., and Straus̀, M.A. 1987. The 'Drunken Bum' Theory of Wife Beating." *Social Problems* 34:213–30.

Kaufman-Kantor, G., and Straus, M.A. 1990. Response of Victims and the Police to Assaults on Wives. Pp. 473–488 in *Physical Violence in American Families: Risk Factors and Adaptations to Violence in 8,145 Families*, edited by M.A. Straus and R.J. Gelles. New Brunswick, NJ: Transaction Press.

Kelly, L. 1989. "How Women Define Their Experiences of Violence." Pp. 114–132 in *Feminist Perspectives on Wife Abuse*, edited by K. Yllo and M. Bograd. Beverly Hills, CA: Sage.

Kelman, H.C. 1972. "The Rights of the Subject in Social Research: An Analysis in Terms of Relative Power and Legitimacy." *American Psychologist* 27:989–1016.

Kempe, C.H. 1977. "Sexual Abuse, Another Hidden Problem." *Pediatrics* 62:382–89.

Kempe, C.H., and Helfer, R.E., eds. 1980. *The Battered Child*, 3rd ed. Chicago: University of Chicago Press.

Kempe, C.H., Silverman, F.N., Steele, B.B., Droegemueller, N., and Silver, H.K. 1962. "The Battered-Child Syndrome." *Journal of the American Medical Association* 181:17–24.

Kiecolt-Glaser, J.K., Fisher, D., Ogrocki, P., Stout, J.C., Spiecher, C.E., and Glaser, R. 1987. "Marital Quality, Marital Disruption, and Immune Function." *Psychosomatic Medicine* 49(1):13–34.

Kitson, G.C., Lopata, H.Z., Homes, W.M., and Meyering, S.M. 1980. "Divorcees and Widows: Similarities and Differences." *American Journal of Orthopsychiatry* 50:291–301.

Kitson, G.C., Sussman, M.B., Williams, G.K., Zeehandelaer, R.B., Schickmanter, B.K., and Steinberger, J.L. 1982. "Sampling Issues in Family Research." *Journal of Marriage and the Family* 44:965–81.

Klaus, P.A., and Rand, M.R. 1984. *Family Violence*. Bureau of Justice Special Report. Washington, D.C.: U.S. Department of Justice.

Knudsen, D.D. 1988. "Child Maltreatment over Two Decades: Change or Continuity" *Violence and Victims* 3:129–44.

Koop, C.E. 1986. Surgeon General's workshop on violence and public health report, Publication No. HRS-D-MC 86-1. Washington, D.C.: DHHS.

Kubler-Ross, E. 1969. *On Death and Dying*. New York: Macmillan.

Kurz, D. 1987. "Emergency Department Responses to Battered Women: Resistance to Medicalization." *Social Problems* 34:501–13.

Kurz, D., and Stark, E. 1989. "Not So Benign Neglect: Use and Abuse of Women in the Health Care System. Pp. 249–266 in *Feminist Perspectives on Wife Abuse*, edited by K. Yllo and M. Bograd. Beverly Hills, CA: Sage.

Landenburger, K.M. 1988. Conflicting Realities of Women in Abusive Relationships." *Communicating Nursing Research* 21:15–20

Langan, P.A., and Innes, C.A. 1986. *Preventing Domestic Violence Against Women*. Washington, D.C.: U.S. Department of Justice.

Larzelere, R.E., and Klein, D.M. 1987. Methodology. Pp. 125–155 in *Handbook of Marriage and the Family*, edited by M.S. Sussman and S.K. Steinmetz. New York: Plenum.

Launius, M.H., and Jensen, B.L. 1978. Interpersonal Problem-Solving Skills in Battered, Counseling, and Control Women." *Journal of Family Violence* 2:151–62.

Lehman, B.A. 1989. "Spanking Teaches the Wrong Lesson." *Boston Globe*. March 13, 1989. p. 29.

Lemert, E.M. 1960. "The Occurrence and Sequence of Events in the Adjustment of Families to Alcoholism." *Quarterly Studies on Alcohol* 21:679–97.

Lerman, L.G. 1981. "Expansion of Police Arrest Power: A Key to Effective Intervention." *Response to Violence in the Family* 4(3):1–19.

Lerman, L.G. 1986. "Prosecution of Wife Beaters: Institutional Obstacles and Innovations." Pp. 250–295 in *Violence in the Home: Interdisciplinary Perspectives,* edited by M. Lystad. New York: Brunner/Mazel.

Lerner, M.J., and Simmons, C.H. 1966. "Observer's Reaction to the 'Innocent' Victim: Compassion or Rejection?" *Journal of Personality and Social Psychology* 4:203–10.

Lichtenstein, V.R. 1981. "The Battered Woman: Guidelines for Effective Nursing Intervention." *Issues in Mental Health Nursing* 3:237–50.

Lizotte, A.J. 1978. "Extra-Legal Factors in Chicago's Criminal Courts: Testing the Conflict Model of Criminal Justice." *Social Problems* 25:564–80.

Loftus, E.F. 1986. "Ten Years in the Life of an Expert Witness." *Law and Human Behavior* 10:241–63.

Loseke, D.R., and Cahill, S.E. 1984. The Social Construction of Deviance: Experts on Battered Women." *Social Problems* 31:296–310.

Lyon, E., Mace, P.G., and Hunt, J. 1989. "The Family Violence Prevention and Response act: Services Provided by the Family Violence Victim Advocates. Final report presented to the Connecticut Commission on Victim Services, Hartford.

Mac Murray, B.K. 1988a. "The Nonprosecution of Sexual Abuse and Informal Justice." *Journal of Interpersonal Violence* 3:197–202.

Mac Murray, B.K. 1988b. Prosecutorial Decision Making and Case Attrition for Child Sexual Abuse: A Qualitative Approach to Case Rejection Decisions." *The Prison Journal* 68:11–24.

Mac Murray, B.K. 1989. "Criminal Determination for Child Sexual Abuse: Prosecutor Case-Screening Judgments." *Journal of Interpersonal Violence* 4:233–44.

Mac Murray, B.K., and Carson, B.A. 1990. "Legal Issues in Violence Toward Children." Pp. 57–71 in *Case Studies in Family Violence,* edited by R.T. Ammerman and M. Hersen. New York: Plenum.

Mahon, L. 1981. "Common Characteristics of Abused Women." *Issues in Mental Health Nursing* 3:137–57.

Marris, P. 1974. *Loss and Change.* London: Routledge & Kegan Paul.

Maryland v. Craig, 110 S.Ct. 3157. 1990.

Martin, D. 1976. *Battered wives.* San Francisco: Glide.

Martin, E. 1983. "Surveys as Social Indicators: Problems in Monitoring Trends." Pp. 677–743 in *Handbook of Survey Research,* edited by P.H. Rossi et al. New York: Academic Press.

Martin, S.E. 1989. "Research Note: The Response of the Clergy to Spouse Abuse in a Suburban County." *Violence and Victims* 4:217–25.

Mayer, A. 1983. *Incest: A Treatment Manual for Therapy with Victims, Spouses and Offenders.* Homes Beach, FL: Learning Publications.

McCormick, C. 1972. *Handbook of the Law of Evidence.* Section 203, n. 31, 489.

McDonald, W.F. 1979. "The Prosecutor's Domain." Pp. 15–52 in *The Prosecutor,* edited by W.F. McDonald. Beverly Hills, CA: Sage.

McFadden, E.J. 1984. *Preventing Abuse in Family Foster Care.* Ypsilanti: Eastern Michigan University Press.

McFadden, E.J. 1986. "Fostering the Child Who Had Been Sexually Abused." *Fostering Ideas* 1:3.

McKenna, L.S. 1987. "Social Support Systems of Battered Women: Influence on Psychological Adaption." Ph.D. dissertation. University of California, San Francisco.

McLeer, S.V., and Anwar, R. 1989. "A Study of Battered Women Presenting in an Emergency Department." *American Journal of Public Health* 79:65–66.

Mederer, H.J., and Gelles, R.J. 1989. "Compassion or Control: Intervention in Cases of Wife Abuse." *Journal of Interpersonal Violence* 4:25–43.

Melton, G. 1984. *Child Sexual Abuse Victims in the Courts.* Hearings before the Senate Subcommittee on Juvenile Justice, May 22, p. 117.

Mercy, J., and O'Carroll, P. 1988. "New Directions in Violence Prediction: The Public Health Arena." *Violence and Victims* 3:285–301.

Mickow, P.O. 1988. "Domestic Abuse: The Pariah of the Legal System." Pp. 407–433 in *Handbook of Family Violence,* edited by V.B. Van Hasselt et al. New York: Plenum.

Miller, B.C., Rollins, B.C., and Thomas, D.L. 1982. On Methods of Studying Marriages and Families." *Journal of Marriage and the Family* 44:853–73.

Miller, D.T., and Porter, C.A. 1983. "Self-Blame in Victims of Violence." *Journal of Social Issues* 39:139–52.

Misener, T.R. 1986. "Toward a Nursing Definition of Child Maltreatment Using Seriousness Vignettes." *American Nursing Survey* 8:1–14.

Mnookin, R.H. 1973. "Foster Care, In Whose Best Interests?" *Harvard Educational Review* 43:599–638.

Moore, D.H. 1973. "Evaluation of Five Discrimination Procedures for Binary Variables." *Journal of the American Statistical Association* 68:399.

Moore, D.M. 1979. *Battered Women.* Beverly Hills, CA: Sage.

Mrazek, P.B. 1981a. "Definition and Recognition of Sexual Child Abuse: Historical and Cultural Perspectives." Pp. 5–16 in *Sexually Abused Children and Their Families,* edited by P.B. Mrazek and C.H. Kempe. Oxford: Pergamon.

Mrazek, P.B. 1981b. "The Nature of Incest: A Review of Contribution Factors." Pp. 97–108 in *Sexually Abused Children and Their Families,* edited by P.B. Mrazek and C.H. Kempe. Oxford: Pergamon.

Mrazek, P.B., and Bentovim, A. 1981. "Incest and the Dysfunctional Family System." Pp. 167–178 in *Sexually Abused Children and Their Families,* edited by P.B. Mrazek and C.H. Kempe. Oxford: Pergamon Press.

Murphy, J.E. 1987. "Prevalence of Child Sexual Abuse and Consequent Experience of Date Rape and Marital Rape in the General Population." Paper presented at the National Council on Family Relations Meetings, Atlanta, Georgia.

Murphy, J.E. 1988. "Child Sexual Abuse: Effects of Parental Interaction on Incidence of Abuse and Effects of Abuse on Later Dating and Marital Relationships." Paper presented at the Midwest Sociological Society Meetings, Minneapolis, Minnesota.

Murphy, S.M., Kilpatrick, D.G., Amick-McMullan, A., Veronen, L.J., Paduhovich, J., Best, C.L., Villeponteaux, L.A., and Saunders, B.E. 1988. "Current

Psychological Functioning of Child Sexual Assault Survivors." *Journal of Interpersonal Violence* 3:55–79.

Myrdal, G., with assistance of R. Sterner and A. Rose. 1962. *An American Dilemma: The Negro Problem and Modern Democracy.* New York: Harper.

Nakashima, J.J., and Zakus, G.E. 1980. "Incest: Review and Clinical Experience. Pp. 109–117 in *Child Abuse: Omission and Commission,* edited by J. Valiant Cook and R. Tyler Bowles. Toronto: Butterworths.

Newberger, E. 1987. "Prosecution: A Problematic Approach to Child Abuse." *Journal of Interpersonal Violence* 2:112–17.

Newberger, E., and Bourne, R. 1978. "The Medicalization and Legalization of Child Abuse." *American Journal of Orthopsychiatry* 48:593–607.

Okun, L.E. 1986. *Women Abuse: Facts Replacing Myths.* Albany, NY: State University of New York Press.

O'Toole, R., and Webster, S.W. 1988. "Differentiation of Family Mistreatment: Commonalities and Differences by the Status of the Victim." *Deviant Behavior* 9:347–68.

O'Toole, R., Gorsuch, K.L., Pisaneschi, R.H., and Stahl, K.A. 1985. "The Seriousness of Family Abuse and Neglect." Unpublished paper, University of Akron, Ohio.

O'Toole, R., Turbett, J.P., Sargent, J., and O'Toole, A.W. 1987. "Recognizing and Reacting to Child Abuse: Physicians, Nurses, Teachers, Social Workers, Law Enforcement Officers, and Community Respondents." Paper presented at the National Conference on Family Violence, University of New Hampshire, Durham.

Pagelow, M.D. 1981. *Woman-Battering.* Beverly Hills, CA: Sage.

Pahl, J. 1979. "The General Practitioner and the Problem of Battered Women." *Journal of Medical Ethics* 5:117–23.

Parkes, C.M., and Brown, R.J. 1972. Health after Bereavement." *Psychosomatic Medicine* 34:449–61.

Parnas, R.I. 1972. "Police Response to Domestic Disturbance." Pp. 206–238 in *The Criminal in the Arms of the Law,* edited by L. Radinowicz and M.E. Wolfgang. New York: Basic Books.

Paulson, M.J. 1978. "Incest and Sexual Molestation: Clinical and Legal Issues." *Journal of Clinical Child Psychology* 7:177–80.

Pearlin, L.I., and Aneshensel, C.S. 1986. "Coping and Social Supports: Their Functions and Applications." Pp. 417–437 in *Applications of Social Science to Clinical Medicine and Health Policy,* edited by L.H. Aiken and D. Mechanic. Brunswick, NJ: Rutgers University Press.

Pedrick-Cornell, C., and Gelles, R.J. 1982. "Elder Abuse: The Status of Current Knowledge." *Family Relations* 31:457–65.

Pelton, L.H. 1981. *The Social Context of Child Abuse and Neglect.* New York: Human Services Press.

Perkins, D.V. 1982. "The Assessment of Stress using Life Events Scales. Pp. 320–331 in *Handbook of Stress,* edited by L. Goldberger and S. Breznitz. New York: Free Press.

Peters, J.M., Dinsmore, J., and Toth, P.A. 1988. *Child Abuse Is a Criminal Offense.* Alexandria, VA: American Prosecutors Research Institute.

Peters, S.D., Wyatt, G.E., and Finkelhor, D. 1986. Prevalence. Pp. 15–59 in *A Sourcebook on Child Sexual Abuse*, edited by D. Finkelhor et al. Beverly Hills, CA: Sage.

Pfohl, S.S. 1977. "The Discovery of Child Abuse." *Social Problems* 24:310–23.

Phillips, L.R., and Rempusheski, V.F. 1985. "Decision-Making Model for Diagnosing and Intervening in Elder Abuse and Neglect." *Nursing Research* 34:134–39.

Pillemer, K.A., and Wolfe, R.S., eds. 1986. *Elder Abuse: Conflict in the Family.* Dover, MA: Auburn House.

Pleck, E. 1989. Criminal Approaches to Family Violence, 1640–1980. Pp. 19–57 in *Family Violence*, edited by L. Ohlin and M. Tonry. Chicago: University of Chicago Press.

Ponzetti, J.J., Cate, R.M., and Koval, J.E. 1982. Violence between Couples: Profiling the Male Abuser. *The Personnel and Guidance Journal* 61:222–24.

Purdy, S., and Nickle, N. 1981. "Practice Principles for Working with Groups of Men who Batter." *Social Work with Groups* 4:111–22.

Radelet, M.L. 1988. Evaluating and treating prisoners so they can be put to death. Paper presented at Psychological Perspectives on the Death Penalty, Symposium of the American Psychological Association, Atlanta, Georgia.

Radloff, L.S. 1980. "Risk Factors for Depression: What Do We Learn from Them? Pp. 93–109 in *The Mental Health of Women*, edited by M. Buttentag, S. Salasin, and D. Belle. New York: Academic Press.

Rein, M., and Miller, S.M. 1967. "The Demonstration Project as a Strategy of Change. Pp. 160–191 in *Organizing for Community Welfare*, edited by M.N. Zald. Chicago: Quadrangle.

Ringwalt, C., and Earp, J. 1988. "Attributing Responsibility in Cases of Father–Daughter Sexual Abuse." *Child Abuse and Neglect* 12:273–78.

Rogers, R., ed. 1989. *Behavioral Sciences and the Law* 7(1).

Rose, K., and Saunders, D.G. 1986. "Nurses' and Physicians' Attitudes about Women Abuse: The Effects of Gender and Professional Role." *Health Care for Women International*, 7:427–38.

Rosenbaum, A., and O'Leary, D. 1981. "Marital Violence: Characteristics of Abusive Couples." *Journal of Consulting and Clinical Psychology* 49:63–71.

Rossi, P.H., and Freeman, H.E. 1985. *Evaluation: A Systematic Approach*, 3rd ed. Beverly Hills, CA: Sage.

Rossi, P.H., Berk, R.A., and Lenihan, K.J. 1980. *Money, Work and Crime: Experimental Evidence.* New York: Academic Press.

Rounsaville, B.J. 1978. "Theories in Marital Violence: Evidence from a Study of Battered Women." *Victimology* 3:11–31.

Runyan, D.K., et al. 1988. "Impact of Legal Intervention of Sexually Abused Children." *Journal of Pediatrics* 113:647–53.

Russell, D.E.H. 1982. *Rape in Marriage.* New York: MacMillan.

Ryan, P. 1984. *Fostering Discipline.* Ypsilanti: Eastern Michigan University.

Ryan, W. 1971. *Blaming the Victim.* New York: Random House.

Saks, M.J., ed. 1986. *Law and Human Behavior*, 10(1,2).

Saltzman, L.E., Mercy, J.A., Rosenberg, M.L., Elsea, W.R., Napper, G., Sikes, R.K., Waxweiler, R.J., and the Collaborative Working Group for the Study of

Family and Intimate Assaults in Atlanta. 1990. Magnitude and patterns of Family and Intimate Assault in Atlanta, Georgia, 1984. *Violence and Victims* 5:3–18.

Sandberg, D.N. 1987. "Child Sexual Abuse: To Prosecute or Not?" *New Hampshire Bar Journal* 29:15–27.

Sarason, B., Shearin, D., Pierce, G., and Sarason, I. 1987. "Interrelations of Social Support Measures: Theoretical and Practical Implications." *Journal of Personality and Social Psychology* 52:813–32.

Saunders, D., and Size, P. 1986. "Attitudes about Woman Abuse among Police Officers, Victims, and Victim Advocates." *Journal of Interpersonal Violence* 1:25–42.

Schuller, R.A. 1988. "The Impact of Social Science Experts in the Courtroom. Paper presented at the Law and Society Association Meeting, Vail, Colorado.

Schur, E.M. 1980. *The Politics of Deviance.* Englewood Cliffs, NJ: Prentice Hall.

Seligman, M. 1975. *Helplessness: On Depression, Development and Death.* San Francisco: Freeman.

Sherman, L.W., and Berk, R.A. 1984. "The Specific Deterrent Effects of Arrest for Domestic Assault." *American Sociological Review* 49:261–72.

Sherman, L.W., and Cohn, E.G. 1989. "The Impact of Research on Legal Policy: The Minneapolis Domestic Violence Experiment." *Law and Society Review* 23:117–44.

Shields, N.M., and Hanneke, C.R. 1983. "Battered Wives' Reactions to Marital Rape." Pp. 132–140 in *The Dark Side of Families*, edited by D. Finkelhor et al. Beverly Hills, CA: Sage.

Shipley, S.B., and Sylvester, D.C. 1982. "Professionals' Attitudes toward Violence in Close Relationships." *Journal of Emergency Nursing* 8:88–91.

Snyder, J.C., and Newberger, E.H. 1986. "Consensus and Difference among Hospital Professionals in Evaluating Child Mistreatment." *Violence and Victims* 1:125–39.

Spivak, H., Hausman, A.J., and Prothraw-Stith, D. 1989. "Practitioners Forum: Public Health and the Primary Prevention Project." *Violence and Victims* 4:203–12.

Spohn, C., Gruhl, J., and Welch, S. 1981–82. "The Effect of Race on Sentencing: A Re-examination of an Unsettled Question." *Law and Society Review* 16:71–88.

Star, B. 1980. "Patterns in Family Violence." *Social Casework* 61:339–47.

Stark, E.F., Flitcraft, A.H., and Frazier, W. 1979. "Medicine and Patriarchal Violence: The Social Construction of a 'Private' Event." *International Journal of Health Services* 9:461–93.

Stark, E.F., Flitcraft, A., Zuckerman, D., Grey, A., Robison, J., and Frazier, W. 1981. *Wife Abuse in the Medical Setting*, Domestic Violence Monograph Series No. 7. Rockville, MD: National Clearinghouse on Domestic Violence.

Steele, B.F., and Alexander, H. 1981. "Long-Term Effects of Sexual Abuse in Childhood." Pp. 55–74 in *Sexually Abused Children and Their Families*, edited by P.B. Mrazek and C.H. Kempe. Oxford: Pergamon.

Stein, T.J. 1981. *Social Work Practice in Child Welfare*. Englewood Cliffs, NJ: Prentice Hall.

Steinmetz, S.K. 1977. *The Cycle of Violence: Assertive, Aggressive and Abusive Family Interaction*. New York: Praeger.

Steinmetz, S.K. 1987. "Family Violence: Past, Present, and Future." Pp. 725–765 in *Handbook of Marriage and the Family*, edited by M.B. Sussman and S.K. Steinmetz. New York: Plenum.

Stets, J.E., and Straus, M.A. 1990. "Gender Differences in Reporting Marital Violence and its Medical and Psychological Consequences." in *Physical Violence in American Families: Risk Factors and Adaptations to Violence in 8,145 Families*, edited by M.A. Straus and R.J. Gelles. New Brunswick, NJ: Transaction Press.

Stewart, L.P., Cooper, P.J., and Friedly, S.A. 1986. *Communication between the Sexes: Differences and Sex-Role Stereotypes*. Scottsdale, AZ: Gorsuch.

Stith, S.M. 1990. "Police Response to Domestic Violence: The Influence of Individual and Familial Factors." *Violence and Victims* 5:37–49.

Straus, M.A. 1974. "Leveling, Civility and Violence in the Family." *Journal of Marriage and the Family* 36:13–29.

Straus, M.A. 1976. "Sexual Inequality, Cultural Norms and Wife-Beating." *Victimology* 1:54–76.

Straus, M.A. 1977. Sociological Perspective on the Prevention and Treatment of Wifebeating. Pp. 194–238 in *Battered Women: A Psychosociological Study of Domestic Violence*, edited by M. Roy. New York: Van Nostrand Reinhold.

Straus, M.A. 1979. "Measuring Intrafamily Conflict and Violence: The Conflict Tactics Scales (CTS)." *Journal of Marriage and the Family* 45:75–95.

Straus, M.A. 1980. "Social Stress and Marital Violence in a National Sample of American Families." Pp. 229–250 in *Forensic Psychology and Psychiatry*, edited by F. Wright et al. New York: New York Academy of Sciences.

Straus, M.A. 1981. "Societal Change and Change in Family Violence." Paper presented at the Conference on Family Violence, University of New Hampshire, Durham.

Straus, M.A. 1983. "Ordinary Violence, Child Abuse, and Wife-Beating: What Do They Have in Common." Pp. 213–234 in *The Dark Side of Families*, edited by D. Finkelhor et al. Beverly Hills, CA: Sage.

Straus, M.A. 1986. "Domestic Violence and Homicide Antecedents." *Bulletin of the New York Academy of Medicine* 62:446–65.

Straus, M.A. 1988. "Primary Group Characteristics and Intrafamily Homicide." Paper presented at the American Society of Criminology, Chicago.

Straus, M.A. 1989. "Assaults by Wives on Husbands: Implications for Primary Prevention." Paper presented at the American Society of Criminology, Reno, Nevada.

Straus, M.A. 1990a. The Conflict Tactics Scales and its Critics: An Evaluation and New Data on Validity and Reliability." Pp. 49–74 in *Physical Violence in American Families: Risk Factors and Adaptations to Violence in 8,145 Families*, edited by M.A. Straus and R.J. Gelles. New Brunswick, NJ: Transaction Press.

Straus, M.A. 1990b. "Injury and Frequency of Assault and the Representative

Sample Fallacy." Pp. 75–94 in *Physical Violence in American Families: Risk Factors and Adaptations to Violence in 8,145 Families*, edited by M.A. Straus and R.J. Gelles. New Brunswick, NJ: Transaction Press.

Straus, M.A., and Gelles, R.J. 1986. Societal Change and Change in Family Violence from 1975 to 1985 as Revealed by Two National Surveys." *Journal of Marriage and the Family* 48:465–79.

Straus, M.A., and Gelles, R.J., eds. 1990. *Physical Violence in American Families: Risk Factors and Adaptations to Violence in 8,145 Families.* New Brunswick, NJ: Transaction Press.

Straus, M.A., and Lincoln, A.J. 1985. "Non-Violent Crime within the Family." Pp. 71–87 in *Crime and the Family,* edited by A.J. Lincoln and M.A. Straus. Springfield, IL: C.C. Thomas.

Straus, M.A., and Smith, C. 1990. "Family Patterns and Primary Prevention of Family Violence." Pp. 507–523 in *Physical Violence in American Families: Risk Factors and Adaptations to Violence in 8,145 Families*, edited by M.A. Straus and R.J. Gelles. New Brunswick, NJ: Transaction Press.

Straus, M.A., Gelles, R.J., and Steinmetz, S.K. 1980. *Behind Closed Doors: Violence in the American Family.* Garden City, NJ: Doubleday.

Straus, M.A., Sweet, S., and Vissing, Y.M. 1989. "Verbal Aggression against Spouses and Children in a Nationally Representative Sample of American Children." Paper presented at the Speech Communication Association Meeting, San Francisco.

Strube, M.J., and Barbour, L.S. 1983. "The Decision to Leave an Abusive Relationship: Economic Dependence and Psychological Commitment." *Journal of Marriage and the Family* 45:785–93.

Sudman, S. 1983. "Applied Sampling." Pp. 145–194 in *Handbook of Survey Research,* edited by P.H. Rossi et al. New York: Academic Press.

Summit, R., and Kryso, J.A. 1981. "Sexual Abuse of Children: A Clinical Spectrum." *American Journal of Orthopsychiatry* 48:237–51.

Tedesco, J.F., and Schnell, S.V. 1987. "Children's Reactions to Sex Abuse Investigation and Litigation." *Child Abuse and Neglect* 11:267–72.

Thoits, P.A. 1982. "Conceptual, Methodological and Theoretical Problems in Studying Social Support as a Buffer against Life Stress." *Journal of Health and Social Behavior* 23:145–59.

Tilden, V.P., and Shepherd, P. 1987. "Increasing the Rate of Identification of Battered Women in an Emergency Department: Use of a Nursing Protocol." *Research in Nursing and Health* 10:209–15.

Tolman, R., and Bhosley, G. 1988. "The Impact of Criminal Justice System Involvement on the Outcome of Intervention for Men who Batter." Paper presented at the American Society for Criminology, Chicago.

Tolman, R., Beeman, S., and Mendoza, C. 1987. "The Impact of a Shelter-Sponsored Program for Men Who Batter." Paper presented at the Conference on Family Violence, University of New Hampshire, Durham.

Topper, A.B., and Aldridge, D.J. 1981. "Incest: Intake and Investigation." Pp. 109–127 in *Sexually Abused Children and Their Families,* edited by P.B. Mrazek and C.H. Kempe. Oxford: Pergamon.

Torres, S. 1987. Hispanic-American Battered Women: Why Consider Cultural Differences?" *Response* 10:20–21.

Truninger, E. 1971. "Marital Violence: The Legal Solutions." *Hastings Law Journal* 23:259–76.

Tyler, A.H., and Brassard, M.R. 1984. "Abuse in the Investigation and Treatment of Intrafamilial Child Sexual Abuse." *Child Abuse and Neglect* 8:47–53.

U.S. Department of Justice. 1984. *Attorney General's Task Force on Family Violence: Final Report.* Washington, D.C.: U.S. Government Printing Office.

Utech, M.R. 1987. "The Concept of Child Abuse: Problems and Prospects in Reporting and Research." Paper presented at the Conference on Family Violence, University of New Hampshire, Durham.

Vissing, Y.M., and Straus, M.A. 1991. "Verbal Aggression by Parents and Psycho-Social Problems of Children." *Child Abuse and Neglect.* (forthcoming)

Vivian, D., and O'Leary, D.K. 1987. "Communication Patterns in Physically Aggressive Engaged Couples." Paper presented at the Conference on Family Violence, University of New Hampshire, Durham.

Wald, M. 1975. "State Intervention on Behalf of 'Neglected' Children: A Search for Realistic Standards." *Stanford Law Review* 27:985–1040.

Walker, L.E. 1979. *The Battered Woman.* New York: Harper and Row.

Walker, L.E. 1983. "The Battered Woman Syndrome Study. Pp. 31–48 in *The Dark Side of Families,* edited by D. Finkelhor et al. Beverly Hills, CA: Sage.

Walker, L.E.A. 1984a. *The Battered Woman Syndrome.* New York: Springer.

Walker, L.E.A. 1984b. "Battered Women, Psychology and Public Policy." *American Psychologist* 39:1178–82.

Walters, C.M. 1985. "Admission of Expert Testimony on Eyewitness Identification." *California Law Review* 73:1402–30.

Wardell, L., Gillespie, D.L., and Leffler, A. 1983. "Science and Violence against Wives." Pp. 69–84 in *The Dark Side of Families,* edited by D. Finkelhor et al. Beverly Hills, CA: Sage.

Watzlawick, P., Beaven, J.H., and Jackson, J.D. 1967. *Pragmatics of Human Communication: A Study of Interactional Patterns, Pathologies, and Paradoxes.* New York: Norton.

Wauchope, B., and Straus, M.A. 1990. "Physical Punishment and Physical Abuse of American Children: Incidence Rates by Age, Gender, and Occupational Class. Pp. 133–143 in *Physical Violence in American Families: Risk Factors and Adaptations to Violence in 8,145 Families,* edited by M.A. Straus and R.J. Gelles. New Brunswick, NJ: Transaction Books.

Weiss, R.S. 1975. *Marital Separation.* New York: Basic Books.

Wells, G.L. 1984. "How Adequate is Human Intuition for Judging Eyewitness Testimony?" Pp. 256–272 in *Eyewitness Testimony: Psychological Perspectives,* edited by G.L. Wells and E.F. Loftus. New York: Cambridge University Press.

Wermuth, L. 1983. "Domestic Violence Reforms: Policing the Private?" *Berkeley Journal of Sociology* 27:27–49.

Wheeler, G.R., and Wheeler, C.L. 1980. "Reflections on Legal Representation of the Economically Disadvantaged: Beyond Assembly Line Justice." *Crime and Delinquency* 26:319–32.

Wheeler, G.R., and Wheeler, C.L. 1982. "Bail Reform in the 1980s: A Response to the Critics." *Criminal Law Bulletin* 18:228–40.

Whitchurch, G.G. 1987. "Linkages in Conjugal Violence and Communication: A Review and Critical Appraisal." Paper presented at the Conference on Family Violence, University of New Hampshire, Durham.

Whitcomb, D. 1985. "Evaluation of Programs for the Effective Prosecution of Child Physical and Sexual Abuse. Draft of final report submitted to the Bureau of Justice Assistance. In D. Whitcomb et al., *When the Victim is a Child*. Washington, D.C.: National Institute of Justice, Cooperative Agreement No. 86-SD-CX-K005, with the Institute for Social Analysis.

Wilber, N. 1985. "Dilemmas of Child Sexual Abuse Reform: The Implementation of Massachusetts Chapter 288." M.A. thesis proposal, Harvard University Graduate School of Education, Cambridge, MA.

Williams, K., and Hawkins, R. 1989. "The Meaning of Arrest for Wife Assault." *Criminology* 27:163–81.

Williamson, J.B., Karp, D.A., Dalphin, J.R., and Gray, P.S. 1982. *The Research Craft: An Introduction to Social Research Methods*, 2nd ed. Boston: Little Brown.

Wolfe, D.A., and Mosk, M.D. 1983. "Behavioral Comparisons of Children from Abused and Distressed Families." *Journal of Consulting and Clinical Psychology* 51:702–8.

Yllo, K.A., and Straus, M.A. 1981. "Interpersonal Violence among Married and Cohabiting Couples." *Family Relations* 30:339–45.

Zellman, G.L. 1990. "Report Decision-Making Patterns among Mandated Child Abuse Reporters." *Child Abuse and Neglect* 14:325–36.

Zimbardo, P.G. 1969. "The Human Choice: Individuation, Reason and Order vs. Deindividuation, Impulse and Chaos." *Nebraska Symposium on Motivation*. Lincoln: University of Nebraska Press.

Zimring, F.E. 1989. Toward a Jurisprudence of Family Violence. Pp. 547–569 in *Family Violence*, edited by L. Ohlin and M. Tonry. Chicago: University of Chicago Press.

Subject Index

Act of violence, 18, 19
Aggression against women
  direct, physical, 116–118, 135
  threat of, 118
  frequency of, 171
  psychological, 118
  effects on victims, 96–97, 118–120
  verbal, 135
  typologies of, 136, 141–142
Anger
  arousal and, 193
  arrest and, 194
Attributions, 42

Bail release decisions, 63
Battered child syndrome, 5
Battered woman syndrome, 8, 102–106
Battering
  psychological responses to, 42

Causal studies, 9
Child protective services, 31, 32
Child sexual abuse, 79, 82–84, 123
  agency reactions to, 126–128
  foster care and, 125–126
  social reactions to, 124–125
Clinical reports, 41
Clinical samples, 17, 23
Community
  samples, 23, 49, 80
  definition of family mistreatment, 49
Conflict Tactics Scale, 21, 116
Criminal justice policy, 64
Criminal justice system
  family violence and, 153, 169–170
  impact of domestic violence law, 177–179
  mode of entry, 193
  prosecution outcome, 193
Crisis Center for South Suburbia, 114–115

Data collection methods, 8
  ethnographic data, 89
  group interviews, 90, 92

hospital chart review studies, 37
longitudinal method, 35
modified factorial survey design, 51
Offender Based Transaction Statistics (OBTS), 65
retrospective accounts, 138
self-reports, 85
storytelling, 90
telephone surveys, 51, 80–83, 86
Date rape, 79
Depression, 44–45
Deterrence, 10, 192

Elder abuse, 6, 37, 58
Ethics in family violence research, 14–16, 81
Evaluation studies, 10, 11, 12
Expert testimony, 101–106

Failure to report abuse, 49
Family characteristics, 24–26
Family privacy, 25
Federal Bureau of Investigation, 13, 20

Gender differences in marital assault, 21
Gender inequality, 26, 31

Health care
  system, 35
  education, 35
  professionals, 38

Incidence rates, 19, 21, 79
Inductive techniques, 92
Intention, 18, 19
Intervention programs
  advocates for victims, 168–170
  Connecticut, 168–170
  effectiveness for men, 120–122
  for child victims of sexual abuse, 125–126
  for male batterers, 114–115
  limitations on advocacy, 171–177
  type of intervention and mothers, 128–131

Just world hypothesis, 38–39

Labeling, 39–40
Laws concerning family violence
  Connecticut, 168
  Illinois, 147
  Massachusetts, 155
Learned helplessness, 44, 106

Marital rape, 6, 79
Murder (homicide), 19, 20, 32

Physical injury
  patterns of, 36
  symptoms of, 36
Physical punishment of children, 20
Police, 17
  knowledge of battered-women
    syndrome, 108
  referrals to domestic violence
    program, 148–150
  responses to domestic violence,
    147–148, 150
Post-traumatic stress disorder, 98
Pretrial release, 63
Prevalence rates, 21, 79, 86
Primary prevention, 18, 31
Problem solving techniques, 43–44
Prosecution
  low rates of family violence cases,
    63
Prosecutors
  adjudication, 161
  and attitudes toward sex offenders,
    159
  case processing and, 160
  in criminal justice policy, 154
  models of policies, 154
  policies toward child sexual abuse,
    156–160
Psychological abuse
  consequences of, 113
  definition, 118
Psychological problem checklist, 116,
  120

Psychopathology, 36
Public health, 35

Qualitative research methods, 7
Quantitative research methods, 7

Rape, 79, 85
Reformation of perpetrator, 192
Removal (from home) of child victim
  factors involved, 131–133
Reprisal by perpetrators, 191
Retaliation by perpetrators, 191

Sample size deficiency, 75
Self-esteem, 45–46
Social isolation
  of perpetrators, 42
  of victim, 86
Social obstruction, 89, 92, 93–96
Social support, 89, 90, 92, 93–96
Social visibility of child and family
    violence or abuse, 10, 57
Spouses of alcoholics, 41
Stress research, 89
Systematic data, 13–14
Stigmatization, 97

Trends in family violence, 31–34

Unsubstantiated reports of abuse, 49

Validation, 94
Verbal aggression
  relationship to physical aggression,
    135–136, 140–142
  types, 138–139
Victim blaming, 9, 39
Victims
  advocates for, 168
Violence
  by parents, 27, 28
  by relatives, 63, 67, 70–71, 74, 92,
    96–97
  by spouses, 27
  norms, 26–28

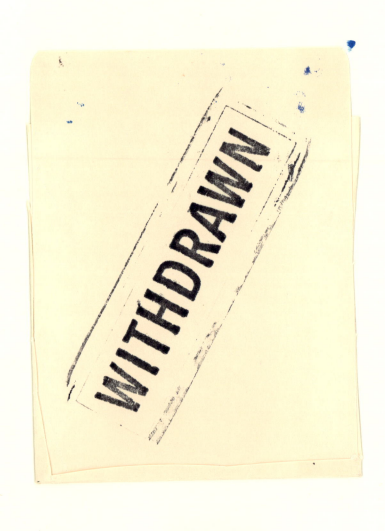